Antique Trader™

Guide to
Fakes
& Reproductions

3rd Edition

MARK CHERVENKA

Published by

krause publications
An F&W Publications Company

700 East State Street • Iola, WI 54990-0001
715-445-2214 • 888-457-2873
www.krause.com

Please call or write for our free catalog of publications.
Our toll-free number to place an order or obtain a free catalog is 800-258-0929
or please use our regular business telephone 715-445-2214.

Library of Congress Catalog Number: 00-111278
ISBN: 0-87349-590-X

Printed in the United States of America

Contents

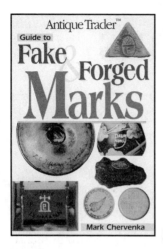

4

Introduction

Dear Friend,

Your decision to purchase (or consider purchasing) this book shows you are concerned about fakes and reproductions. That is good. You have joined thousands of others who want clear, direct information on separating old from new.

By far, the vast majority of reproductions are easy to separate from old originals. Do not let others tell you that it's not. Once you see new and old side by side, even beginners find new confidence. Experienced dealers will add to what they know.

That is why there are 1,036 photos and drawings in this 368 page book. Most photos are close ups clearly showing how new and old differ. Just viewing the photos and reading captions will probably answer most questions. There is a detailed text for additional background.

Readers of past editions say they now buy or sell with greater confidence. Because their risks are reduced, they say they enjoy their hobby or business more.

For you to get maximum benefit from this book, please keep these simple suggestions in mind. First, there are many, many more reproductions than can fit in this book. What's shown is only a fraction of what's out there.

Second, there are always exceptions. Never use one single test to determine age. There are many variations among originals as well as reproductions. The most typical examples of both are used for comparison.

Third, apply the guidelines only to the specific piece discussed. A clue that tells you a butter dish is old, may not be the test for the sugar bowl in the same pattern.

And, finally, many items honestly sold as legitimate reproductions only become fakes when their age is misrepresented by an unethical seller.

Mark J. Chervenka
editor/publisher
Antique & ‘Collectors Reproduction News
The monthly newsletter on fakes and reproductions since 1992

Art Glass

Reproduction of Victorian mother of pearl (MOP) art glass cruet made in Murano, Italy, ca. 1975-85.

Reproduction fairy lamp made to imitate Burmese, a type of Victorian art glass that shades from pale yellow to soft pink.

Due to its high value, art glass is a frequent target of reproductions, especially fake and forged marks and signatures. When evaluating a suspect piece, you should consider many factors including: 1) shapes known to be original; 2) glass quality and finishing; and 3) any markings and signatures and how they were applied.

• Shape–Shapes and patterns of major companies like Steuben, Lalique and others are fairly easy to document in original catalog drawings. Steuben shapes obviously should not have Tiffany signatures. As you'll see in the following pages, though, original shapes are being copied, so shape alone should not be used as your only test of age.

Many original pieces, particularly Steuben, include shape numbers in original markings. If a shape number is present, it should agree with the original catalog shape of the same number. But again, this is a general rule; some forged marks on copied shapes do include the correct shape number. However, many forgers are careless and make up shape numbers at random when applying fake marks.

Nearly all Steuben designs 1903 to 1932 are recorded with their original shape numbers. Any shape with a Steuben mark should logically match up with a recorded known shape. Comparing suspected pieces to originals in catalogs, pattern books, and other references is a good way to catch many art glass reproductions.

• Glass quality and finishing–The vast majority of all authentic 19th and early 20th century art glass has a polished or ground out pontil (see next page). Pontils on the reproductions are rarely ground out or polished. If you encounter a piece marked or signed with the name of a well-known art glass maker, such as Tiffany, Steuben, etc., and the piece does not have a ground pontil, it is almost certain to be a forgery.

On the other hand, a ground pontil is not a guarantee of age. Forgers now are polishing out rough pontils on reproductions. It has also become common to buy new studio glass made in an Art Nouveau style–such as Orient and Flume, Lundberg Studios or others–polish out those legitimate marks, and add forged marks of old companies like Tiffany, Steuben, or Loetz (see photo next page). Even though pontils can be added, it is still a good idea to check for a polished pontil. With rare exceptions, if a piece doesn't have a polished pontil, you really don't need to bother with any other tests.

• Markings–Fake marks are now so common they should never be used as a single test of age or authenticity. It has become more important than ever to know and understand what original marks are appropriate for the pieces to which they are applied and how original

Art Glass

The majority of blown art glass is removed from the blow pipe with a pontil rod.

The rod has a small dab of hot glass on the end, which is joined to the blown glass.

Then, the blown glass is sheared off the blow pipe. Now, held on the pontil rod, the blown glass receives its final shape and decoration. After decorating, the pontil rod is snapped or "cracked" off, leaving a pontil mark or "scar" where the rod was attached. On good quality pieces, the pontil mark is ground out and polished.

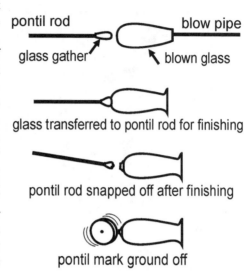

pontil rod   blow pipe

glass gather   blown glass

glass transferred to pontil rod for finishing

pontil rod snapped off after finishing

pontil mark ground off

marks and signatures were made. In other words, learn which marks were used during what years and which should be acid-etched, which wheel-engraved, and which appear only as paper labels.

Most forgers use modern tools that make their work quick and easy, not necessarily historically accurate. That's why you often see pieces never originally marked suddenly appear with marks. Original Burmese by Mt. Washington Glass Co., for example, was never

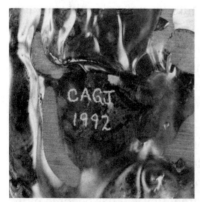

Dated 1992 mark in pontil of new iridescent studio glass made in Art Noveau style.

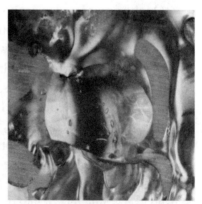

New mark ground out at glass repair shop. Now ready for forged mark of Steuben, Tiffany, or Loetz.

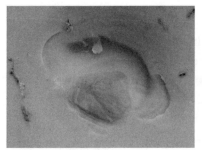

Typical rough pontil; also called open, cracked, or scarred pontil.

Roughly ground pontil. Grind marks highlighted by pencil rubbing.

Close-up view of typical polished pontil.

Pinched, or tooled pontil, leaves a particularly small mark.

permanently marked. The only documented marks on this ware are rarely found paper labels. Any form of permanent mark, such as acid stamped or engraved, is a forgery.

Be especially wary of all acid etched marks. Rubber stamps can be made from all kinds of artwork such as logos, trademarks, letterheads and patent applications that appear in reference books on antiques. These rubber stamps are then used to apply liquid acid to new glass, as well as genuine old glass that was never originally marked. Such marks are fantasy marks; no originals ever existed. Frequent targets of acid etched forgeries include Tiffany, Loetz, and Gallé. None of those firms ever used acid stamps to apply original marks. Knowing how original marks were applied is one of the best ways to protect yourself against forgeries.

Burmese

Original Burmese was made by the Mt. Washington Glass Co. beginning in 1885. It was later made under license in England by Thomas Webb and Sons. Burmese shades from a yellow body to a salmon pink towards the edges and rims.

Authentic Burmese and other internally shaded 19th century art glass, such as amberina, peachblow, etc., are made from *heat sensitive* glass formulas. Burmese, for example, after being blown and worked, would be entirely yellow. The pink shading was produced only by exposing selected areas to a higher temperature. The key ingredient to any heat-sensitive glass is gold. The exact color the reheated areas change to depends on what other ingredients are in the batch. The soft yellow color of Burmese was produced by uranium oxide.

Keep these guidelines in mind when evaluating a piece of Burmese:

1) All authentic 19th century Burmese has a smooth polished pontil (although it will be satinized on acid finished Burmese). The great majority of reproduction pontils are not polished. Although some reproduction pontils have been just recently ground out, this is still a good first test.

2) The majority of the Italian reproduction Burmese has narrowly ridged handles and feet. Most original handles and feet are smooth. When old handles and feet are ridged, the ridges are very broad and wide (see illustration opposite page).

3) Swirled streaks in the glass body are a sign of a reproduction

New covered butter or cheese dish, 8¾-inch dia. Poorly blended colors, narrowly ridged knob. Made in Italy, ca. 1980s.

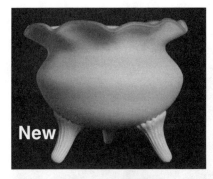

Italian Burmese footed bowl with narrowly ridged feet. New bowl imitates original Mt. Washington catalog shape #129.

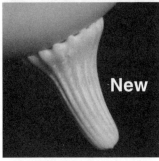

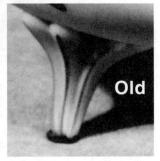

Narrow ribbing on the feet from the reproduction above. This narrow ribbing is typical of the Italian reproductions.

When ridges appear on original Burmese, the ridges are broad and widely spaced, unlike the new Italian pieces.

(see below). Original Burmese is one, homogeneous body that comes from the furnace all yellow. Only when it is reheated do some areas change into pink. New Burmese glass is often, but not always, mixed from two separate colors, pink and yellow. This often produces streaks and swirls in the body glass that are never found in original Burmese.

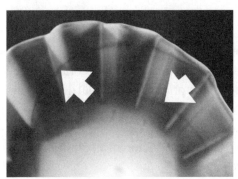

Many pieces of new Burmese show swirls and streaks in the glass when held to the light. Internal flaws like these are extremely rare in original Burmese.

Art Glass

Three pieces of reproduction Burmese made in Italy from 1970 to 1980. An 8-inch vase (left) with applied decoration, rough non-polished pontil. Bulbous hobnail 10-inch pitcher and matching 7-inch cruet (right). Hobs on authentic pitcher continue under the base; the base is flat on the reproduction. No original hobnail cruet was ever made. Note the narrowly ridged handles on both the pitcher and cruet.

4) The very edge of rims on Italian Burmese are nearly transparent (clear glass). Sight along the rim and you'll see a line of what appears to be clear frosted glass.

5) Most original Burmese has softer texture due to acid finishing. The majority of reproductions have a coarser texture from sandblasting.

6) Original Burmese will fluoresce under black light. However, the Italian reproductions *also fluoresce* because they contain uranium. Remember, uranium causes the fluorescence, not age. Black light is helpful to eliminate the more obvious fakes but is not a 100% guarantee of age.

It is also becoming more important to carefully inspect decorated Burmese pieces. Genuinely old but originally undecorated pieces are now being painted to bring higher prices. All original decorations are fired on; many recent paintings are not. Black light may be helpful in spotting recently applied decorations.

A group of Murano reproductions of Victorian art glass is shown in the catalog on the opposite page.

Fine Replicas of Antique Satin Glass Handmade in Italy

Peach Blow • Burmese • Aqua or Pink Quilted Satin

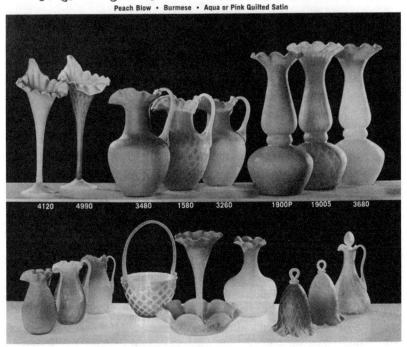

Partial catalog page from reproduction wholesaler ca. 1980 showing Murano copies of Victorian art glass. Includes Burmese, mother of pearl (MOP), satin glass and peachblow.

Murano reproduction, ca. 1980, of rainbow striped mother of pearl (MOP). Red "Made in Italy" label on left. Imported by Koscherak Bros., whose blue and silver label is on right.

Top view of toothpick at left. Note the semi-circular crimps. This crimp is found almost exclusively on the 1970-80s Murano copies.

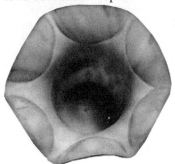

13

Lalique

Rene Lalique (1860 to 1945) was one of the most successful artists/designers of all time. Lalique began commercial production of his own glass around 1905, which continued until his death in 1945. The glass business was carried on by his son Marc, who died in 1977, and then his granddaughter Marie-Claude Lalique. The business still operates today as Cristal Lalique. Many of the original pre-1945 designs remain in production.

There are several considerations when evaluating Lalique. There are genuine Lalique pieces made after 1945 with forged pre-1945 marks; new glass (especially from the Czech Republic) with forged marks that copy Lalique patterns; and pre-1945 glass by other manufacturers with forged Lalique marks.

Virtually all authentic Lalique glass is marked. Pieces made before Lalique's death in 1945 were marked "R. Lalique," usually followed by the word "France." After 1945, the "R" was dropped and the mark was simply "Lalique, France." The single letter R is commonly forged on current Lalique to suggest a piece was made before 1945. Pre-1945 clear Lalique fluoresces a soft yellow-green to yellow under long-wave black light. Clear Lalique made after 1945 does not fluoresce. Since 1980, Lalique engraved marks have also included the ® symbol, which was never used before 1980. If the initial "R"

New copycat frosted glass perfume bottle made in Taiwan. Frequently seen with forged marks. Stopper made with double flower.

Original Deaux Fleurs Lalique perfume marked "R. Lalique." Re-issued after 1945 without "R." Original stopper is a single flower.

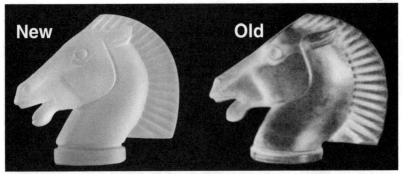

New frosted clear glass horse head made today in Czech Republic, left. Original, ca. 1929, Lalique "Longchamps" hood ornament, right. Czech piece has been in the market since the early 1990s. There are also new Czech copies of other Lalique hood ornaments including Lalique's Victoire and Vitesse. The new piece is gray and chalky, with obvious mold seams.

appeared with that symbol, it would automatically be a forgery.

New Art Deco-styled glass made today in the Czech Republic is frequently sold as "unmarked" Lalique or sold with forged Lalique marks. Most is inferior in quality to Lalique. One quick test of quality is to look for mold seams. Mold seams are almost impossible to find in genuine Lalique. Seams on the inexpensive copycat pieces are usually very obvious. Most original Lalique has at least some polishing, either on the base or top rim. The look-alike pieces are generally frosted all over.

Glass from other manufacturers made before 1945 seldom passes the quality tests described above. Forged marks on Lalique imitations made before 1945 have the same general problems as the other typical forgeries shown here.

Most Lalique was pressed and therefore does not have a pontil. Glass is uniformly high quality without flaws.

Lalique marks have included the registered symbol, an R in a circle, ®, since 1980. This symbol is virtually unknown in pre-1945 Lalique marks.

Art Glass

New frosted glass 17-inch lamp, left, with molded mark "Made in France." New 5-inch frosted glass vase with nudes, right, made today in Czech Republic, no mark. These and other similar new pieces are frequently found with forged Lalique marks.

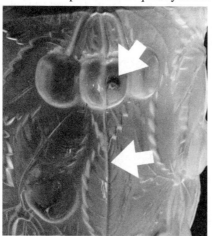

New ca. 1990s 7-inch Czech frosted glass vase with cherries, right, made from original 1930s mold. New production has obvious mold seams (left arrow) and unmelted impurities in glass (top arrow).

Obvious mold seams on most new Czech pieces continue down body on to the bottom rim.

New 5-inch vase with forged Loetz signature. Gold oilspot iridescence.

Loetz

Johann Lötz never owned a glass business. The iridescent glass known by his name was made at a glass house started by his widow, Susanna, in 1851. She named the business "Johann Lötz Witwe" (the widow of Johann Lötz). The business began making common objects, but turned to art glass in 1879 when Johann's grandson, Maximilian Von Spaun II, took control of the business.

The firm became best-known for iridescent glassware in the Art Nouveau style, similar to Tiffany and other makers. Sometime around the turn of the century, spelling of the business name was changed to Loetz. Pieces for export, if marked, usually read "Loetz, Austria."

Far more iridescent Loetz was originally unmarked than either Tiffany or Steuben. Before Loetz prices began rising in the 1990s, many original pieces of Loetz had forged signatures of other more valuable makers like Tiffany. Now that Loetz has risen to the same price as other makers, many variations of forged Loetz marks are in the market.

There are so many fake marks, it's hard to show typical examples of forgeries. In this case, it's easier to show the original marks.

Loetz, Austria
wheel engraved

First, no original Loetz mark was acid-etched; any acid-etched Loetz mark is a forgery. With the exception of one style of paper label, all original marks are wheel-engraved, as shown here.

Virtually all old Loetz has fire-polished rims and ground, usually polished, pontils.

Steuben

Steuben Glass Works was founded in 1903 in Corning, New York. Led by Frederick Carder, the firm began making iridescent glass in the Art Nouveau styles similar to Tiffany. Steuben continued to make high-quality colored art glass until 1932. In 1932, colored glass was discontinued and Steuben turned to producing clear crystal only, which remains the glass it makes today.

Reproductions are getting more sophisticated and are now frequently made in original shapes (see vase on opposite page). Forged Steuben marks are also improving and often include model numbers that correspond to the original shape.

Generally, original iridescent Steuben Aurene should feel silky smooth over the entire surface. Many reproductions have rough, pitted surfaces that feel coarse. Original iridescence is consistent over the entire surface. That means the underside of the base looks about the same as the sides of a vase. Many reproductions will not have iridescence on the undersides of bases.

Virtually all original Steuben pontils are polished. Most reproductions with forged marks have rough pontils. It is not unusual, though, for unethical sellers to polish out new rough pontils to create an imitation of an original piece. Marks on legitimate new studio glass in Art Nouveau styles–like Orient and Flume, Lundberg Studios, and others–are also frequently ground out before applying forged marks.

Be sure to hold up all pieces to a light. The great majority of reproductions have internal flaws in the glass. In ordinary light, these

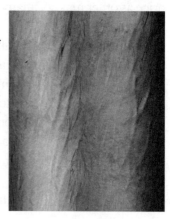

Close up view of surface of Steuben fake shown on opposite page. The glass below the iridescent surface is wavy and rough. Area shown about actual size.

Steuben

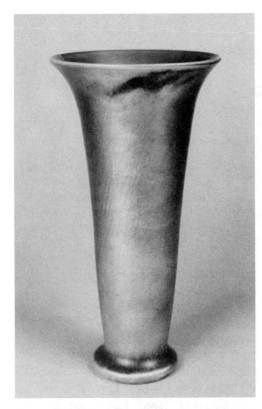

New 11-inch vase. Gold iridescent finish over opal glass body similar to original Aurene and Calcite. New vase is a copy of the original 2564 shape.

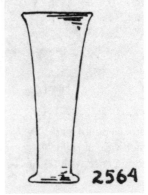

Original #2564 shape vase, as shown in 1903 to 1932 Steuben shape book.

Forged signature "Aurene," followed by model number "2564." Note large broken pontil mark (arrow). Signature applied with modern carbide tool leaving smooth sided engraving.

flaws are hidden under iridescence or other surface decorations. Held to the light, bubbles, streaks, and folds are easily seen. These types of flaws are virtually never found in original art glass.

Tiffany

Forged signature "Tiffany Favrile 3343B." Note large broken pontil mark. The forgery appears on the new 11-inch vase at right. The surface of the new vase is blue iridescence with flashes of gold highlights.

Louis Comfort Tiffany (1848 to 1933) was a leading designer of the Art Nouveau period. He is perhaps best known for his art glass and table lamps, but also designed jewelry, metalwork, textiles, pottery and complete interiors. Although his name appears on most objects, Tiffany himself never worked on any glass or lamps. All work was performed by highly skilled artisans according to Tiffany's designs.

Before about 1890, most objects were custom-made for special commissions in Tiffany's interior design business and marks on those pieces varied greatly. After 1890, more goods were made for the general public, and those are the majority of pieces in the market today. All production of Tiffany products ended in 1938.

Tiffany's companies operated under various names over the years, and these are reflected in the marks. There are so many Tiffany marks that it is particularly important to understand which marks were originally used on the various materials. Some original marks appear only on metal, others only on glass. Some of today's forgeries are trademarks that only appeared on legal documents and were never used as marks.

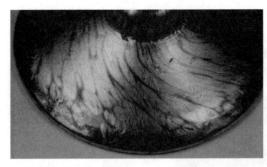

Iridescence on new Tiffany is often very inconsistent. This foot is swirled, while the sides are streaked and the top is clouded.

But again, marks are commonly forged and can't be used as a test of age. Overall quality is a much more reliable indication of authenticity.

The most common Tiffany reproductions with forged marks are iridescent pieces. As discussed previously, new iridescence generally has a very inconsistent finish. This includes random mirror-like reflections in otherwise satin or matte surfaces or patches or irregular patterns of iridescence. In the example above, there is oil-spot iridescence on the foot, pronounced vertical streaks on the sides and a cloudy swirled effect around the top third of the vase.

There are numerous spots where the iridescence is very thin and the base glass shows through. Random streaks, runs, drips and cloudiness are common. These variations are not controlled or part of a deliberate decoration or effect.

The vast majority of iridescent Tiffany originals show an even deposit of color that is silky smooth to the touch and evenly consistent over the entire surface. Flaws, such as bubbles, drips or runs, in iridescence are virtually unknown in genuine Tiffany.

Original glass is also of the highest quality. Hold an original up to the light and you'll virtually never see internal bubbles, folds or streaks in the body glass. New glass reproductions commonly have such flaws, although they are hidden by the iridescent surface. Virtually all originals will have ground pontils and with fire-polished top rims.

Original engraved marks appear on Tiffany blown glass made from 1893 to 1928. There is a tremendous difference found among original engraved marks. Some are illegible, others are in beautiful flowing script. Marks on original iridescent pieces are almost always rotary-engraved. Some pieces were marked with only a diamond tip

Art Glass

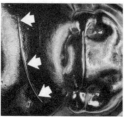

Reproduction scarabs usually have numerous flaws, such as the large crease shown above. News surfaces are often pitted and irregular.

Reproduction 5-inch solid glass iridescent scarab paperweight. Very similar to Tiffany original. Frequently found with forged marks.

New iridescent three-dimensional glass scarabs are widely available at stained glass supply stores. These new pieces are often set in new sterling and gold mountings and sold as original Tiffany scarab jewelry.

but these are mostly semi transparent pastel pieces. Most engraved marks include model numbers or date codes (see chart on next page).

Large, poorly spaced, badly proportioned or awkwardly located marks are always suspect. Original engraved marks are usually only three-sixteenths to one-quarter inch tall on even the largest pieces. All acid-etched Tiffany marks on art glass are fakes.

Authentic LCT monogram paper label. Embossed gold printing on green background on white paper. Original labels are only about 3/8-inch diameter. Shown here on polished pontil with authentic engraved mark. Note the small size of original engraved letters (arrow).

Tiffany Glass Date codes

These are typical date codes found on Tiffany glass. Marking was very sporadic. Use these dates only as rough guides. There are many exceptions. Marks before 1892 used numbers only. After 1893, letters were added before the numbers as prefixes. Letters were added after the number as suffixes after 1906.

	#1 to #9999 = 1892-1893	sf- F 1911
	pr- A or B 1894	sf- G 1912
pr=prefix	pr-C or D 1895	sf- H 1913
sf=suffix	pr- E or F 1896	sf- I 1914
	pr- G or H 1897	sf- J 1915
EXAMPLES:	pr -I or J 1898	sf- K 1916
E-2458=1896	pr- K or L 1899	sf- L 1917
789-Q = 1922	pr- M or N 1900	sf- M 1918
	pr- O or P 1901	sf-N 1919
	pr- Q or R 1902	sf- O 1920
	pr- S or T 1903	sf- P 1921
	pr- U or V 1904	sf- Q 1922
	pr- W or Y 1905	sf- R 1923
	sf- A 1906	sf- S 1924
	sf- B 1907	sf- T 1925
	sf- C 1908	sf- U 1926
	sf- D 1909	sf- V 1927
	sf- E 1910	sf- W 1928

Cameo Glass

New mold-blown 6½-inch vase with raised glass
Gallé signature. Polished blue raspberries on yellow.

Reproduction cameo glass marked Gallé has been in the market since at least 1993. Until recently, it was thought that Gallé was the only significant mark appearing on cameo reproductions.

Since mid-1999, however, marks from other well known original cameo glass manufacturers have been appearing on reproductions of both French and English cameo glass. These include Thomas Webb, Daum Nancy, Richard, Legras, Muller and Schneider.

Many buyers–believing cameo reproductions were marked Gallé only–never suspected other marks were being copied and paid

Group of cameo reproductions, 4 to 8 inches tall. Signed in raised cameo, from left to right, Richard, Thomas Webb, Muller.

significant prices for reproductions with names of other makers. This chapter reviews the many names now found on cameo reproductions and discusses techniques to detect the new pieces.

Many new marks are virtually identical to original marks in size, appearance and method of manufacture. Like the originals they copy, most new marks are in raised lettering formed by removing the surrounding background. There is so much variation among genuine marks that attempting to compare any one specific original mark to a suspected mark is of little practical value in separating new from old.

Generally, most new marks are placed in locations far more conspicuous than original marks. Most marks on reproductions of French cameo, for example, are located somewhere in the top half of the piece on which they appear. The vast majority of original marks were much more subtle and less obvious, typically appearing around the bottom of a piece usually in the lower third.

The position of the mark and the appearance of the mark are relatively easy to change, so signatures and marks alone are not a reliable test of age or authenticity. A better indication of age is revealed by examining the quality of the glass itself and how skillfully

Cameo Glass

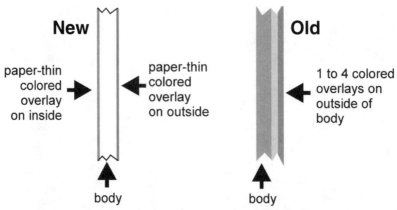

the glass was worked and formed into the final product.

The types of glass used for the great majority of cameo reproductions can be divided into three broad categories: those with single colored bodies; those with clear bodies; and those with spattered or mottled glass bodies. The best quality reproductions are those with multi-layers of single colored glass made in Eastern Europe, either the Czech Republic or Romania. Cameo reproductions with clear colorless bodies, spattered or mottled glass bodies are almost always made in China, Japan or Taiwan.

Types of new glass bodies

Many persons are surprised to learn the bodies of most cameo reproductions are clear colorless glass, not the colored glass they appear to be. In virtually all the new cameo from China, Japan and Taiwan, the color is only a paper thin colored glass flashing applied over a clear colorless body glass. The flashing is applied over both sides of the reproductions, inside and out. As light passes through the outer colored flashing, the color is diffused throughout the body, giving the appearance the body is also made of colored glass.

So how do they get the multicolored effects? In a way most casual buyers would never think to check. The area behind the pattern is ground out. By removing the colored flashing on the inside of a piece, more light streams through the pattern than the surrounding areas making the pattern appear as another color. You can usually feel the ground-out area by reaching down behind the pattern with your finger.

Another way to detect the new clear glass bodies is to hold

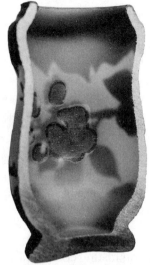

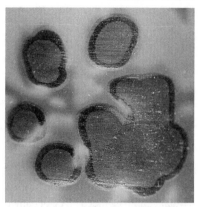

Close up view of grinding behind the design on inside of new cameo vase shown at left.

New cameo vase cut in half showing clear glass body and colored overlays on both inside and outside. Note grinding behind design.

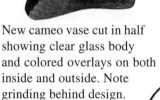

Many pieces of new cameo can be detected by feeling the inside wall with your finger. New pieces are ground out (concave) behind the design. Old pieces will be smooth.

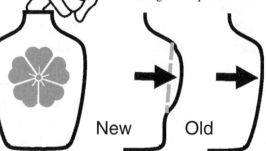

New   Old

a suspected piece under a strong light. In most pieces, the paper thin colored overlays are almost always nicked or accidently touched with the grinding wheel. The strong light inside will usually show spots of clear colorless glass that escapes through and nicks or scratches in the colored outer layer. This method requires close observation; most of the spots are typically only one-eighth to one-sixteenth of an inch.

Original cameo glass is typically constructed of a relatively thick

Cameo Glass

Mottled glass bodies like this are a virtual guarantee that a piece of cameo is new. As seen held against a strong light.

Streaks of contrasting color in the body glass are another sure warning sign of a cameo reproduction.

body of colored or clear glass with layers of contrasting color applied to the outside of the piece only. The only vintage cameo glass ground on the inside are one-of-a-kind, specially executed pieces. No standard production acid cutback vintage cameo glass was ever ground on the inside.

Another clue to new cameo is spattered and mottled glass. Bodies of the reproductions have colored opaque spots, streaks and swirls in translucent colored or colorless glass bodies. New spattered and mottled bodies typically have one or more solid colored overlays applied to the outside only (no colored layer on the inside). No grinding behind the patterns on the inside.

The great majority of original cameo bodies are virtually always a single color throughout the body, not spattered or mottled. The only authentic pieces frequently found with multicolored bodies were made by Daum. However, the glass in Daum pieces is generally so well blended together there is usually no clear line or boundary between pieces, bits or streaks of glass within the mottled body. In the reproductions with spattered and mottled bodies, it is easy to see individual and separate pieces of glass suspended in the body.

The best quality cameo reproductions have bodies of a single color glass almost identical to vintage originals. These pieces are generally from the Czech Republic or Romania. Quality is very high and many of these pieces are nearly the technical equal of originals and can be very difficult to detect.

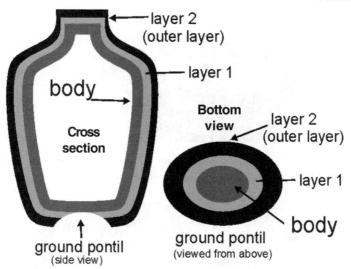

Ground pontils expose the various layers of glass in original cameo glass pieces. Reproductions rarely have ground pontils; see examples next page.

 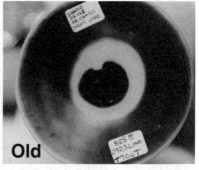

Typical new cameo base. Slightly depressed but without ground pontil.	Original cameo base; ground pontil reveals layers of different colors.

Typical rough base found on new cameo glass. No polished pontil.	Base of typical old cameo glass. Ground out multicolored pontil.

Cameo Glass

Sheared off rim on new cameo leaves rim flat. Old rims are fire-polished or wheel-ground with a rounded-over profile.

Cross-section of sheared flat new rim.

Cross-section of rounded-over old rim.

One of the ways to detect many of these better pieces is to check for a polished pontil. If a piece of cameo is marked with the name of a well-known English or French maker and it doesn't have a ground pontil, it is almost certainly a reproduction. The only general exceptions to this rule are miniatures (under 2") and some later Art Deco pieces which had the entire bottoms cut flat to give an angular geometric look.

Typical pontils in original cameo glass generally, but not always, show more than one color. This is because grinding the pontil will cut through the outer overlay(s) exposing each layer of glass. Most pontils on original cameo have a dull finish because they were already ground when the glass was acid finished. Some reproductions have slightly depressed areas in the bases, but these should not be confused with ground pontils.

It's also important to check the top rim. The top rim on many new pieces of cameo are simply sheared or ground flat. Virtually all top rims on vintage cameo are finely rounded over, not perfectly flat. The only exception to this rule would be an original piece that had a damage ground out of the top.

Although detail in originals is still better in general, the gap between new and old is closing fast, especially between East European copies and originals. Fine detail in old pieces was used to create a sense of depth. This was done primarily by manipulating the thickness of the overlays. Using multiple acid cuttings, a single thick overlay could actually appear multicolored because thicker areas would appear darker than more deeply cut areas. Designs on the majority of reproductions are sandblasted with the design controlled by a stencil. This often leaves noticeable awkward gaps formed by small tabs necessary to hold the stencil together.

When examining the glass in a suspect piece of cameo, keep these warning signs in mind. You probably are looking at a reproduction if: 1) area behind the pattern is ground out; 2) clear glass body is covered by paper thin colored glass flashing; 3) body is spattered or mottled glass; 4) no ground pontil and a sheared or ground flat top rim; 5) signature is unusually large and placed in a conspicuous place.

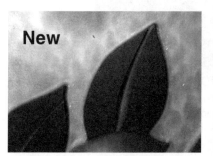

Simple background, sharp edges and broad cuts are typical of late 1980s cameo reproductions.

Great sense of depth and soft edges of typical original cameo glass.

By the late 1990s, detail on reproductions had greatly improved.

Cameo Glass
Signatures on cameo reproductions

Marks from virtually all original 19th and early 20th century cameo makers are being used on reproductions. Due to space restrictions, it is impossible to show all of the fakes. The examples shown here will give you a sample of what is in the market.

Marks alone are not a reliable test of authenticity. Details of glass construction, discussed in the previous pages of this chapater, are better tests of quality and age.

New raised glass signatures of Muller (left) and Schneider (right).

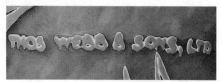

Raised glass "THOS WEBB & SONS, LTD" mark now appearing on reproduction cameo glass.

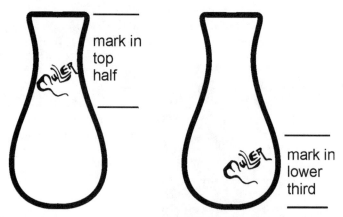

mark in top half

mark in lower third

New marks are much more prominent than originals. Most marks in original French cameo are in the lower third of an object. New marks are generally very prominently placed in the top half of pieces.

Reproductions marked Gallé and TIP were first made in Romania about 1993. It is very high quality and well made. TIP is Romanian meaning "type" or "in the manner of." TIP was a legal warning that the piece was not genuine Gallé, but "in the style of Gallé." Many times the TIP mark was explained away as a "student" of Gallé or a gallery that sold Gallé glass. Many of these pieces have had the TIP ground off, leaving only the Gallé mark.

TIP and Gallé marks are usually fairly close together as shown, right, on this typical TIP-Gallé mark. The exact position, size and appearance vary from piece to piece.

TIP tip TIP

Some typical TIP styles. No TIP mark was ever used on pre-1930 cameo.

New cameo lamp, fish decoration, marked Gallé. Made in China. Note large prominent signature on shade. Base also marked.

Cut Glass

New 14-inch cut glass pitcher from Turkey. Price: $45 from antique reproduction wholesaler.

New cut glass has been widely reproduced since the 1950s. It is so widespread at shows, auctions, shops and malls, that even experienced dealers and longtime collectors may have trouble telling new from old.

Reproduction cut glass is most frequently represented as being made during the American Brilliant Period, a span of years from about 1880 to shortly before World War I. During this time, American cut glass was the finest in the world. It was made of the highest quality glass and cut with the finest and most imaginative patterns. Nearly the entire surface was cut or decorated. New patterns and polishing techniques gave the glass never before seen sparkle and reflections which came to be called "brilliant." Unless specifically stated otherwise, all references in this

New 12-inch cut glass vase from Czech
Republic. Wholesale $55; 24% lead.

New cut glass vase from Czech
Republic

chapter to authentic cut glass will mean cut glass of the American Brilliant Period (ABP).

The focus of this chapter is on mass-produced reproductions made to imitate genuine cut glass in the $50 to $1,000 range. Individually made elaborate forgeries of rare and expensive cut glass valued at more than $5,000 are not included (although some of the same guidelines apply).

Separating old and new

The new mass produced cut glass can generally be detected by tool marks, composition of the glass (detected by black light), certain basic shapes, cutting techniques and evidence of normal wear.

• Wheel marks–Rough cuts on authentic ABP glass were made with *steel* or *iron* wheels with abrasives dripping down from a hopper above the cutting frame. These cuts were then smoothed at *stone* wheels and finely polished with wood and cork wheels. Eight inch bowls in relatively simple patterns might take a total of 10 to 20 hours of labor.

New cut glass, by contrast, is mass produced with high-speed *diamond* wheels. Embedded with industrial diamonds, these wheels cut 10 to 20 times faster than the old iron and steel wheels

Cut Glass

Close-up of grooves and rough surface made by diamond wheel.

Close-up of grooves and rough surface made by diamond wheel.

Close up of smooth cut in old glass made with iron or steel wheel.

that used dripping abrasives. In tests and demonstrations sponsored by the American Cut Glass Association, even elaborate ABP patterns were produced in only a couple hours time using diamond wheels. Most new glass cut with diamond wheels goes directly to polishing and finishing after its first cutting. The smoothing step used in ABP pieces is generally eliminated in present day reproductions.

Diamond wheels cut so quickly and easily that modern cutters can generally make even long cuts in one pass. This produces virtually continuous unbroken parallel ridges and grooves the length of the cut. The areas between the ridges also frequently have a *pebbled or textured* appearance. In the vast majority of new cut glass, these marks are never polished out and remain in the finished piece when it is offered for sale. These marks can be seen by the unaided eye but are easier to study with the aid of a magnifying glass or 10X loupe.

Old ABP glass cut with iron and steel wheels, on the other hand, may show some faint cutting lines but not the prominent ridges left by modern diamond wheels. Virtually all traces of tool marks have been polished out of ABP glass. If there are some faint lines present in ABP, they tend to be short and broken because they are the result of *multiple passes* with the old wheels, not long continuous passes as with diamond wheels.

Diamond wheels were not in existence until World War II when they were developed to speed up production of war goods. Any piece cut with a diamond wheel could not possibly be from the ABP and must logically have been made in the second half of the 20th century. While it is possible to polish out ridges left by diamond wheels, the added labor expense generally takes away any profit gained from selling the piece as genuine ABP. Besides, there are several additional guidelines to help detect new cut glass besides marks left by cutting tools.

• Teeth–Although we now admire ABP cut glass for its decorative value, we often forget its original function was to serve lemonade, hold sugar for your coffee or carry fruit salad. Authentic ABP cut glass logically had to withstand reasonable amounts of handling, washing and storage.

In contrast, almost all reproductions are made as decorative objects; after all, they're antiques, right? Their new construction and design are almost always illogical with the function or purpose of the original antique they seek to imitate. This is most obvious with the teeth in cut glass reproductions.

Whether tall, wide, short or deep, virtually all new teeth come to very sharp points. This style is a characteristic of new eastern European cut glass and was never used on ABP cut glass. Authentic ABP teeth are rounded or squared off. The edges of some ABP teeth are even beveled, tooth by tooth.

Teeth on original ABP are blunted for two very practical reasons: safety and appearance. Sharp points on teeth would knock off at the slightest touch with a ladle or serving spoon, sending

Cut Glass

Teeth on new cut glass are cut to a dagger-like point.

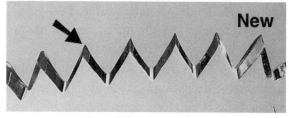

New

Pointed teeth on new plate, twice actual size.

New

Typical old ground teeth; twice actual size.

Old

Beveled edges on blunted teeth. Beveled edges are a sign of extra work, found on some but not all ABP.

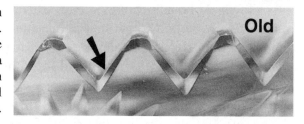

Old

chips of glass into the strawberries or ice cream. After a couple of dinners, the chipped and missing points would look a sorry sight indeed. Designers of original cut glass prevented those problems by eliminating sharp teeth. Even those original teeth that appear pointed are seen to be blunted when viewed under magnification.

• Details of quality–Other clues to a reproduction are found in the small details related to overall quality. Pinhead size and larger bubbles, for example, are rarely found in ABP cut glass, but are fairly common in new cut glass. Large bubbles in old blanks caused the piece to be discarded, or the pattern was

Poorly planned typical new cutting with pattern running out beyond rim.

deliberately cut over the bubble to hide it.

Patterns should also remain within logical boundaries. It's common in new cut glass to find overlaps in patterns where elements of one design intersect, overcut, or run over elements of another design. In many pieces, entire segments of the pattern are eliminated because they run off the edge of a blank due to poor planning. Such poor work wouldn't have been tolerated in the ABP. Grossly out-of-round circles, stars with wobbly irregular points, unbalanced patterns, and crossover cuttings are all signs of new work.

• Signs of normal wear–Another feature of genuine ABP cut glass hard to duplicate in new cut glass is normal wear. In other words, if a piece of glass is represented as being 100 years old, it should logically show some evidence of that age. Decanters, cruets, jars, etc., should show wear where the stoppers and

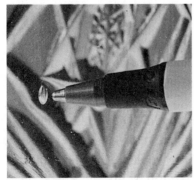

Above, large bubbles are common in new cut glass.

Poorly cut star overlaps other parts of the pattern.

Artificial wear

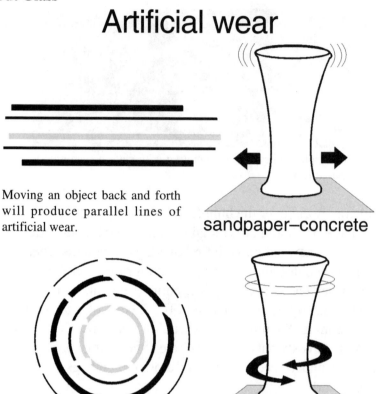

Moving an object back and forth will produce parallel lines of artificial wear.

sandpaper–concrete

Twisting an object back and forth on a rough surface will produce lines of artificial wear in concentric circles.

sandpaper–concrete

lids rest on the body. Serving pieces such as bowls, trays, relishes, etc. should show wear on *inside bottoms* as well as on their bases or feet. Even essentially stationary pieces such as vases and candlesticks had to be cleaned or dusted and should show some wear on the base or feet.

Normal wear appears as lines of *random* width, direction, depth, and length. Normal wear occurs over many years with each bump, knock or jiggle, an entirely separate event producing unique individual marks (a scratch, chip, scuff, etc.). The only source of repeated wear should be at a point of constant contact,

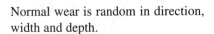

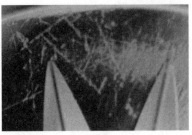

Normal wear is random in direction, width and depth.

Random lines of normal wear. Areas of heavy normal wear show up as frosted white patches.

such as a foot or a high spot on the bottom of a bowl, for example. Areas of repeated wear in genuinely old pieces tend to show up as frosted patches or spots. Under a 10X loupe, you can see that even these areas are formed by many (tiny) random scratches

Artificial wear, because it is generally applied all at one time, almost always shows a definite *pattern*. Moving an object back and forth over a rough surface, for example, produces a pattern of parallel lines. Twisting an object produces a pattern of concentric circles. Tools, such as a wire brush or rough grinding wheel, will also leave a definite repeated pattern. If the majority of scratches seem to run the same direction, are about the same depth and run about the same length, it is almost a sure sign of artificial aging.

Although it is possible to find a genuinely old piece that has been "put away" and shows no wear, it is not likely.

• Shapes– Genuine ABP cut glass was made in literally thousands of shapes. Rather than try to learn authentic shapes, you would be better off learning to recognize a few shapes that are almost a virtual guarantee of a reproduction.

Probably the easiest shape to recognize as new is the so-called "helmet-shaped" one-piece basket. This is a European shape virtually unknown during the ABP. It is, however, almost the only basket shape shown in antique reproduction wholesale catalogs since the late-1940s. Authentic ABP baskets were made of *two pieces* of glass with a *separate* handle *applied* to the body.

Cut Glass

New

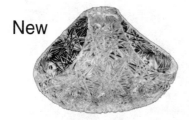

New

Old

One-piece helmet-shaped baskets are almost exclusively a European shape. Only a handful of orignal ABP basksets are known in this shape. Any basket in this shape is virtually guaranteed to be a reproduction. Shown here in clear (top) and ruby overlay (below).

Almost without exception, ABP baskets are made of two pieces as shown here. There is a separate body below and a separate *applied* handle. The applied handle is just another example of the extra work and detail that went into genuine ABP cut glass, as opposed to the quickly-made modern cut glass.

Only a handful of authentic ABP baskets are known to exist in the helmet shape; they are exceedingly rare, costing thousands of dollars. As a general guideline, *all helmet-shaped* cut glass baskets should be considered new.

Another shape that must be on the wholesalers' bestseller list is the so-called "biscuit jar." Like the helmet basket, this veteran has appeared unchanged in the catalogs since the late 1940s. It is basically a straight-sided cylinder 8 to 10 inches high with a flat lid. The lid is fitted with a solid glass knob; an inner rim fits down into the base. This shape is a modern design; no similar shape in these large dimensions was ever used during the ABP.

The closest similar shape in genuine ABP cut glass was the *cigar jar*. Although these old jars are also straight-sided

There is no old ABP counterpart to new straight sided 8- to 10-inch "biscuit" jars with solid glass knobs.

The only remotely similar old jar shape is the cigar jar. However, all these jars have *wide hollow* knobs, not solid knobs.

cylinders, their knobs are *wide* and *hollow,* not round and solid like the new biscuit jar. In addition to clear, the new jars are widely available with colored overlays such as ruby, green, and cobalt.

• Blanks–In general, blanks of new cut glass show much more variation in thickness within a single piece than old blanks. Bases will be thicker than side walls, one side of a plate will be thicker than the opposite side, etc. This is especially noticeable in plates, tumblers, and some bowls; the smaller the size, the more noticeable the differences.

Many bottoms of new tumblers and plates are frequently twice the thickness as old blanks of similar shape. The center of the new thicker blanks also frequently, but not always, forms a high spot. There is some debate as to exactly why this occurs.

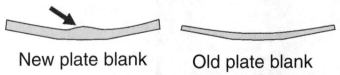

New plate blank   Old plate blank

Many new plate blanks are often twice as thick as old plate blanks. Most new plate blanks have raised centers (arrow).

Cut Glass

Some persons believe the extra thickness is a deliberate attempt to make new glass more closely resemble the weight of old. Others believe irregular thickness is only another sign of the poor quality typical of the new cut glass.

New tumbler. Sides are about one-eighth inch thick; base is about one-half inch.

• Marks–Never base your judgment of age or quality on marks. Fake and forged acid signatures and marks are widespread in cut glass and applied to both new and genuinely old but originally unmarked pieces. Fake marks on new cut glass can usually be caught by applying the guidelines on quality and construction details listed above. Catching new marks on genuinely old ABP cut glass is somewhat tougher.

One way to catch many forged marks on old but originally unmarked ABP glass is to examine the mark with a 10X loupe. If a piece is truly old, it will have some signs of wear. Many careless forgers place their new marks over normal wear. When acid is applied over an old scratch, the acid tends to flow through the scratch and fills the scratch. In other words, you'll have a frosted scratch (see illustrations opposite page).

• Black light tests–Virtually all authentic ABP cut glass fluoresces green with some yellow under long-wave black light. Small

Forgery of acid-etched Libbey mark. Acid etching fluid is applied with a rubber stamp. The stamp was made at an office supply store.

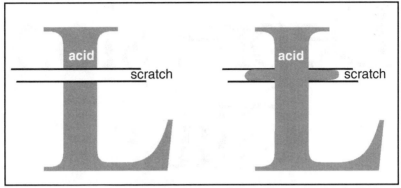

A genuine acid mark applied at the time of manufacture has logically been subjected to the same wear as the piece to which it was applied. Scratches from normal authentic wear pass through the mark as well as the glass (left). Therefore, any scratch passing through genuine marks should not be frosted...the scratch was made after the acid was applied. Many forged marks are applied to old but originally unmarked pieces. If a new acid stamp is applied over a scratch already on the old piece, the acid frequently flows into the scratch (right).

lights of low wattage may only fluoresce rims and bottoms; larger more powerful lights will fluoresce larger areas. The darker the room, the more obvious the fluorescence. Nineteenth and early 20th century cut glass from other countries may or may not fluoresce. Until the mid-1990s, many cut glass reproductions fluoresced pink, purple, or white or appeared to have no reaction. Cut glass made in Turkey since the mid-1990s fluoresces yellow sometimes with a slight greenish cast.

Although black light is an important test, it should not be your only test. Be sure to look at the shape, signs of wear, and overall quality before making a judgment of age.

The potentially confusing fluorescence of the Turkish glass proves that buyers must *never rely on only one test* to determine age. As many tests as possible should be used before making a judgment as to age.

The most important clues to a possible reproduction are: 1) grooves left by a diamond wheel; 2) lack of normal wear; 3) dagger-like teeth; 4) shapes that were never made during the ABP; 5) blanks with illogically thick areas; 6) obvious flaws in the blank and irregularities in patterns; and 7) incorrect fluorescence.

Depression Glass

Depression glass has been widely reproduced since the 1970s. Reproductions include rare patterns and colors such as Royal Lace cobalt blue, as well as everyday standards such as pink Cherry Blossom.

The most reliable way to catch the reproductions is to compare details in the molded pattern. Unfortunately, there is no one single test that can be used across all the patterns, colors, and shapes. Eliminating the fakes is pretty much a piece-by-piece process, requiring comparisons to the originals you'll find in the following pages.

That said, here are some very broad rules of thumb about Depression glass reproductions.

• Almost all new pieces feel slick or greasy to the touch due to a high sodium content in the glass formula that attracts moisture and dust.

• Many pieces will not function for the purpose they were supposedly created. New spouts often don't pour correctly; knobs and handles can be difficult to grasp.

• Color alone is not a good test of age. Colors change with the glass batch. The best test is to compare molded details.

• Some new glass has a strong vinegar-like odor.

It is very important to apply guidelines to only the piece being discussed. Don't assume the test for tumblers is the same for shakers. Don't assume the same test can be used for other patterns.

Adam

Original: Jeanette Glass Co., 1932 to 1934.

Reproductions: Made since the 1980s. Only the butter dish is known to be reproduced.

Turn the base upside-down. Notice the four arrows in original pattern point to the sides of the base. Arrows in reproductions point to the corners of the base.

Cameo   Ballerina/Dancing Girl

Glass in new shakers is about twice as thick as the old. Pattern in new very faint.

All toy and child-size Cameo is new. No originals were ever made in this size.

Original: Hocking Glass Co., 1930 to 1934. Also called *Ballerina* or *Dancing Girl.*

Reproductions: The only reported full-size Cameo

47

reproduction is the shaker. New shakers have been found in cobalt blue, green, and pink.

There are many pieces of new child- or toy-size Cameo. All original pieces of this pattern are full (adult) size. No original child sizes were ever made, so no toy or child sizes are authentic.

The majority of new Cameo child-sized pieces are made by Mosser Glass of Cambridge, Ohio. Mosser calls these pieces the *Jennifer Line* made in pink, yellow, and green. Child-size Cameo is also being made in Taiwan and China.

Cherry Blossom

Original: Jeanette Glass Co., 1930s.

Reproductions: Reproductions have been on the market since 1973. The majority of new pieces have been made in Japan, Taiwan and China. New colors include pink, green, red, transparent blue, Delphite, cobalt blue and a variety of iridized (carnival) finishes.

Reproduction Cherry Blossom has been made or is being made in the following known shapes:

> berry bowls, 8½-inch and 4¾-inch
> butter dish, covered
> cake plate (on three feet)
> cereal bowl, 5¾ inches
> child/toy sizes in cup, saucer, butter, sugar and creamer
> cup and saucer
> pitcher, 36-ounce all over pattern (AOP), scalloped foot
> plate, 9-inch dinner
> shakers
> platter, 13-inch, divided
> tray, 10½ inches, two-handled, sandwich
> tumbler, all over pattern (AOP), scalloped foot

Basic differences in new and old

As a general rule, most Cherry Blossom reproductions can be identified by poorly shaped cherries and leaves. Old leaves have a realistic appearance with serrated (saw-tooth) edges and veins that vary in length and thickness. New leaves commonly have perfectly straight and uniformly even veins that form "V"-shaped grooves. Original cherries usually give an illusion of a rounded three-dimensional ball-shaped figure; many new cherries appear to be only a flat circle. Differences between old and new patterns are generally greater in earlier 1970s reproductions than in more recent reproductions.

Several green reproductions do fluoresce. This includes a new butter dish, tumbler, cup, and several other shapes, so don't use black light as your only test of age.

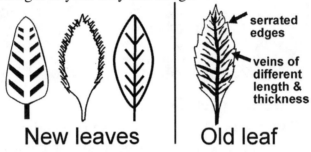

Original Cherry Blossom leaves look real. They have irregular saw-tooth edges and both large and small veins. Reproduction leaves usually have smooth or feathery edges. New veins are generally straight-sided "V"-shaped grooves or regularly spaced lines.

Berry bowl, 8½-inch

Made new in pink, green and cobalt blue (cobalt was not an old production color). Turn the bowl over and look at the bottom. There are nine cherries in the bottom of the old, arranged in groups of four, two and three. The nine cherries in the new bowl are arranged in groups of four, one and four. Edges of old leaves are serrated; new are smooth. (These tests are for the 8½-inch size only, not the 4¾-inch size.)

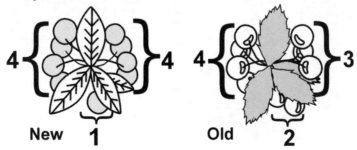

Berry Bowl, 4¾-inch

New 4¾-inch berry bowls were confirmed in summer 2002. Bottoms of the new bowls have very faint detail; bottoms of originals are very sharp (see examples below). Don't let anyone tell you these new pieces are made from "worn" or "reworked" molds.

New   Old

Butter dish (covered)

Child/toy size: This is a fantasy item; no original child's butter dish was ever made. All pieces now on the market are new.

Full size: There are at least two styles of reproductions. The 1970s reproduction has a very crude pattern in the base. A later reproduction has an improved pattern in the base, but the branch stops short of the rim. The original base has realistic leaves and cherries with a branch that extends from rim to rim.

All reproduction lids made so far have a smooth band separated from the rest of the lid by a single line. On old lids, the band is separated by two lines.

New

First reproduction base (left) has unrealistic flat cherries and fishbone-type veins in leaves. New lid (above) has single line around rim.

New

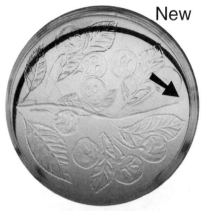

Second reproduction base (left), has improved pattern, but note that the branch stops short of the rim. Lid (above) has single line around rim.

Old

Original lid has two lines around bottom rim of lid. Original base has realistic cherries and leaves; the branch touches both sides of the rim.

Cereal bowl

The circle in the bottom of the new cereal bowls is 2 inches in diameter; the circle in the bottom of old bowls is 2½ inches.

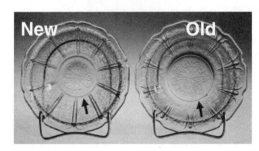

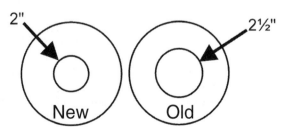

Cake Plate (on three feet)

There is a raised ring on the bottom side of the cake plate. On earlier reproductions, the pattern is misaligned where it crosses the ring (below left). Current reproductions have corrected this problem, and the pattern is now in alignment. However, the surface of the new cake plate is often pitted, and leaves and cherries are still poorly formed.

New

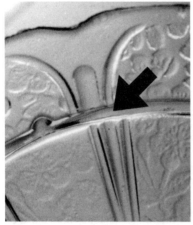

Old

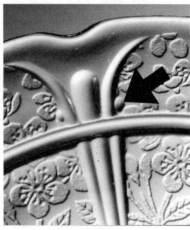

The pattern in the first reproductions of the three-footed cake plate is misaligned where it crosses the outer ring.

Pattern in original cake plate maintains alignment as it crosses outer ring.

Pattern is corrected in latest cake plate reproductions, but new glass is very rough with many bumps and pits.

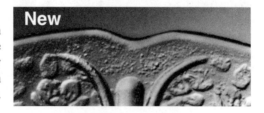

Cake plate turned upside-down to show raised ring. Arrow points to area shown in close-ups above.

Cup

The pattern in old cups is very realistic. Each old twig ends in a blossom, with the blossom touching the twig. In new cups, there is a considerable gap between blossoms and twigs. In old cups, the pattern fills almost the entire bottom; in new cups, the pattern is faint and weak. Leaves on old cups look like leaves; leaves on the new cups look like arrowheads or barbs.

New

Faint, crude pattern in the bottom of new cup.

Blossoms don't touch twigs. Leaves are not realistic (curved arrow).

Old

Strong, detailed pattern fills bottom of old cup.

Blossoms and twigs touch. Realistic leaves (curved arrow).

New   Old

Pitchers and tumblers

The all-over pattern (AOP), scallop foot pitcher and tumbler have been reproduced since the 1970s. The easiest way to tell old from new pitchers is to turn the pitcher over and look at the design on the bottom. Now, count the cherries: old pitchers have nine; new pitchers have only seven. Leaves and cherries on new pitchers are also poorly designed with lots of open space. Leaves and cherries on the old are realistic and cover almost the entire bottom surface. New pitchers are slightly smaller in size.

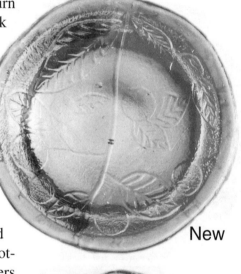

New

The easiest way to detect the new tumblers is to look at the lines around the smooth band in the top rim. Old have three bands; new tumblers only one.

Old

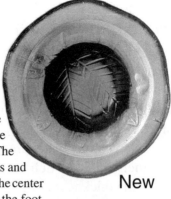

New

New Tumbler Style A

Introduced mid-1970s, continued to be made through 1990s. This style has only a single line around the smooth band in the top rim. The design in the foot has the typical new leaves and cherries. The pattern in the foot is mostly in the center with lots of open space around the edge of the foot.

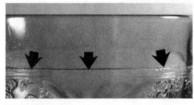

New

New Style B

This style does in fact have three lines around the top rim, but the lines are not continuous. They are strongest above the design panels but disappear completely over the rib between panels. The design on the foot is also very weak and usually found in the very center only. This style was made in pink, green, and Delphite Blue. Style "B" was made around 1980 and was reported when it first came out by H.M. Weatherman in *Price Trends 1981*.

Old

Original

Three distinct continuous lines separate the smooth band from the pattern below. The design in the foot is sharp and almost fills the entire base.

Plates and saucers

New dinner plates and sau-cers have a raised mold seam around their top rims. Seam lines in old were removed, leaving a smooth surface.

New dinner plates are about 1/4-inch thick, which is about twice the thickness of old dinner plates. New saucers are about the same thickness as old.

New   Old

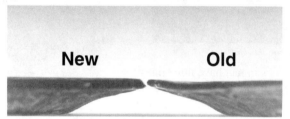

Comparison of thickness between new and old dinner plates.

Shakers

Only a handful of authentic shakers are known. The high price for originals has brought thousands of reproductions into the market.Top rims of old shakers (see Top Views) are scal-loped with curves. The top rims of new shakers appear like four separate squared-off tabs. Almost one-third of the new shakers are solid glass in the bottom. Old shakers have much less glass.

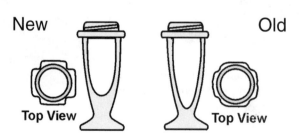

New   Old

Top View   Top View

Tray, divided

The new 13-inch divided tray is very similar to the original piece, with a good copy of the original pattern. The best clue to age is the thickness of glass in the bottom.

Glass in the bottom of new trays is nearly ½-inch thick. That means if the glass is thicker than a stack of five nickels or six pennies, the tray is new.

New

Sandwich tray, two handled

Hold the tray with the handles at the sides. In all new trays, the branch in the center runs left to right, in line with the handles. New leaves have unrealistic grooves for veins. New trays are somewhat heavier than old.

In the vast majority of old trays, the branch runs top to bottom, with the handles at the side. However, some documented old trays have been found with the branch running side to side. If in doubt, look at the leaves. All old trays have realistic leaves with naturally appearing veins and serrated edges.

New   **Old**

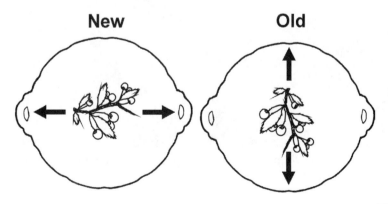

Child/toy-size Cherry Blossom

New pieces of child's Cherry Blossom were among the first pieces of Depression glass to be reproduced. The reproductions began appearing in the early 1970s.

There were only five shapes made originally in the child/toy size. These were: creamer, sugar, plate, cup and saucer. All the original shapes have been reproduced.

One of the most widely seen reproductions is a child/toy-size covered butter dish. All of these pieces are fakes; no child/toy-size butterdish was ever made in the original production.

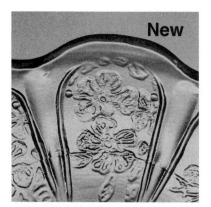 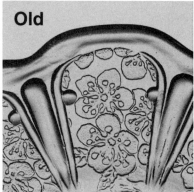

Pattern detail in child/toy-size plates. Old is sharp and distinct with natural appearance. Note clearly defined flower petals in old.

 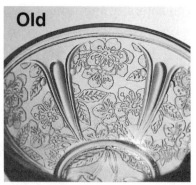

Details of cups. Old pattern very sharp and clear. Pattern in reproduction cups is blurred and has wavy lines.

New **Old**

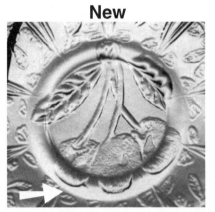

Detail of cup rings in saucers. The cherry and leaf pattern extends out beyond the raised cup ring in new child/toy-sized saucers. The entire pattern is within the cup ring of old saucers.

Floral (Poinsettia)

Original: Jeannette Glass Co., 1931 to 1935. Original colors include amber, crystal, delphite, green, pink, red, and yellow.

Reproductions: New shakers are appearing in cobalt blue, dark green, pink and red. Shakers in cobalt blue, dark green and red are obvious reproductions because those colors were never used in original production. The new pink shakers, however, are very close in color and pattern to the originals.

The easiest difference to detect is in the way the glass threads are molded. In old shakers, there is a ¼-inch horizontal gap

New **Old**

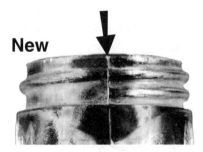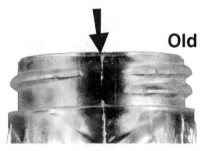

Threads in new shaker cross the mold seam.

There is a ¼-inch gap in old threads where they cross the mold seam.

Depression Glass

between the raised threads along the mold seam. No old thread goes over this mold seam. In the new shakers, there is no horizontal gap between the threads at the vertical mold seam. The new threads cross over the vertical mold seam. The threads look slightly different on the front and back sides of both new and old, and each is illustrated below.

New shakers also tend to have more glass at the bottom, but this can vary. Checking the threads is a more reliable way to catch the new pieces.

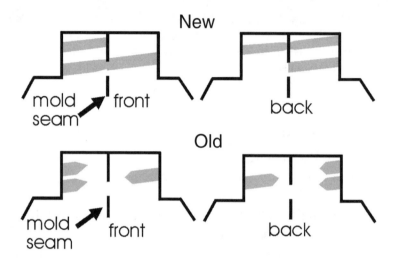

New

mold seam   front   back

Old

mold seam   front   back

Florentine #1 (Poppy #1)

Original: Hazel Atlas Glass Co., 1932 to 1935.

Reproductions: This pattern has been reproduced in shakers in a number of colors. The best test is to look at the flowers. The original flower has seven distinct blossoms; the reproduction appears as a single large blossom.

New   **Old**

Florentine #2 (Poppy #2)

Original: Hazel Atlas Glass Co., 1932 to 1935.

Reproductions: Cone footed 7½-inch pitcher and 4-inch footed tumbler. New colors include a blue often mistaken for the rarest original color, which is ice blue.

New   Old

Center of foot on new tumbler is plain. Old base has pattern

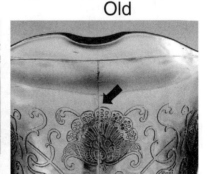

New   Old

In the new pitcher, the pattern meets at the mold seam under the pour spout.

In the old pitcher, the pattern is divided in half (split) by the mold seam under the pour spout.

Iris (Iris and Herringbone)

Original: Jeanette Glass Co. The original factory name was Iris, but now commonly called Iris and Herringbone. First made in clear crystal 1928 to 1932. A limited number of shapes were made in crystal in the 1950s and vases were produced into the 1970s.

Reproductions: Include beaded edge 4½-inch berry bowl, coaster, 6½-inch footed tumblers, candy dish and 10-inch dinner plate.

There are several key features that separate old and new 4½-inch berry bowls. Perhaps the most obvious is the pitted frosted surface of the new flowers (see opposite page). This frosted surface is on the new flowers only; not any other part of the new bowl. The surface of original flowers (see opposite page) is perfectly smooth and clear.

The new candy dish is easy to spot because there is no rayed pattern in the bottom of the piece. Vases were reissued in the 1970s and are the same as vases produced in earlier years.

Generally, molding on originals is much sharper and crisper. This means the original Herringbone pattern catches more light and sparkles and appears brighter than on the reproductions.

Berry bowl, 4½-inch

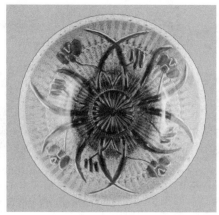

Original 4½-inch beaded edge Iris berry bowl, clear crystal.

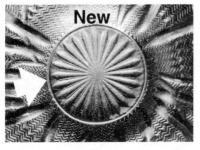

The new 4½-inch berry bowl has a distinct circular line around the hobstar in the bottom. It is wide enough to run a fingernail into as viewed from outside bottom.

The hobstar in old bowl is not surrounded by a line. A circle is formed where the Herringbone pattern stops. There is no impressed line.

Coaster

The Herringbone pattern in all old coasters has a sharp border for a full 360 degrees around the iris in the center. The pattern in new coasters is weak overall but completely missing in the lower left (6 o'clock to 8 o'clock). Coasters shown as viewed from above.

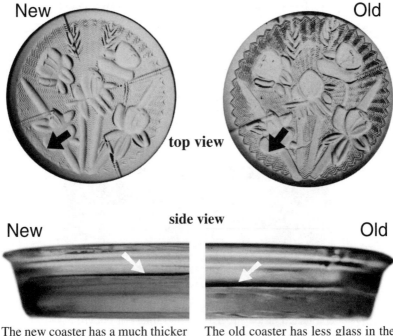

The new coaster has a much thicker bottom, about 1/4-inch thick.

The old coaster has less glass in the bottom, not quite 3/16-inch thick.

Depression Glass

Plate, 10-inch dinner

The outermost edge of the pattern in new 10-inch dinner plates is formed by an unbroken ring of sharp points with the point facing the outer rim of the plate. The outermost edge of the pattern in old plates is a series of groups of points. The groups of points in old plates faces in towards the center of the plate.

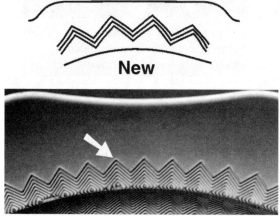

The pattern of new plates ends in perfectly connected saw teeth, or pyramid shapes, pointing towards the outer rim.

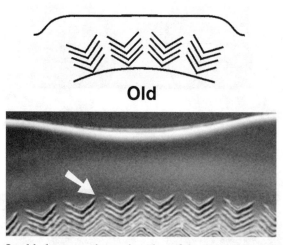

In old plates, angles at the edge of the pattern are not connected at the tip. The angled lines, or chevrons, point towards the center of the plate.

Tumbler, 6½-inch footed

Look at the rays around the base of the tumbler. In new tumblers, there is a distinct gap between the end of the ray and the ring around the center of the foot. In the old tumbler, the rays extend to the center ring. New rays are also much sharper to the touch than old rays.

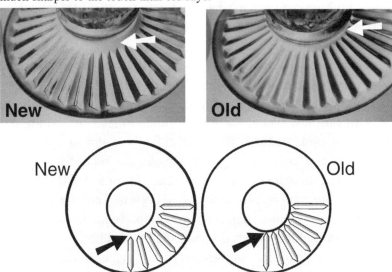

The pattern on both old and new 6½-inch footed tumblers appears twice around the sides–once on the front and again on the back. The pattern is identical front and back in the old tumbler. The pattern in new tumblers is different from front to back.

Reverse side of pattern in new tumbler does not have the pointed leaf.

Pointed leaf behind flower bud is on both sides of old tumbler.

Madrid

Original: Federal Glass Co., 1932 to 1939.

Reproductions: There are two groups of modern Madrid. In 1976, Federal changed the pattern name to Recollection and began making new pieces. The first new pieces of Recollection were easily identified because pieces were dated in the mold with the year "1976."

But then, Federal Glass went bankrupt, and the rights to the design were acquired by Indiana Glass. Indiana Glass discontinued dating the glass and that has caused problems for collectors.

So far, new pieces have been made in five colors: amber, blue, clear, pink, and teal. Teal, a greenish-blue almost aqua color, is the only new color not originally made. The other four colors– amber, pink, blue and clear–were all used for the 1930s Madrid.

The situation is further confused because Indiana Glass has also introduced many shapes never originally made, such as the cake stand, goblet, covered candy dish and others. Don't mistake these items for rare or unlisted pieces just because you can't find them in a book.

Known shapes reproduced to date include: covered butter dish, dinner plate, grill plate, luncheon plate, creamer, open sugar, shaker, cup, saucer, goblet*, vase*, hurricane lamp*, pedestal covered candy dish*, footed cake stand*, footed fruit stand/dish*, 9½-inch bowl, 10-inch oval vegetable bowl, 7-inch soup/cereal bowl, and candleholder. (Items marked with an asterisk* are shapes never made in original 1930s Madrid.)

The Madrid pattern has been renamed Recollections and is marketed by Indiana Glass Co. Many new shapes are similar to the 1930s Madrid, including the butter dish shown here in the new box.

New shapes

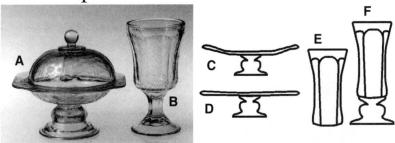

Some of the new Recollection shapes never made in the original Madrid: pedestal candy dish (A), goblet (B), pedestal fruit stand (C), pedestal cake plate (D), flat sided tumbler (E), flat sided vase (F). Several new pieces are made by simply joining two shapes. The new cake plate is made by joining a plate with the candleholder; the vase is made by joining a new tumbler and candleholder; the candy dish joins a butter dish and candleholder.

Candleholders

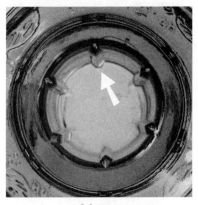

New	**Old**
Top view of socket in new candleholder. There are ridges around the new candle socket.	Top view of socket in old candleholder. The inside of old candle socket is smooth, no ridges.

The overall shape of new and old candleholder is the same. Only the socket is different.

Butter dish

Knob on lid of new butter dish has *vertical* mold seam

Mold seam on old butter dish knob runs *horizontally*.

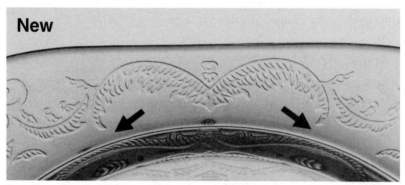

Top view, new butter dish base. Tips of the decorative scroll stop short of the rim in which the lid rests.

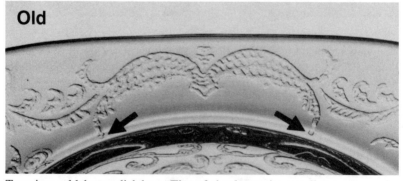

Top view, old butter dish base. Tips of the decorative scroll stop pass under the rim in which the lid rests.

Creamer

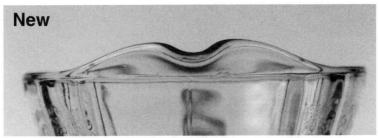

Spouts on new creamers *rise above* the top rim.

Spouts on old creamers *dip below* the top rim.

Cup and sugar

The easiest way to detect new cups and new sugars is to examine how their handles joined the bodies. Looking at the inside of a sugar bowl or cup, the lower part of old handles forms a tear drop shape. The same area in new handles form an oval.

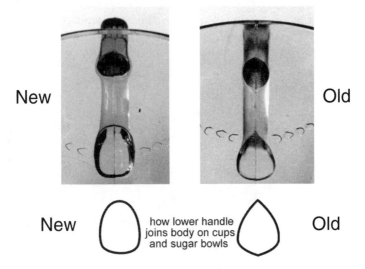

New   Old

New   how lower handle joins body on cups and sugar bowls   Old

69

Plates, grill

New grill plates have only two sections or compartments. Original grill plates have three sections.

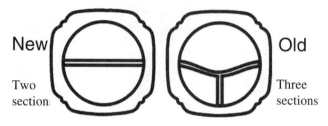

New — Two sections

Old — Three sections

Plates, dinner

Dinner plates can be dated by examining the beaded swag under the scroll design in the corners.

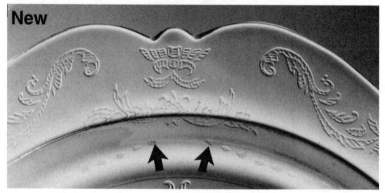

Beaded swag has a ½-inch or more gap under scroll in corner.

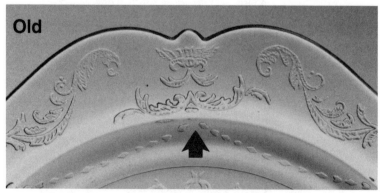

Virtually no gap in beaded swag on old dinner plate.

Shakers

The new shaker is a squat barrel shape. There are two styles of old shakers. Both are *slender, vertical shapes*: one footed, the other with a flat bottom.

Soup/cereal, 7-inch bowl

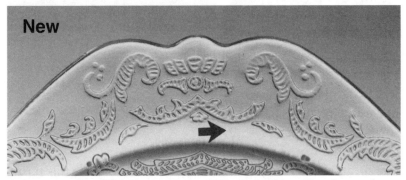

The scroll design in the corner of the new 7-inch soup/cereal bowl *stops* almost one-quarter inch away from where the bowl begins.

The scroll design in the original 7-inch soup/cereal bowl goes up to the edge of where the bowl begins.

Mayfair (Open Rose)

Original: Hocking Glass Co., 1931 to 1937.

Reproductions: Mayfair has been widely reproduced since 1977. Many reproductions are in colors that were never made in the 1930s. The best way to separate old from new is by studying differences in pattern details.

Cookie jars

Original cookie jars were made in pink, blue, green and yellow. Reproductions have been made in many colors, including pink, green, amethyst, cobalt blue, and red.

The easiest way to identify a new cookie jar base is by examining the bottom. If you turn an old jar upside-down, you'll find a raised circle created in the manufacturing process. This circle measures about 1¾ inches in diameter but can vary in

Mayfair cookie jars

size. Bottoms on new jars are smooth and do not have this raised circle.

Bottom of new Mayfair cookie jar is smooth and flat; no molded ring like old jar.

Bottom of old Mayfair cookie jar has a molded circular ring about 1¾-inch diameter.

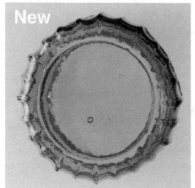

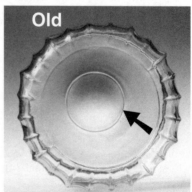

The knobs on old lids are eight sided. It has four long sides connected by four short lines in the corners; new lids have only six sides. You can remember the difference by comparing the shape of the knob to the shape of the lid. The old knobs and old lids each have eight sides.

Another difference between old and new lids is in the scroll-like border on the sides of the lid. On old lids, this line is nearly flat on either side of the center "V." In new lids this line has curves on either side of the center "V."

It has generally been thought that old green jars fluoresce

Knobs on cookie jar lids-top view

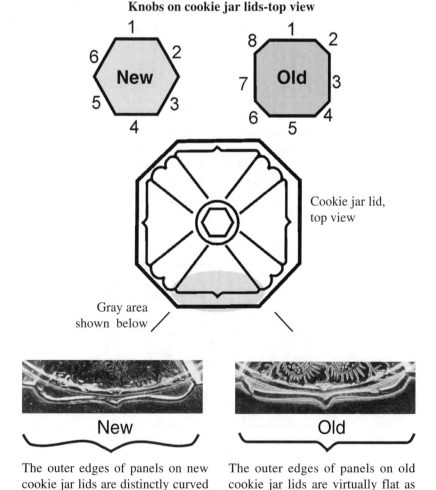

Cookie jar lid, top view

Gray area shown below

New

Old

The outer edges of panels on new cookie jar lids are distinctly curved as they extend out from the center.

The outer edges of panels on old cookie jar lids are virtually flat as they extend out from the center.

under long wave black light and new green jars do not. This may have been true once but may not be true now. We have several recent samples of new green Depression glass that does fluoresce. So, use the black light test with caution.

Pitcher, 6-inch

New

Old

New spout extends about 1/2-inch beyond the body. The space between new handle and pitcher body is very tight, hardly large enough for fingers to pass through. New pitchers do not have a circular mold mark in the base.

Old spout nearly flush with body. The opening between the old handle and pitcher body is comfortably wide enough for fingers. All old 6-inch pitchers have an offset circular mold mark in the bottom, about 2½-inch diameter.

Tumblers, 3½-inch

no band

raised vertical ridges

smooth band

pattern inside panels

New   Old

Old tumbler has a smooth band around the top rim. In old tumblers, the flower pattern is inside a panel. New tumblers are missing the smooth band and the flower pattern is surrounded by raised ridges, not set in a panel.

Shaker

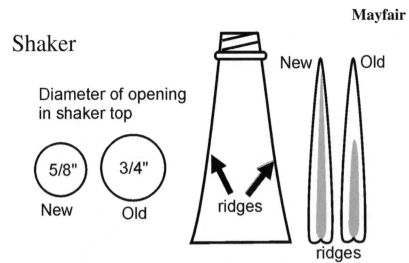

Diameter of opening
in shaker top

5/8" New   3/4" Old

New   Old

ridges

ridges

The inside opening of old tops is 3/4-inch diameter; opening in new tops is only 5/8-inch diameter. The ridge on the four corners in old shakers goes about halfway to the top; ridge in new goes all the way to the top.

Shot glass, 2½-inch

New   Old

On the original shot glass, there are two small branches on the flower stem. There are no branches on the flower stem of the new shot glass. The glass in the bottom of new shot glasses is also thicker than the glass in the bottom of old shot glasses.

Miss America

Original: Hocking Glass Co., 1935 to 1938.

Authentic colors include crystal, green, ice blue, jadeite, and ruby red.

Reproductions: Miss America has been reproduced since the late 1970s. Reproduction shapes include water pitcher (without ice lip), 4½-inch 10-ounce tumblers, covered butter dish and shakers. New colors include crystal, cobalt blue, green, ice blue, pink, and red/orange.

You can use your black light on clear pieces. Original clear crystal Miss America will fluoresce yellow-green under longwave black light. The new clear will not. Be sure to apply the guidelines below only to the specific shape discussed.

New

New butter dish

Detail of pattern

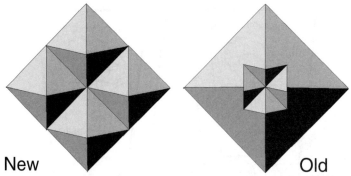

New   Old

In general, the pattern diamonds on original Miss America are sharper than on the reproductions. The original pattern is composed of a four sided pyramid with the top removed. On reproductions, there is much greater space between the points at the top of the pyramid, giving the appearance of four separate pyramids.

The pattern on originals also tends to remain sharp and clear even when it follows curves, changes from large to small, and where the pattern meets handles, rims, and bases. The pattern in reproductions frequently becomes distorted, fades out, or becomes blurred around curves and changes in size.

Butter dish

There are at least two styles of new butter dishes. Turn over the lid and look through the base of the knob. In all original lids, the knob will appear as a clear, sharp, multifaceted star. The first knobs appear as a blob-shaped star; the second reproductions appear as a flower-petal star (see photo at right).

Second style reproduction knob from inside of lid.

Also use your finger to check the area directly below the knob inside the lid. Glass bulges downward (convex) on new lids; glass bends towards the knob (concave) on old lids.

Base of butter dish knobs

New   New   Old

As seen from inside lid.

Butter dish knobs

Glass directly below the knob on all new lids bulges downward (convex). Glass under all old lids bends towards the knob (concave).

Shakers

The main difference between old and new shakers is the glass thickness and shape of the glass inside the shaker. On new pieces, the open area is only about 2 inches deep and is almost

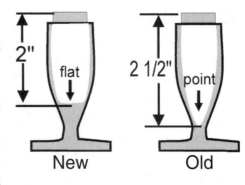

always flat at the bottom. Open areas in original shakers are about 2½ inches and taper to a point.

Tumblers

All old tumblers have four vertical mold seams evenly spaced around the sides. Old tumblers also have a mold seam around the entire bottom rim. The bottom of original tumblers is recessed less than ¼ inch. There are at least two styles of new tumblers.

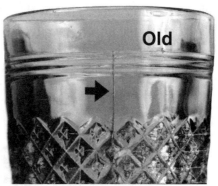

Old tumblers have four vertical mold seams.

All old tumblers have a mold seam around the entire bottom rim (arrow). The bottom on old tumblers is recessed only slightly, less than ¼ inch (pencil).

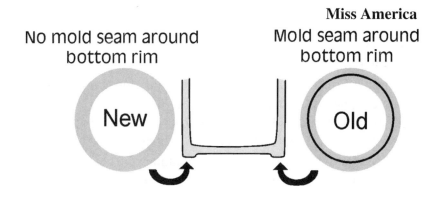

No mold seam around bottom rim

Miss America
Mold seam around bottom rim

New | Old

Tumblers
cross sections of bottoms

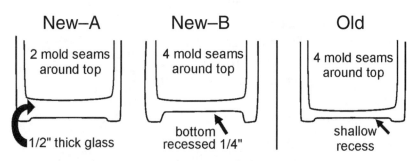

New–A | New–B | Old

2 mold seams around top

1/2" thick glass

4 mold seams around top

bottom recessed 1/4"

4 mold seams around top

shallow recess

Comparison of glass thickness in the bottom of tumblers and how deeply the bottom is recessed below the rim.

Water pitcher

On old water pitchers, there is a bulge or "bump" in the rim directly above the handle. This feature is missing on the reproduction pitchers. So far, only the regular water pitcher has been reproduced; the ice lip water pitcher has not been copied.

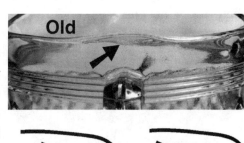

Old

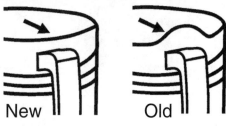

New | Old

Princess

Original: Hocking Glass Co., 1931 to 1935. The majority of original Princess was made in green, pink, topaz and apricot. Some originals were made in blue, but this color is very rare. Original blue Princess has been found in only four shapes: cup, saucer (identical shape as sherbet plate), cookie jar, and grill plate.

Reproductions: New Princess includes the covered candy jar, 9-inch plate and shakers. Reproductions are available in a wide range of colors including blue.

Candy jar, covered

Old

The easiest way to detect the new bases is to look at the foot. The underside of the foot of original jars is divided into panels that radiate out from the center. The foot of the new jars is smooth and plain.

New lids are best detected by viewing the knob from directly overhead. There are four straight-sided sections to new knobs; only two straight-sided sections to old knobs. The flat disc on which the knobs rests is 2 inches in diameter on old lids; only slightly over 1¾ inches in diameter on new lids.

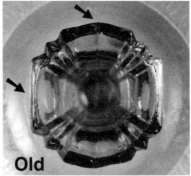

New | Old

Looking down from above, old knobs have two larger sections that are straight-sided and two larger sections that are curved. All four of the larger sections of new knobs are straight-sided.

New

Old

Candy jar base as seen from bottom. Original base is rayed with panels. The new base is plain without panels.

Plate, 9-inch

Nine-inch dinner plates in blue have been reproduced since early 1998. No original nine-inch plate was ever made in blue. Any plate in blue is therefore a reproduction.

New plates have an obvious mold seam around the rim; old plates do not have a raised

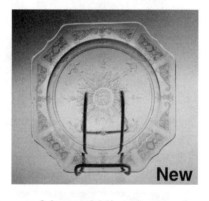

New

seam. Some old plates do have a very faint mold line that can be seen but it is virtually never raised high enough to be felt. Mold seams on the new are obvious and easily detected. Don't do just

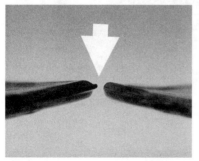

New plates have mold seam around edges. Old plate rims are smooth.

a spot check; examine the entire rim.

The point of the scallop in the corner is sharper in new plates than old plates. Scallops in old plates meet in a gentle bump. New scallops dip deeper and form a sharper point where they meet.

"Beads" at the tips of

Depression Glass

scrollwork in old plates have a texture; the new beads are plain. This is best seen holding the plates up to the light.

Scallop in corner of new plate meets in sharp point. New scallops dip deeper than old.

Scallops in old plates meet in a gentle bump. The scallops are more shallow than scallops in new plates.

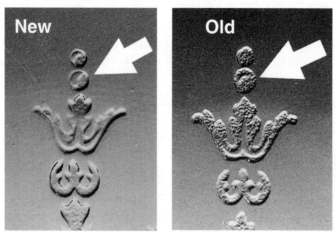

The beads around the scrollwork pattern in original plates are textured. Beads in new plates are smooth.

Royal Lace

Original: Hazel Atlas, 1934 to 1941.

Reproductions: Three shapes in blue Royal Lace are now being reproduced: the cookie jar, 9-ounce tumbler, and 5-ounce juice glass. The juice glass was the first to appear, showing up in the summer of 1996. The jar and larger tumbler began appearing in mid-1997. In 1998, the cookie jar started to be made in other colors including pink and green. Reproduction cookie jars sell for under

New Royal Lace cookie jar.

$15; both sizes of new tumblers are less than $4 each. Generally, new cobalt blue pieces are usually, but not always, a darker blue than originals.

Cookie jar

Pay particular attention to lids, as they are the most valuable part of the cookie jar. Genuine old jars are easier to find than old lids, so be alert for new lids on old jars.

All old lids have a single mold seam that splits the lid in half. There is no mold seam on the new lids.

Depression Glass

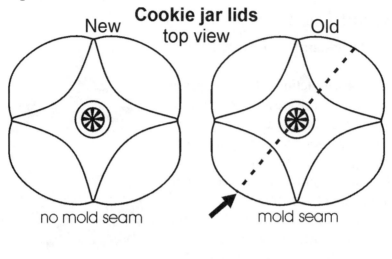

Cookie jar lids top view

New — no mold seam

Old — mold seam

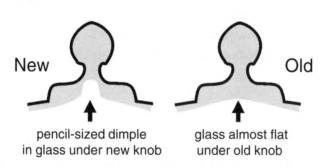

New — pencil-sized dimple in glass under new knob

Old — glass almost flat under old knob

The bottom of the base of the new cookie jar is smooth and plain.

The bottom of the base of the old cookie jar has a plunger mark.

New

Top of new pattern is flat, almost a straight line.

Old

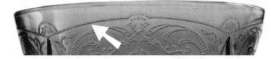

Top of original pattern is curved with pronounced dips.

New   **Old**

The glass in the sides and bottoms of the new tumblers is generally about two to three times as thick as originals.

Old 5-ounce juice glasses have a geometric design molded in the bottom (right). Bottoms of new juice glasses are plain (left).

Sandwich

Original: Hocking Glass Co., 1939 to 1964.

Reproductions: The bulbous cookie jar has been reissued by Anchor Hocking only in clear crystal. The smaller barrel shape is a new shape made overseas with the Sandwich pattern. It is made in a wide variety of colors.

The original Hocking cookie jar is 9¼ inches tall; imported reproductions are 7¼ inches tall; the Anchor Hocking reissue jar is 10¼ inches tall.

New   New   Old

Sharon (Cabbage Rose)

Original: Federal Glass Co., 1935 to 1939.

Reproductions: Include covered butter dish, candy jar, cheese dish, shakers, and sugar and creamer.

Butter dish

The best test for lids is to examine the knob. On old lids there is only about ¼ inch between the bottom of the old knob and the top of the lid. It's very hard to get your fingers under the

knob of an original lid. The gap under the knobs on new lids is about ¼ inch.

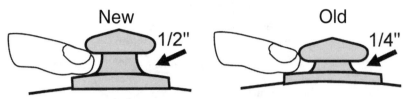

There is a much larger gap under the knobs of new lids. The gap under the knob in new lids is about ½ inch. The space under the old knob is ¼ inch.

The age of butter dish bases can be determined by the ridge in which the lid fits. The ridge in which the lid sets in old bases is very shallow, only about the depth of a dime. The ridge in new bases is much deeper, about three or more dimes in depth.

Candy jar

The easiest way to catch a new base is to measure the foot. The foot on reproductions is almost a full ½ inch smaller.

The lids require closer inspection. Begin by locating a mold seam in the raised circle under the knob. Check its alignment with the bars in the pattern.

The foot on the original base is 3¼ inches in diameter. The foot on the new base is considerably smaller, less than 3 inches in diameter.

Depression Glass

Top view
raised disc under knob

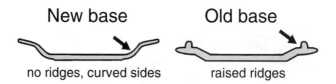

New   Old

mold seam

To test lids, look down on the lid from above. The seam line on the raised circle under the knob in old lids is aligned with two of the bars in the pattern; the seam in new lids is at an angle to the two bars in the pattern.

Cheese dish

The cheese dish, both new and old, uses the same lid as the butter dish. You can use the same test for butter dish lids to check the lids found on cheese dishes.

The key difference in cheese dish bases is that original bases have a raised molded ridge to hold the old lid. The new base is bowl-shaped without a raised ridge.

New base   **Old base**

no ridges, curved sides   raised ridges

Creamer and sugar

The knob in the old sugar lid has a mold seam around the middle. There is no seam around the new sugar knob. Look inside the bowls of the creamer and sugar where the handles join the bodies. In old sugars and creamers, the joint looks like a pointed oval or teardrop shape. In new sugars and creamers, it looks like a circle or very rounded oval.

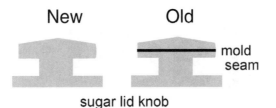

sugar lid knob

The knob in the old sugar lid has a horizontal mold seam around the middle. The new sugar knob does not have a horizontal mold seam.

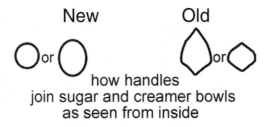

how handles
join sugar and creamer bowls
as seen from inside

Shaker

Each panel in the pattern has a single rose bud at the top of the panel. In old shakers, this is a realistic looking flower with three realistic leaves with veins.

In new shakers, the top flower cluster looks more like a four-bladed pinwheel than a realistic flower.

Jadite

Reproduction jadite made in China. From left: ball jug, tumbler, cannister. New jadite is also being manufactured in the United States.

Reproduction jadite, a pale green opaque glass, has been mass produced in both China and the United States since 1999. Some new pieces are shapes never made originally, or fantasy items, and are fairly easy to spot. But other new pieces are very similar to vintage shapes made by original makers such as McKee, Jeanette, Anchor Hocking and others. As we discuss these pieces, we are using "jadite" as a generic term to mean any opaque green glass. "Jade-ite" with a capital J and a hyphen, is the registered brand name of opaque green glass made by Anchor Hocking.

The great majority of original American jadite was made from the 1930s up through the 1950s. Although most original jadite was

Original packaging for one of the new jadite lines made in China. Front of salad plate box and side of box for covered bowl.

made for home kitchens– such as shakers, bowls, storage jars, etc.– original table settings were also made for home use, as well as institutional use in hotels and restaurants.

Most, but not all, new jadite is being produced in new molds. Although many new pieces from these new molds appear similar to originals, molded details can be used to separate new pieces from originals. No known new pieces have yet been made from original Jeanette molds; the only known original McKee mold in production is the double-ringed rolling pin.

In late 1999, Anchor Hocking and Rejuvenation Hardware attempted to reissue Hocking's Jade-ite restaurant line from original molds. Quality was so poor the project was abandoned. The only known shape to surface in any numbers from this experiment was a coffee mug, found in very limited areas of the United States. This cup

New

This new jadite rolling pin is made by Fenton. It has been sold through the Martha Stewart mail order catalog since late 2000 and possibly other distributors. Opaque pink was also available. This piece is made in the original 1930s McKee mold now owned by Fenton. Some new Fenton pins are slightly lighter in color, but color also varies in originals. Some, but not all, new pins show some streaking and swirls in the glass. The new Fenton pins are marked, but the mark is extremely hard to find. These pins are produced by blowing. During blowing and finishing, the Fenton mark is almost always badly blurred and sometimes disappears almost completely. The Fenton mark (shown above) on this new pin is virtually impossible to read. Original McKee jadite pins can sell for $1,000 and up. New pins are $40.

Jadite

New jadite batter bowl in swirl pattern. No old swirl pattern batter bowl in jadite is known. New batter bowl weighs in at slightly over 4 lbs., 8 inches dia., 5 inches tall.

Old

9779-9779½—4 x 4 in. Sq.
Ref. Jar & Cover—**C-G-P**

Above, new jadite jars from China in Crisscross patern, 5, 7, 9 inches. No vintage Crisscross jars were made in jadite. Original Hazel Atlas crisscross 4-inch jar shown upper left.

is permanently dated "2000" and is no problem to collectors.

Perhaps more confusing is new jadite made in genuinely old molds originally owned by Imperial, Westmoreland, Cambridge and others. Although those companies never made jadite glass ca. 1930-50s, new jadite coming from their molds often has the original company mark molded in such as Westmoreland. Some of these old molds date back to the 19th century and are for distinctly Victorian era shapes such as figural animal covered dishes, cake stands, salt dips, mustard pots and others. Such early shapes were never associated with original jadite produced in the mid-20th century, ca. 1930-50s.

One of the largest retailers of new jadite is the Martha Stewart

New jadite ball pitcher. Sold for $19.95 at the local Target store. New pitchers have been selling on eBay for up to $200 and more. Made in China.

New ball pitchers have a very obvious raised seam on handle as shown here. Seams on old pitchers are nearly perfectly smooth.

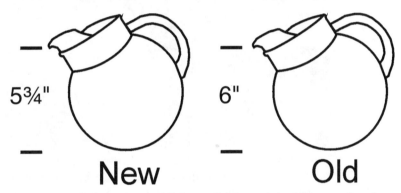

5¾" New

6" Old

New Pillar Optic pitchers are slightly smaller than originals. Base to lip of new pitcher is 5¾ inches. Original Pillar Optic pitchers measure 6 inches from base to lip.

mail order catalogs and online shopping sites. Almost all of the Stewart jadite is from L.E. Smith Glass Co. Some, but not all, of the Stewart pieces are permanently marked in the mold. Typical markings are "Martha by Mail" or "MBM" in raised letters or the raised capital letter S in block type or raised capital letter S in cursive, or script. This letter does not stand for Stewart, but L.E. Smith which makes new jadite for Stewart. New marks are reviewed at the end of this chapter. Fenton also makes jadite for Stewart (see page 91).

Another large distributor of new jadite is Rosso Glass. Many, but far from all, of its new jadite pieces carry a molded trademark of the letter R in a keystone. Much of Rosso's jadite is made in genu-

Jadite

New jadite round shaker, left, is a close copy of original jadite 6 oz. shaker by Jeanette, right. Sizes are virtually identical, about 4¼ inches tall. The key difference is the top, see close-up below.

Top of new shaker has a distinct neck between the shaker body and the beginning of the threads. Original Jeanette shaker has virtually no neck between threads and body. New shakers, $8 pair.

inely old molds. These include Westmoreland reamer shapes and animal covered dishes, Imperial Candlewick tableware and a wide variety of kitchen styled glass including mortar and pestles, toothpicks, shakers and other early shapes. Rosso also developed and is the leading distributor of new jadite with new decals.

Other new jadite can be found at Target department stores and Cracker Barrel, a national restaurant chain which sells antique reproductions in its lobbies.

Blue opaque glass

Blue opaque glass was made about the same time as jadite. The primary original makers of opaque blue glass were the same companies which produced jadite: Anchor Hocking, McKee and Jeanette. McKee's blue was sold under the trade name Chaline.

New jadite 4½-inch eight-sided shakers, holding about 3 ounces. Available with various colored decals and names of condiments. No vintage jadite shakers were ever made in this shape.

Jeanette called its blue Delfite. Anchor Hocking sold a line of blue dinnerware called Turquoise Blue, a name collectors frequently use to refer to all opaque blue by Anchor Hocking.

At the time of this writing, there are far fewer reproductions in blue opaque glass than in jadite. However, you need to be aware that blue is being reproduced and more could appear at any time.

General Guidelines

There is no one single test to reliably separate new jadite and opaque blue from vintage pieces. Generally, many new pieces have a slick, greasy feeling . Embossed detail is often poor and mold seams can be obvious. Pits and broken bubbles can also be a sign of the low quality glass commonly used to make new jadite. These flaws are more obvious in reproductions from China. New jadite by American makers such as Fenton tend to be quite good quality.

Currently, there are no jadite or opaque blue reproductions with old company marks. But that doesn't mean marks are a guarantee of age. Marks on both new and old jadite can be so faint as to be practically invisible, especially on the new Rosso and old McKee.

Your best tests of age are a close examination of glass quality, inspecting mold details of originals, and knowing what shapes were originally made in jadite or opaque blue.

The number of jadite reproductions keeps growing and it's impossible to show them all. We have selected a cross section of new examples most often confused with original shapes.

Jadite

New flat-sided jadite bodies by Rosso Glass. Available with various decals and names of condiments. Syrup tops also available. Shaker bodies faintly marked with the Rosso trademark on bottom.

Comparison of new flat sided shaker to old McKee and Jeanette square shakers. Top opening in Jeanette is only 1-1/4 inches, which makes it easy separate from the other two shakers which have top openings of 1-5/8 inches. New square shaker is closest in appearance to McKee original. Although a large percentage of old McKee shakers are marked, many marks are very faint and hard to see. The best test for age is to look at the bases and necks.

Original McKee jadite flat sided shaker has a horizontal mold seam near the base. New flat sided jadite shakers have a stepped raised base.

New 3-piece jadite shaker set with bulbous 3¾-inch shakers. Shakers available with names of many different condiments. No old counterparts in original jadite.

New 4¼-inch jadite butter tub. Made by Mosser Glass and permanently marked with M molded in base. See last page in this chapter for marks on new jadite.

New jadite 10-inch dia. cake stand. Marked in small raised letters "Martha by Mail" along bottom rim.

Jadite

9778-9778½—¼ lb. Butter &
Cover—**C-G-P**

9781-9781½—1 lb. Butter &
Cover—**C-G-P**

Original crisscross pattern covered butter dishes by Hazel Atlas.
Made only in clear, pink, blue and green transparent glass. Some
original crisscross butters were made with a fired-on pale green
paint but no originals were ever made in true jadite.

Lid of new jadite crisscross butter dish with word "Butter."

Complete new jadite crisscross butter dish.

New crisscross bases have tab handles; original crisscross bases
do not have handles.

New jadite butter dish made in original Candlewick mold.
Original Candlewick was never made in jadite.

New jadite one-cup measure made from
original Westmoreland mold.

New jadite 4½-inch tumbler. No
old pieces like this are known.

New jadite reamer from original Westmoreland mold. Original
reamer in this shape never made in jadite.

Jadite

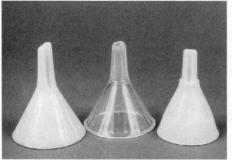

Jadite is one of the colors new glass funnels are made in. Left, jadite 4-oz.; center, 4-oz. vaseline; right, jadite 2-oz.

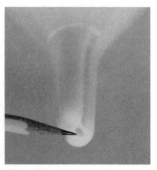

New funnel spouts are almost solid glass.

New jadite salts are made in a wide variety of shapes such as the heart and octagonal shapes shown here.

New jadite mortar with clear glass pestle. Mortars made in 2- and 4-oz. sizes. Some have decals with names of ingredients.

Laurel Fire-King

Original: Made by Fire-King, a division of Anchor Hocking glass, from 1951 to 1965. The most common colors are gray, peach lustre and ivory white. Ivory is less common and the rarest of all Laurel colors is Jade-ite, Fire-King's brand name for its pale green opaque glass, commonly called jadite. So far, the only confirmed authentic piece of Fire-King Jade-ite Laurel is an 8-ounce cup. No authentic saucer or other shapes in jadite Laurel are known.

Reproductions: At this time, only the Laurel jadite cup and saucer are reproduced.

There are several features that separate old from new. First, the new saucer does not have a molded cup ring. Both new cup and saucer have strange marks molded in the bottoms. So far, none of the new numbers match any Fire-King catalog numbers.

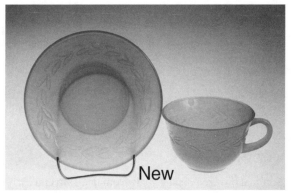

New Laurel cup and saucer in jadite.

New

Old

New Laurel saucers do not have a cup rim; the center of the plate is smooth.

Old saucers have a cup rim molded into the center. (No genuine Laurel saucers were ever made in jadite.)

New

Old

Mark on new Laurel saucer. Note that the numbers are reversed. Similar markings appear on new cup.

An authentic Fire-King mark on an original peach-colored Laurel saucer. (No genuine Laurel saucers were ever made in jadite.)

Jadite

New jadite animal covered dishes made from late 19th and early 20th century molds. No covered animal dishes were ever made in 1930-50s jadite.

Molded letter R in keystone of Rosso Glass.

Molded letter M mark of Mosser Glass.

Molded letter S mark of L.E. Smith Glass.

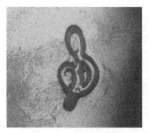

Molded script style letter S mark of L.E. Smith Glass.

Molded mark, Martha by Mail, appears on some pieces of new jadite sold by Martha Stewart. The Stewart jadite is made by a variety of manufacturers including L.E. Smith and Fenton.

Blue opaque glass

The new batter bowl is probably the most confusing piece in new blue opaque glass. Anchor Hocking made a very similar piece for its Fire-King line of Jade-ite and Turqoise Blue. All original pieces have the Fire-King trademark molded into the base.

New opaque blue glass batter bowl; 5 inches tall, 10 inches from spout to handle. New price $29; original blue Fire-King can sell for $250+.

New 12-inch dia. blue opaque glass ribbed bowl. A close, but not exact, copy of bowls in two Anchor Hocking patterns, Manhattan and Park Avenue. No original bowls in those patterns were made in opaque blue.

New four-piece setting in opaque blue similar to Anchor Hocking's Turquoise Blue Fire-King made 1956-58. Virtually all original pieces have Fire-King trademark molded on reverse. New pieces are unmarked.

Transfer Ware

Ironstone, Flow Blue, Blue Willow, Staffordshire

Many new pieces of blue transfer are copying unusual 18th and 19th century shapes. This is a reproduction of a rare shaving basin or barber bowl. The crescent shaped opening was held against a man's neck during shaving.

Flow Blue, Blue Willow, Ironstone and Staffordshire are all names of various wares decorated with underglaze transfer designs, the majority in cobalt blue. Although limited reproductions of all those types have been made for many years, new blue transfer ware now occupies entire pages of reproduction wholesale catalogs. Several American wholesalers each sell over 40 new shapes; one English supplier offers nearly 100 pieces.

Many new pieces have patterns identical, or at least very similar, to authentic 19th century patterns. These old-appearing patterns are applied to new pieces made in 19th century shapes

Blue Willow   **Flow Blue**   Ironstone

Reproduction transfers are virtually exact copies of old original patterns. Shown here are new Blue Willow, Flow Blue and multicolored ironstone.

such as tea caddies, toothbrush holders, pitcher and wash basins and others. Almost all the reproductions are also marked with symbols, trade names and words found in original 19th century marks.

In other words, it is increasingly common to find new blue transfer ware with original patterns on 19th century shapes with marks of well-known 19th century manufacturers. Knowing just a few basic differences between new and old will help you detect and avoid the great majority of these confusing copies.

New two-piece 12-inch high chamber pot, or slops bucket; 12-inch dia. Decorated with Flow Blue style transfers.

Transfer Ware

New 8-inch biscuit jar. Multi-colored transfer similar to original 19th century Ironstone.

New 18-inch platter, multicolored transfer.

We need to begin our discussion with a quick review of the transfer process. Decorating ceramics with printed transfers was developed in the middle of the 18th century as a substitute for expensive hand painting. Low cost, mass-produced transfer ware made decorated china affordable to middle-class families.

Here are the basic steps in transfer printing. First, the design is engraved into a sheet of copper which could either be flat

New 12-inch dia. plate with multi-colored transfer similar to original Ironstone.

New 8-inch Blue Willow sugar pot. Factory "distressed" background is tinted brown to suggest age and wear.

New 6½-inch food mold in Flow Blue. Inside of mold shown above. No old Flow Blue food molds are known.

or mounted on a roller. A separate engraving is fitted to each shape. Next, for Flow Blue, Blue Willow and similar wares, a blue pigment is deposited in the engraved design on the copper sheet. Transfer paper, which resembles tissue paper, is then pressed against the copper and the pigment is transferred to the paper. The paper with the pigment is now applied to the unglazed china. The paper is either soaked off in water or burned off at a low temperature leaving the design in blue. The china is now covered with a clear glaze and fired at high temperature. This basic system produces the characteristic blue underglaze decorations found in the blue transfer ware discussed in this article.

Why was blue used? Cobalt blue was the best and least expensive pigment capable of withstanding the high temperatures of 18th and 19th century kilns. Blue was also the color of

New Flow Blue two-piece reamer. No originals known.

Transfer Ware

Two new shapes in Blue Willow that have no old counterparts. Left, 5-inch hatpin holder; right, 4½-inch oil lamp. The new hatpin holder shape is sold with many different decorations and marks.

decoration used in expensive hand painted porcelain imported from China. From a distance, factory-made blue transfer resembled porcelain used by the rich and famous.

Under the broad generic term, "blue transfer," are many subcategories based on patterns such as Flow Blue, Blue Willow and Staffordshire Blue. All were made by essentially the same transfer process previously discussed. Blue Willow refers to a pattern based on a Chinese love story featuring the lovers on a bridge. Staffordshire, or Historical, Blue features patterns based on important landmarks, scenes from history or literature and commemorative events.

Of all the blue transfer ware, only Flow Blue was made slightly different than the other blue transfer wares. The ink and ceramic blanks of Flow Blue were deliberately designed to allow the ink to "flow," or spread, into the blank. The spreading ink creates the typical blurred or distorted Flow Blue effect.

While most of the new pieces are in blue only, some transfers are also available in multiple colors. Most of the multicolored transfers are similar to handpainted decorations found on

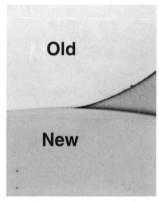

Virtually all new blue-transfer pieces have a blue or blue-green tint in the background. Originals are nearly white.

Wide unglazed standing rims are a virtual guarantee of a reproduction. This new rim averages about ¾ inch.

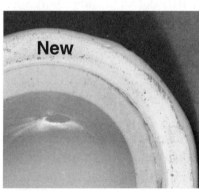

Typical new lid with unglazed rim. All surfaces of original lids are glazed.

authentic 19th century Ironstone, not necessarily blue transfer ware. The multicolored pieces are included in this article because they share many of the same new marks and are constructed in the same manner as the blue-only pieces.

With few exceptions, shape is not generally a very reliable clue to age. Many reproductions are copied from original 19th century shapes like chamber pots, toothbrush holders, sugar jars, and even rare shapes like the shaving basin shown at the beginning of this chapter.

The exceptions are the fantasy shapes, shapes and forms never made in the 19th century. Typical fantasy shapes include pieces like the Flow Blue reamer and Blue Willow oil lamp shown

Transfer Ware

The vast majority of reproductions with blue transfers are slip cast. This process leaves holes where new handles meet the new body. Originals were made with solid handles which do not leave holes. Some reproductions made since the mid-1990s also have solid handles so you need to use several tests for age.

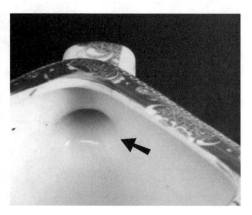

in this chapter. As a general rule, be suspicious of any shapes you can't find in a reference book.

Other exceptions are not so easily detected and require specialized knowledge. Original Ringtons Tea teapots, for example, are a low, oblong shape. New Ringtons teapots, the one shown here and a similarly shaped new teapot with a longer spout not shown, are unlike any original shape. Fortunately, the new Ringtons Tea items can be detected by other features such as glaze, construction and marks.

For example, virtually all vintage blue transfer wares are fully glazed. This includes inside and outside surfaces and top and bottom rims and rims of lids. This is logical for practical daily use–unglazed areas would permit water to get behind the glaze and destroy the surface. Dirt and grease could also penetrate unglazed areas and make dinnerware impossible to clean. Reproductions aren't made for practical use, though; they are made as "antiques," objects to be looked at, not used. That's why the vast majority of new blue transfer pieces are not glazed in critical areas.

With rare exception, most reproductions have broad, unglazed standing rims. It is not uncommon on even relatively small shapes, such as hatpin holders, to have unglazed rims ½- to ¾-inch wide. Despite having glaze over their new marks, the glaze does not extend to the new flat standing rims. The vast majority of originals are fully glazed and rest on very narrow, raised stand-

New examples

Reproductions of Ringtons Tea Blue Willow have been in the market for at least 20-30 years. The new mark above left is just one of many old-appearing marks that appear on various new jars and teapots, two of which are shown here.

Old examples

Original Ringtons Tea marks almost always include "Maling Ware" in the mark. It appears in script at the bottom of the example on the left. Almost all original Ringtons pieces also have an RT monogram mark under the lid.

ing rims seldom wider than 1/8 inch, sometimes only 1/16 inch on small items.

Unglazed rims on news lids are especially obvious. It is not unusual for new lids to have a ½-inch wide unglazed rim. The top rims in new teapot bodies are also usually unglazed. Apparently, any area which doesn't show in the reproductions is left unglazed. All the items with lids shown in this article–chamberpot, reamer, tea jars, etc.–have wide, unglazed rims on their lids with matching wide unglazed rims on which they rest.

Transfer Ware

New glazes on the majority of the reproductions generally have a definite blue to blue-green tint. Glazes on original 19th century blue transfer wares in good condition generally have white backgrounds without a strong color tint. Originals that do have a tint are usually off-white or gray, not the obvious blue-green of the reproductions. The blue-green tint is most obvious on the earthenware-bodied reproductions made in China since the

New 10-inch Flow Blue pitcher with Art Nouveau-style flowing vines and flowers.

mid-1990s. Many Japanese-made reproductions in true porcelain show virtually no tint.

One final factor to consider when evaluating construction is to inspect all handles, knobs and finials. These features on originals are solid; they were made as separate pieces and attached to the main body. Many, but not all, reproductions with blue transfers are made by slip casting. Slip cast pieces are made in a one-piece mold which includes handles, knobs and finials as part of the overall piece. Slip cast handles, knobs and finials are hollow; there will be a hole where they join the body or a lid. This is particularly true of reproductions from Japan and Europe. Recent imports from China do have separately applied solid handles, knobs and finials like originals. That is why it is always important to use several tests before making a judgment on age and authenticity.

The majority of new marks are either direct copies of originals or based on the general appearance of originals. Perhaps the most striking difference between new and old marks is size. Many

Many new marks are exceptionally large, up to 2 to 3 inches. Most original marks are typically much smaller, usually no more than 1 inch across.

new marks average 2 to 3 inches across regardless of the size of the piece on which they appear. Virtually no original mark approaches those dimensions. Most authentic marks on 19th century blue transfer wares are rarely over 1 inch. In other words, old marks are almost always about the size of a quarter, virtually never larger than a half-dollar. Any mark larger than a half-dollar is extremely suspicious and almost certain to be new.

The next most obvious group of new marks are those which include modern symbols such as trademark (™), registered trademark (®) and copyright (©). Any mark with those symbols is almost certainly to have been made since the 1950s, definitely

E & C Challinor, one of the most confusing new marks. Virtually an identical copy of an original 19th century mark. This new mark is 2½ inches wide; old mark is rarely over 1½ inches wide. Most, but not all, original Challinor marks also include "England."

Transfer Ware

Be suspicious of marks that do not include a country, factory or pattern name. Generic names such as Staffordshire and Ironstone are no guarantee of age.

Modern mark of Mason's Ironstone is similar to 19th century mark except for use of © copyright mark.

made after 1900, usually not used until the 1920s at the earliest. Those symbols are particularly useful when dating the products of legitimate potteries that are in business today under the same name as their Victorian founders such as Masons, Ridgway, Royal Doulton, and others. Other obviously modern terms to avoid are "detergent proof," "oven safe," "dishwasher safe," and, of course, "microwave safe."

The next test is to look for generic names in the mark. No one ever walked into a 19th century china shop and said, "Excuse me, my good man, kindly direct me to the Flow Blue." Flow Blue, Historical Staffordshire and others names, are generic terms coined by modern antique collectors. Such terms were never used in original 19th century marks. These words have been included in fake marks to suggest age and quality.

The only exception is "Ironstone," which was originally a late-18th century trade name. By the mid-19th century, however, it entered the language as a generic term and has continued in that use to the present day. Original 19th century marks with "Ironstone" virtually never appear without a company name, such as "Mason's," "Woods & Sons," etc.

The absence of key words in a mark is a valuable clue to age. For example, virtually all authentic 19th century blue transfer wares–with the exception of Blue Willow–are marked with the country of origin and company name. Marks on most, but not all, authentic 19th century Flow Blue, Historical Staffordshire and Ironstone also include pattern names. Pattern and company names were an important part of original marks because they helped customers order replacements and add to a service.

With few exceptions, marks on reproductions have no country of origin and no company name. The vast majority of new pieces are from China and that country's name usually appears as a removable paper label which is quickly removed in the secondary market. Marks with no country of origin, pattern name or company name are almost certain to be of recent manufacture.

New 8-inch covered box shown closed, above, and open, left. Shape copied from a 19th century toothbrush holder. Unglazed rims on lid and base are typical of most reproductions.

New 1-inch Flow Blue platter. Latin motto surrounded by classical figures. Bluish-green tint to background; large 3-inch new mark on back.

Nippon

New   Old

New 1999 reproduction 7½-inch biscuit jar on left is a direct copy of the original shown on right. Both have raised gold decoration with pink roses. New jar is unmarked; original jar has an authentic Nippon mark.

Japanese porcelain made for export to the United States from 1891 to 1921 is called "Nippon" porcelain because the word "Nippon" was on each piece. The word Nippon was required by the McKinley Tariff Act of 1890. This law stated that all manufactured goods imported to the United States be marked with the country of origin. Since Nippon was the Japanese word for the country of Japan, porcelain made there for the U.S. market was marked Nippon to comply with the new law.

American trade officials accepted Nippon as the name of the country of origin until 1921. At that time, it was ruled that Nippon was a *Japanese* word. Since the law required the country of origin to be an *English* word, the use of Nippon was forbidden from 1921 on.

The period between the passage of the McKinley Act in 1890 and the English word ruling in 1921 is the only time Nippon appeared in authentic marks. For years, this knowledge was an easy rule of thumb collectors used to their benefit. Any mark with Nippon had to be made before 1921 when the word was banned from

116

New 8-inch vase, gold trim. Same shape also made in 12-inch size.

New 9-inch chocolate pot, trimmed in cobalt blue and raised gold.

any goods imported into the U.S.

This rule was generally true until the 1970s when reproductions of porcelain marked Nippon began appearing. What began with relatively-easy-to-detect fake marks developed into more advanced forgeries in the 1980s. By the late 1990s, reproduction importers were selling new porcelain with marks virtually identical to marks found on genuine pre-1921 originals. In 1999, importers began offering Nippon reproductions that not only carried what appeared to be original marks but also decorations and shapes almost identical to originals.

So how do you separate old from new?

Top view of new tea strainer, raised gold trim, 5-inch diameter.

Nippon

The first reproductions, 1970s to 1997, are relatively easy to detect by examining the mark. The most common marks used on reproductions of this period are the maple leaf mark and "M" in wreath mark. An original circa 1891 to 1921 green "M" in wreath mark is shown at the top of the opposite page. Original marks are transfers (decals). Sizes of original marks vary.

Below the original are the various fake wreath marks that have appeared on the reproductions. With the exception of the most recent new wreath, there are substantial differences between new and old. The wreath is upside-down on two, the letter in the center has been replaced by an hourglass and a "K." Similar differences are readily apparent in the other marks shown in the following pages.

The decorations and blanks of the first reproductions looked more like German and English Victorian designs (with mostly large flowers) than patterns used on authentic 1891 to 1921 Nippon. Gradually, new designs have become more like originals and now include fairly accurate copies of floral patterns, landscapes and garden scenes. New trim now features raised gold and enamel jewels that closely resemble the quality of many originals.

Nippon reproductions made since 1999 are much more difficult to identify. Many new pieces are now direct copies of old shapes and original patterns. The vast majority of previous reproductions carried lookalike Nippon marks that were relatively easy to identify and warned buyers of an item's recent manufacture. These latest reproductions are unmarked, thus removing one clue buyers had to help detect previous Nippon fakes and copies. With these latest pieces now in the market, buyers should be very suspicious of any

New 5-inch sugar shaker. One of the most convincing reproductions.

Old

Original green
wreath mark,
used 1891-1921.

New

New mark, circa 1997, virtually
exact copy of original.

New

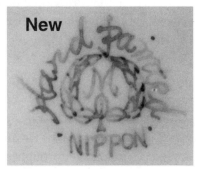

New mark, ca. 1996.

New

New mark, ca. 1996.

New

"K" in center rather than "M,"
wreath upside-down, ca. 1993.

The earliest fake mark, circa
1970 to 1980s. Hourglass
rather than "M" in center,
wreath upside-down.

New

Nippon

unmarked Nippon. If the piece is marked, carefully compare the mark to known originals.

The quality of the latest reproductions has improved so much that many pieces in old shapes and old patterns are becoming harder to detect even for experienced buyers. Many new pieces now have some type of raised gold decoration very similar to old. Color combinations are also similar, including the use of very convincing cobalt backgrounds and cobalt borders.

As fake marks become better and more original patterns are copied, buyers will need other ways to judge age and authenticity. Here are some of the ways to guard against buying a piece of reproduction Nippon:

1. **Check the mark**–Although new marks are getting better, there are still more than 20 years of Nippon reproductions in the market that have fake marks.

2. **Check the glaze**–The high-gloss glaze on most, but not all, new pieces is noticeably rougher and not as smooth as originals. Also inspect the insides of pieces. Many new pieces are not entirely glazed on the inside; originals, of course, are completely glazed.

3. **Compare the thickness**–Most new pieces are much thicker than old, sometimes twice or more as thick.

4. **Compare the weight**–New pieces are generally much heavier than old. This is due to not only their thicker construction but a difference in the raw materials.

5. **Examine the gold trim**–New gold is generally one of two types: a copper-colored gold that usually has lots of bumps and loose particles; or, a brassy yellow gold with a highly reflective almost mirrorlike finish. Original gold never has loose debris suspended in it and is virtually never highly reflective. If you see your reflection in the gold, it is almost certainly new.

6. **Don't rely on one test**–Never base your decision of age on one test alone. Use several cross-checks. Most reproductions fail several tests.

7. **Beware of fantasy shapes**–Learn the basic shapes of original Nippon. Many reproductions like the oyster plate and kerosene lamp were never made in original Nippon porcelain.

Covered 6-inch jar, surface
encrusted with raised gold.

New 6-inch hatpin holder,
raised gold decoration.

Oyster plate, 9-inch dia. A
fantasy shape, no original
Nippon was ever made as
an oyster plate.

New 9-inch kerosene lamp with
exact copy of authentic Nippon
wreath mark. No original lamp like
this was ever produced. The font
and base are *glued* together. Under
long wave black light, the glue
shows up as a yellowish white line
around the joint. The inside of the
new font is unglazed. If it were
actually used as a kerosene lamp,
the kerosene would be absorbed
into the porous unprotected clay.
This particular example is shown
without a brass collar for a burner.

Nippon

Original raised gold and pink roses pattern on authentic Nippon-era creamer. This original pattern now appears on a large number of reproduction shapes including the wall vase shown below.

New pattern, left, is very similar to raised gold discs, enamel pearls, and pink roses pattern shown on old creamer above. The new pattern appears on this 9-inch wide new wall vase, right. No authentic Nippon-era wall vase is known in this size or shape. Old-appearing green wreath Nippon mark on base.

New covered dish; tray is about 11 inches across.

New 3½-inch
shaving mug,
raised gold trim.

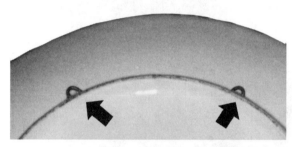

Some Nippon
reproductions have
features typically
found in originals.
This new plate has
wire hanging loops
just like originals.

New 8½-inch gold-encrusted jardinière.

*Special thanks to Joan Van Patten for her generous sharing
of information, photos and support. Joan is the author of the*
Collectors Encyclopedia of Nippon *series.*

Staffordshire

Reproduction cricketers typical of new Staffordshire figures now being made in China. Virtually identical in shape and size to original cricket players. Height slightly over 10 inches. Price $24, pair.

Staffordshire dogs are perhaps the best known symbol of the Victorian era. A wide variety of new dogs like these above have been reproduced since the 1940s.

Staffordshire pottery to most collectors means portrait statues of humans, especially famous Victorians, and a variety of animal figurals, especially dogs. A pair of dogs on the fireplace mantel is nearly an official symbol of the Victorian era.

"Staffordshire pottery," with a lowercase letter "p" in pottery, is a generic term which refers to ceramic wares produced in the general area of Staffordshire County, England. Staffordshire County had large deposits of potting clay and coal and became a center for making pottery in the late 18th century. There were six main potting towns in Staffordshire County including Tunstall, Burslem, Stoke-on-Trent, Fenton, Hanley and Longton.

Regardless of which company made it, all brightly decorated white clay figural pottery from this region, made ca. 1840 to ca. 1912, has come to be called Staffordshire. Although companies of this region also made huge amounts of transfer decorated wares, those tend to be identified by more specific factory names rather than general terms. For this chapter, our discussion of Staffordshire pottery will be limited to the figural wares.

The great majority of original Staffordshire figures were inexpensive wares made for modest country cottage parlors rather than as works of art for stone mansions. Pieces were intentionally designed to be very shallow from front to back because they were used primarily on fireplace mantels. In the pottery trade these figures were commonly called "chimney pieces" and "flat backs."

Figures were primarily made by relatively unskilled labor, many working at home on a piece rate basis. Low production costs meant the pottery could be sold very cheaply at open air markets and small village shops. Figures were so low in price that they were also given as prizes at fairs and carni-

Staffordshire

Made in China reproduction 10-inch figure of Sir Colin Campbell. Direct copy of Victorian original. Multicolored decoration on white background, overall crazing of surface. Price $16.

vals. Like other low cost mass produced items, original 19th and early 20th century Staffordshire figures are very rarely marked with company name or decorator's signature.

Reproductions of Staffordshire portrait statues and dogs have troubled the collectors market since the 1940s. Many models became staple items in reproduction importers catalogs and have remained the same down to the present day.

The best way to separate old and new is by construction details. Original Victorian figural Staffordshire almost without exception was made in press molds. In this process, damp strips of clay were pressed by hand into two or more mold parts. After dry-

Reproduction inkwell with dogs. Note "cauliflower" trim. Wholesale price $10.

Victorian press mold

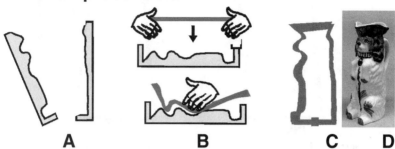

A　　　　　　**B**　　　　　**C**　　**D**

(A) plaster mold in two or more parts is made of model; (B) damp strips of clay called "bats" are pressed into the mold parts by hand. After drying, the formed clay was removed from the mold and joined together forming a hollow clay figure ready for decorating (C). Decorated final product (D). With few exceptions, almost all Victorian-era figural Staffordshire was made in press molds.

Slip mold

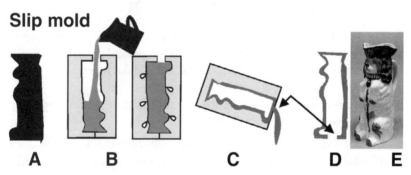

A　　　　**B**　　　　　**C**　　　　**D**　　**E**

Slip–which is clay and water mixed to a consistency of cream–is poured into a plaster mold through hole (A). Water from the slip is absorbed by the plaster mold (B) which forms a shell of clay next to the pattern on the mold wall. Excess slip is poured out (C) leaving clay shell in the shape of the mold behind. When the clay shell is removed it has one or more holes where the slip was poured in and out (D). Decorated final product (E).

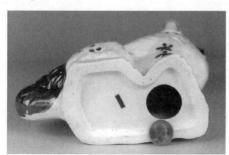

Typical hole left by slip casting method of production in the base of new Staffordshire dog. Casting holes vary in number and diameter. Usually dime-size or larger.

127

Staffordshire

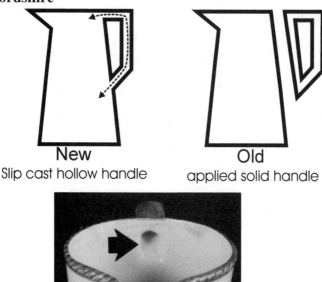

New
Slip cast hollow handle

Old
applied solid handle

Slip casting produces holes in the walls of pitchers where the hollow handles join the body. Old handles were made as solid pieces and applied separately leaving the inside walls of pitchers smooth and without holes.

ing, the clay was removed from the molds and joined together (see illustrations).

There are basically two types of construction used in Staffordshire reproductions: 1) items made by slip casting, and 2) items made by hand.

Slip casting refers to a production method where clay and water, or slip, is poured into plaster molds. As the plaster absorbs water from the slip, a layer of clay builds up on the mold walls. Excess slip is poured out of the mold leaving a hollow shell of clay inside the mold.

On figures and statues, the hole(s) where the slip was poured in and out leaves a telltale mark on the bottom of the final product. Casting holes are generally about dime-size or larger. Any piece with these holes is virtually certain to be a reproduction.

Casting holes, of course, should not be confused with firing holes. A firing hole is a small hole used to vent hot gases and air to prevent hollow items from exploding when heated in the kiln.

Firing holes are rarely much larger than 3/16 of an inch maximum. The other common sign of slip cast production is a hole where handles and trim meet the main body. Slip cast pitchers are made with the handle as part of the same mold that forms the pitcher body. When the slip is poured in, the handle and body are formed as one piece. This produces a hollow handle which forms a hole in the pitcher where the handle joins the pitcher body. Handles on original Victorian era Staffordshire pitchers were solid separate pieces and attached to the separately made pitcher body. Any pitcher represented as Staffordshire with a hole where the handle joins the body is, again, virtually certain to be a reproduction.

Prior to 1996, the majority of Staffordshire reproductions were slip cast and, with a little study, were relatively easy to detect. Since 1996, however, Staffordshire has been made in China by hand, not slip casting. Without the telltale casting holes in bases or hollow handles, the new Chinese pieces are somewhat more difficult to detect but still have obvious clues to their recent manufacture.

One of the more obvious clues is a dark colored spray applied at the factory for an "antique" appearance. This gives each piece a dark sooty look commonly associated with pieces exposed to smoke over long periods of time. No soap and water

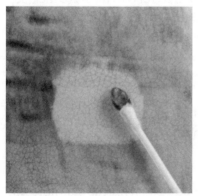

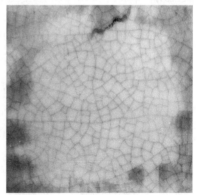

New Chinese pieces are sprayed with a dark overglaze. This is easily taken off with acetone (fingernail polish remover).

The entire surface of the new Chinese pieces are crazed with dark black lines. Crazing *is not* a reliable indication of age.

Staffordshire

Handpainted detail on the new Chinese pieces is quite good. This closeup is of the eyebrows of an Admiral Nelson figural pitcher.

will remove this spray. It is only removed with paint thinner or acetone, a primary ingredient in fingernail polish remover. Perform this test in undecorated, inconspicuous areas such as the back or base.

Another clue to the Chinese-made Staffordshire is the intentional factory crazing to simulate age. Each and every piece the author has examined has a dark crazing over the entire surface. A dark pigment has been rubbed into the crazing to produce deep dark lines over the entire piece. Crazing in any pottery, Staffordshire or others, is never a guarantee of age or authenticity. Crazing in authentic Staffordshire is more random and broadly spaced. Only damaged originals tend to the have the deep dark crazing lines found on the reproductions.

New figures also frequently have a rough surface overall with numerous pieces and patches of grit. With the exception of an occasional piece of debris from firing, the overall surface of originals is smooth to the touch.

The new Chinese Staffordshire is currently being offered by all the large reproduction importers, as well as a number of general mail order catalogs.

Special tips on dogs

No other Victorian-era collectible—with the possible exception of Currier and Ives prints—has been so heavily and steadily reproduced as the simple-faced Staffordshire cottage canines. Reproduction dogs have apparently changed very little

| Typical new reproduction. Holes in base from slip casting, no individual brush strokes in paint, mirrorlike gold trim. | Original press mold dog with solid base, obvious single brush strokes in paint and dull gold trim showing normal wear. |

over the years. Dogs in catalogs of reproductions from the 1990s are virtually identical to dogs shown in similar catalogs from the 1940s through the 1960s.

The only notable exception is the lack of Chinese reproductions of dogs; most of the Chinese pieces are copies of well known collectors pieces, not the more generic dogs. Although there are always exceptions, the following article offers some general guidelines to help separate 20th century copies from pre-1900 originals.

First, old dogs, like the vast majority of all other original Staffordshire, were made in press molds. Almost all the new figures are made in slip molds and have dime-size or larger holes in the base.

Other specific points and areas to inspect on dogs are:

Paint and Decoration—Old pieces generally show at least some fine strokes of a paint brush; modern pieces are often colored by swabs or sponges. Most old dogs show at least some painting on the back side; many new pieces have no painting on the back. Old dogs also generally show more molded detail especially in tails, legs, ears and hair (see photos next page).

Staffordshire

New

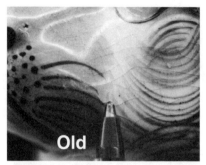

Old

Paint on most reproduction dogs is simply daubed on with sponges or rags with very few brush strokes.

The majority of original dogs clearly show paint applied with individual brush strokes.

Gold Trim—Old gold nearly always shows some wear; new gold usually shows none. Most old gold is relatively soft colored with a dull luster; much of the new gold has a mirrorlike highly reflective surface. If you can see your reflection in the gold, it is always certainly new (see photos opposite page).

Side by Side Comparison—Although many old dogs were originally sold and have survived in pairs, they are very seldom *exactly* the same. Slight variations will exist in size, painting, mold detail, and normal wear. Reproductions, on the other hand, are frequently identical matches. Be suspicious of a pair of dogs

New

Old

Many new dogs have no paint on the back. This example doesn't even have a gold-trimmed collar.

The great majority of old dogs have at least some paint and some gold trim on the back side.

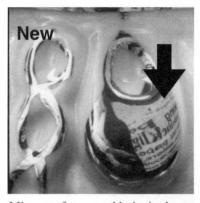

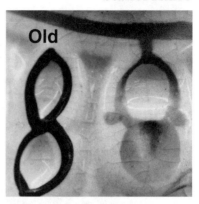

Mirror surface on gold trim is almost a guarantee of a reproduction. You can read a newspaper reflected in this new padlock.

Typical old gold on this original dog is dull and not reflective. Original gold almost always shows some normal wear.

that match perfectly in every respect.

Under the Base—In addition to holes left by slip casting, the base can provide other information. Does the glaze on the bottom match the glaze on the rest of the piece? Glaze on old pieces is usually the same over the entire figure. Glaze on many new dogs, however, is intentionally "aged" or "stressed" on normally exposed areas but frequently unaltered on the under side.

Keep in mind that Staffordshire dogs have been reproduced for many years. Reproductions of the 1920s and 1930s—now 80 to 70 years old—may show some confusing signs of wear.

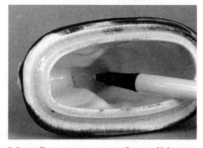

Covered box. Deep dark crazing lines, bright reflective gold trim.

Most figures on tops of new lids are almost always hollow. Original figures would have been made as solid separate figures and applied to the separate lid. The lid and figures have been slip cast in the same mold in one operation.

Delft

All of these 16-inch diameter "Delft" platters are from antique reproduction wholesalers; no old counterparts in these designs were ever made

"Delft" has traditionally been a term to describe earthenware coated with a white tin glaze, handpainted with blue decoration, and fired at a low temperature. This type of ware was first made in Italy in the 15th and 16th centuries as an attempt to imitate the white-bodied *porcelain* then being imported at great cost from China. Early decorations were similar to those on Oriental samples. By the mid-19th century, production had spread into Europe.

The word Delft is taken from the Dutch city of Delft, which became one of the leading manufacturers of white-bodied ware with bold blue decorations. Delft made from the mid-19th century forms the majority of authentic pieces in the antiques market today. It is a hard-bodied material, not the soft-bodied material of earlier 16th and 17th century Delft. Although not entirely accurate, the term Delft today is commonly used to describe almost any blue-decorated ceramics with Dutch scenes.

New Delft has been offered virtually without a change since the early 1960s. Current wholesale price for 16-inch plaques is $16 to $20 each.

Generic Delft plaques and plates like the one shown above have been offered in antique reproduction wholesale catalogs virtually unchanged for more than 30 years. The great majority of the reproduction Delft pieces in the market do not have any old counterpart. They are entirely fantasy pieces invented for interior decorators and antique reproduction wholesalers.

Over the years, reproduction Delft has carried a number of backstamps and marks that deliberately suggest the pieces are much older than their recent manufacture. Most of these new marks, however, are also fantasy marks with no old authentic counterparts.

Separating new from old is fairly simple. First, as a general rule, any mark that includes the word "Delfts" with an "s" is new–that is, less than 30 to 40 years old. Three of the most commonly found new marks are shown on the next page. Always beware of generic names used in marks, such as Delfts, Staffordshire, Flow Blue, etc. Such words are used by collectors to describe *categories* of wares, not specific companies. Reproduction

Dot pattern of printed transfer on "Delft" reproduction. Virtually all genuine 19th century Delft made is handpainted.

Delft

manufacturers try to capitalize on that name recognition with marks incorporating those words.

Another way to separate new from old is based on how the pieces are decorated. All old pieces of Delft–mid-19th century through the 1920s–have *handpainted* decoration with obvious brush strokes. The imitations made for interior decoration and reproduction trades are *transfer-decorated* and do not show brush strokes. Most transfers are made of dots and lines (see close-up photo). Examining the decoration with a 10X loupe will clearly show what method of decoration was used.

Reproduction Delft is one of the most widespread reproductions. It appears in paid admission antique shows to farm field flea markets. Usually, the only difference is the asking price. Prices at "better" shows are generally $250 to $500 for the large plaques; open air entrepreneurs seem to be content with a more modest $50 to $100. Current wholesale for new 16-inch plaques is $16 to $20.

Modern mark, mid-1970s to late 1980s. Note use of word Delfts. Mark reads "Royal Sphinx Maastricht, Made in Holland, Delfts." Signature under Sphinx is "P. Regout." This new mark is loosely based on an original turn-of-century Maastricht mark shown below.

MADE IN HOLLAND

Ca. 1890 to 1920s mark of De Sphinx pottery of Maastricht, Holland. Founded by Petrus Regout (P. Regout) 1836. Made a variety of transfer-decorated ceramics.

New mark, used since late 1980s.
Word "Delfts" removed. This mark
is on a wide variety of
reproductions like Blue Willow,
Pink Luster, Imari, Flow Blue, etc.
Appears in a wide variety of colors.

New mark from 1960s to 1970s.
Note use of word Delfts. Mark reads
"Made for Royal Copenahgen by
Boch." Stamped in dark blue ink.

Facsimile signature found on many reproductions of
Delft. Signature is applied as a transfer, not
handpainted.

RS Prussia

RS Germany, RS Suhl, RS Poland

New swan-handled 10-inch vase, marked R.S. Suhl. Poppy flower transfer decoration on good quality porcelain. Wholesale price in 1997, $27. Same shape also made in 14-inch size. Appears with various new marks.

Reinhold Schlegelmilch's initials, RS, appeared in various marks on fine German porcelain for almost 100 years, 1869 to 1956. Probably today's most desired pieces are those originally marked RS Prussia. Other sought-after marks include RS Germany, RS Suhl, and RS Poland.

RS Prussia marks have been widely forged and copied since the late 1960s. New RS Suhl marks appeared in the early 1990s followed by fake RS Germany and RS Poland marked pieces in 1998.

Reinhold Schlegelmilch started his porcelain factory in the city of Suhl (in what is today Germany, then called Prussia) in 1869. The vast majority of original production was lightweight, high quality, porcelain for use on middle class tables. The primary market was late 19th and early 20th century America where most RS porcelain was sold.

Original decorations–whether portraits, flowers, landscapes, animals, birds–were almost always transfers (decals). Handwork, if used, was primarily to blend the edges of the transfer images into the background and apply gold or enamel trim. All transfer decorations were over the glaze. Distinctive blanks featured molded designs of flowers, fruits, icicles and geometric shapes. Values of authentic pieces are based on a combination of blank, decoration and mark.

Most original marks were applied fairly late in the production process. They were protected by only a light glazing and subject to wear. The basic authentic RS marks are the so-called wreath marks. Keep in mind there are *many other* authentic marks that include additional words and symbols. For our discussion, we are looking at only the wreath marks because they are the ones being reproduced.

Not all original RS porcelain is marked, and there are tremendous price differences between marked and unmarked examples. A marked piece will bring five to ten times the amount of an unmarked piece. Even when a piece is a known RS blank with a known RS decoration, if it is unmarked, it brings far less. This wide price difference has led to the widespread forging, copying, and reproduction of marks.

There are several categories of new marks, including: 1) new marks on old but unmarked genuine RS pieces; 2) new marks

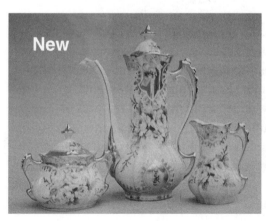

New coffee set with new green and red RS wreath mark. All pieces with gold trim. Coffeepot is 10 inches high. From reproduction importer.
Photo courtesy Joan Van Patten

RS Prussia

Original RS wreath marks

| ca.1870-1918 | ca.1900-1917 | ca.1912-1945 | ca.1948-1956 |

Approximate dates for the various authentic RS wreath marks used on Schlegelmilch porcelain made between 1870-1956.

on old porcelain from other manufacturers; 3) new marks on various kinds of new porcelain; and 4) mass-produced reproductions with close copies of old marks applied at the reproduction factory. The first three groups are generally small scale do-it-yourself home projects or semiprofessional artists. But by far the largest source of new marks are antique reproduction wholesalers who import thousands of pieces with marks that resemble originals.

Individually applied fake and forged RS Prussia marks have been around since the late 1960s. New marks individually applied by do-it-yourself forgers frequently leave tell-tale clues. The surface surrounding these marks is often higher than the mark. This is caused by adding material or glazing to cover undesired marks or blend in the new mark. It's a good idea to run a fingernail across any suspect mark to check the surface for differences. Another good test is to use a long-wave black light, which can catch many attempts at reglazing the bottom to seal in a new mark.

Mass-produced reproductions with RS Prussia marks applied at the factory followed in the early 1970s. New marks shown in this chapter are broad examples of the wide variety of new marks you may encounter. Rather than try to memorize all the new marks, concentrate on learning the basic features of authentic marks. Once you understand the key elements of original marks, you should be able to catch most fakes and forgeries.

Original shapes are also being directly copied by reproduction importers. Buyers now face not only new marks that look old but shapes that look old as well. Shape or mold blank is no

Reproduction muffineer copied from old shape. New RS wreath mark.

This original muffineer, mold #781, served as model for the reproduction.

Reproduction 5-inch pitcher with faked wreath mark. The shape is a close copy of 19th century original shown at right.

This 5-inch pitcher is original mold #640. It was used as a model for the reproduction shown at left.

Photos of both originals on this page courtesy of Joan Gaston, author of *Collectors Encyclopedia of RS Prussia* series published by Collector Books, P.O. Box 3009, Paducah, KY 42002; 1-800-626-5420.

Checklist for RS Prussia marks

Use this chart to help identify typical new, fake, and forged RS Prussia marks.

New Old

Old

"a" filled in, no period   **a** | **a.**

top does not extend to left   **P** | **P**

"i" not dotted   **I** | **i**

top of "R" not closed   **R** | **R**

Old

Original RS Prussia marks, ca. 1870 to 1918, have red letters, a red star, and red outlines to the wreath. Leaves in the wreath usually appear green. Red areas can look rusty brown; sometimes entire mark may be green.

longer necessarily a guarantee of age or authenticity.

Original RS porcelain is thin, lightweight, and translucent (light will pass through it). Keep in mind, however, that translucency is *not* a guarantee of age but only a quick test of whether an item is true porcelain. If you find an RS Prussia mark on an item that is not translucent, be very alert and inspect the item thoroughly. Remember that forged marks can be put on almost any piece, new or old.

Original RS porcelain is also smooth and glassy to the touch in undecorated areas. A number of the cruder reproductions made of pottery and not true porcelain have unglazed bottoms. Insides

Red and green decal. Sold in sheets of 140 in late 1960s. Produced in America.

Red and green transfer in current use (1998) on reproduction imports.

Red and green handpainted forgery, ca. early 1990s on genuinely old but unmarked pieces.

Fake RS marks appear on a wide variety of reproductions including this new 8-inch porcelain plate. No original RS porcelain was ever produced with this decoration. The artist signature and date "Bouchee 1759" appears in the lower left of the scene.

RS Prussia

Reproduction 11½-inch pitchers from the early 1990s that resemble original RS shapes. Sold with a variety of new marks including RS. Handpainted decoration.

of some new pitchers and vases are also unglazed.

Other enhancements

Sometimes, fakers will remove less desirable and less valuable decorations from genuine RS pieces and add decorations more in demand. Original decorations can be removed by sanding or can be hidden under a layer of new paint. Then, the more expensive transfer–such as an animal or portrait–is added. Of course you could also encounter a piece where both a new mark, as well as a new decoration, have been applied.

One of the best ways to catch recently applied transfers is to hold the object to the light with the decoration facing you. Look for traces of the original transfer, which may appear as dim outlines or shadows behind the new transfer. Black light can also be helpful to detect new paint over original transfers and borders where new transfers meet the original surface.

New crude RS Germany mark, left, appears in blue-green paint. Original mark, right, is green or blue.

Left, new 5-inch hatpin holder with fake RS Germany mark. Right, new 4½-inch hatpin holder with fake RS wreath mark. Shape on right appears with many new marks including Nippon, Flow Blue, Blue Willow and others.

In the new mark, the letter "L" is uppercase with no period after it. The old Suhl has a lower case "l" and a period at the end. The letters, star, and outer edges of the wreath are red; the inside of the wreath is green.

New mark is handpainted in orange/red paint. Original mark is a transfer with the words "Made in (Germany) Poland" around the bottom. All lettering is red. This is the most recent of all the genuine RS marks. It was used after World War II, ca. 1948 to 1956.

Black Memorabilia

There are reproductions of black memorabilia in just about every category of collecting: cast iron, toys, kitchen items, textiles, wood, etc. It's impossible to list or show them all in the space available so we have limited our selection to some of the more confusing items. Although there is a tremendous variety of reproductions available, there are some general rules of thumb that are useful to keep in mind.

Ceramics

Virtually all original 1930 to 1950s Japanese ceramic pieces have at least some cold painted overglaze decoration. Most all originals show at least some wear to the paint. The vast majority of ceramic reproductions of those pieces are decorated entirely underglaze with no signs of normal wear.

Function

A great number of pieces sought by black memorabilia collectors were originally made for routine everyday use around the house, especially kitchen items. If an item was meant for food storage, it should be glazed inside. Shakers should have filling holes that make practical sense. Spouts of pitchers and teapots should allow liquid to pass smoothly.

Paper

Be particularly wary of any item that includes images on paper. Now that almost everyone has a home computer, scanner, and color printer, the number of do-it-yourself forgeries has exploded. It's relatively simple to scan an original image in a reference book, alter it, print it out, and apply it to genuinely old recipe boxes, toys, clock faces, and other items.

Banania

New Banania 6-inch ceramic bowl.

Banania was a European brand of chocolate powder popular during the 1920s primarily in France and Belgium. The Banania trademark is a black man wearing a fez and the word "Banania." The African theme represents the source of early 20th century European cocoa, which was from Ghana and the Ivory Coast.

So far new Banania pieces include a 6-inch ceramic bowl with the black man's face in relief (raised) and two metal canisters. One canister is marked Farine (flour); the other Épices (spices). Each is seven inches tall.

All the new pieces sell for about $20 retail. New piece are marked with the letter "C" in a circle, ©, the modern copyright symbol.

Early 20th century genuine Banania items do not generally include the © symbol.

New Banania tin containers. Left, Épices (spices); right, Farine (flour).

Butler decanter

Reproduction ceramic decanter. Virtually identical in overall shape to original.

Original 1950s decanter made in Japan. Both old and new are about 7½ inches tall.

The bottle in the new butler's right hand has a perfectly smooth surface with no molded details. The paint is mostly a solid block of color.

The original bottle has molded lines of a wicker basketweave pattern. These fine lines are individually painted in a dark color.

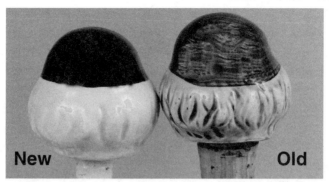

New   Old

The fringe of hair molded into the old stopper (right) is much sharper and more detailed than the hair molded into the new stopper (left). Also notice the obvious brush strokes in the bald scalp of the old stopper which do not appear in the new stopper.

Ceramics marked Nippon

A Pennsylvania reproduction wholesaler sold a number of ceramic pieces with a fake Nippon mark. The mark appears in red lettering. It is shown here with the other removable labels exactly as it was purchased from the wholesaler. The mark appears on the glazed toothpick holder and boy on alligator shown here. No originals like this were ever marked Nippon.

Fake Nippon mark on ceramic pieces below.

New toothpick (left) and child on alligator (above) are fantasy pieces marked Nippon.

Gold Dust Soap

Three new Gold Dust Soap containers with artificial aging: 5-inch orange box; 7½-inch red box; 4½-inch diameter orange cannister.

Gold Dust Soap packages are widely sold in antiques malls, markets and shows. Sellers say buyers like the nostalgic look of the containers. Of course, the two black children in the artwork also help make sales.

But if the original Gold Dust Soap company had actually sold all the packages that bear its name, the company's sales would be greater than General Motors or Microsoft. Gold Dust packaging has been so heavily reproduced that modern copies far outnumber the old originals. It's easy to prove the reproductions are new.

Here's how: The easiest test is to use a long-wave blacklight. Modern cardboard and papers used in the new pieces fluoresce bright white; old pieces do not. Just shine your light anywhere not covered with ink. It is not necessary to view the reverse side of the paper or cardboard. Any unprinted edges or scratches through the ink will work fine.

Another test is to examine areas of "aging." True aging discoloration is caused by the paper absorbing moisture, dirt, grease and other particles. "Aging" discoloration in the

"Handwritten" country store price is actually printed. It appears on the upper left of every 7½-inch box.

reproduction is created by *printing* ink to resemble aging. Use a 10X loupe to examine any suspected discoloration. If you see fine lines, groups of round dots, or any other regular pattern, you are looking at the dot pattern of modern printing. Authentic aging from moisture or sunlight, of course, has no such patterns.

Other "flaws" and "handwritten" marks are also *printed* to simulate age. Many of these flaws and marks show up in exactly the same spot on similar-sized packages. The "handwritten" price, for example, shown above, appears on all the 7½-inch packages in the same place.

The new packages come filled with soap. Don't think the package is original because of its contents.

Expose any non-printed surface like these edges to black light. New cardboard fluoresces bright white.

Open area in letter "O." The brown "aging" is created by printing light brown ink in regular pattern easily seen with a 10X loupe.

Coon Chicken Inn

Coon Chicken Inn was the name of a small chain of restaurants that used the image of a black American with a bell hop cap as its trademark.

Scott Farrar, grandson of the original Coon Chicken Inn founder, and other collectors helped prepare this short history of the original restaurants.

The Coon Chicken Inn business was founded by Maxon Lester in 1925 in Salt Lake City, Utah. In 1929, another Coon Chicken Inn was opened in Seattle, Washington, and another in Portland, Oregon, in 1930. The restaurants operated until 1957 when the business closed. Since then, Coon Chicken Inn plates, menus, matchbooks, toothpick holders, cups, bowls and all other forms of items with the well-known trademark have become highly collectible.

One of the most common myths about the Coon Chicken Inn restaurants is that they were forerunners of Sambos Restaurants (which closed in the late 1970s). There is no connection between the two. The slogan "Nationally famous coast to coast" appears on some originals, but there were only the three locations–Salt Lake City, Portland and Seattle.

About the glass tumblers and ashtrays, Farrar said: "As the grandson and somewhat historian of the family of M.L. Graham, it is my belief that all glass tumblers are fakes. In all the original artifacts that we have of my grandparents' inns, there never was a glass tumbler or glass ashtray. I have seen many of them; I even bought a couple as a novelty. I have also bought Coon Chicken Inn money clips and rings, again definitely reproductions."

New Coon Chicken Inn glass tumblers are found with both a Libbey mark and an Anchor Hocking mark.

Paper items with Coon Chicken Inn advertising are particularly vulnerable to reproductions. Although the fan shown in this chapter is a commercial product mass produced by reproduction wholesalers, similar paper products are just as easily made with personal computers and image editing software.

A Bull Durham tobacco advertisement (right) was used to make the fantasy Coon Chicken Inn hand fan (above). The words "Coon Chicken Inn" and a fictitious menu were added to the reverse.

New clear glass tumbler marked Anchor Hocking (molded anchor). Lettering and image in black, red, and blue. "Coon Chicken Inn–Nationally Famous Coast to Coast." About 4½ inches high. Other new tumblers exist in colors of brown and "Coon Chicken Inn" is spelled out in the teeth of the bell hop.

New Coon Chicken Inn money clip. Silver-finished metal. About 2½ inches.

New clear glass ashtray. Colors and lettering match tumbler shown above. About 4½ inches.

Kitchen ceramics

Pearl China

Pearl China range-size shakers. New and old shown side by side. New lack the detail and lifelike facial expression found on originals.

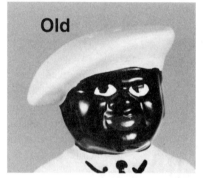

New shaker shows lack of detail typical of Pearl China reproductions. Note the more natural eyes and the more realistic hat of the old shaker.

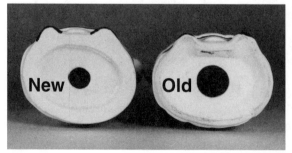

Filling holes on the reproduction are about the size of a dime. Filling holes on originals are about the size of a quarter.

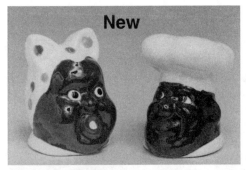

A slightly better quality reproduction set of shakers. Good molded detail in faces, but no sign of wear, all underglaze decoration. No marks.

Typical reproduction shakers. Little molded or painted detail in faces. All decoration is underglaze, no paint wear, no country or factory mark

Typical old shakers, 3 inches tall. Cold-painted overglaze decoration shows normal wear. Nice molded and painted detail in faces. Marked Japan on base.

Bisque finished ceramic reproductions. Shakers (center), are 3½ inches tall. Small pieces are thimbles. No original thimbles like these were ever made. No mark.

New bisque finish ceramic "toothpick holders." Same mold as new shakers with a hole cut in the back. All pieces like this are new. No mark.

String holders

New string holders are commonly sold as old. The vast majority of old pieces have overglaze cold-painted decoration; decorations on new are almost always underglaze.

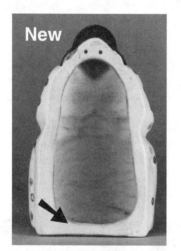 

The short ridge in back of the new holder can't keep a ball of string inside the holder. Backs in old stringholders are higher.

Typical new underglaze decorated piece compared to typical overglaze decoration on original string holder.

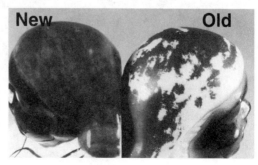

New 7-inch string holder of cast resin or heavy plastic. Old copyright date of 1941 molded on reverse. Painted decoration of red dress, yellow scarf, white apron. Distressed antique finish looks old.

Majolica

New 10-inch humidor, above left; new 11-inch humidor, above right. The inside surfaces of new humidors are not glazed. All old original majolica humidors are fully glazed inside. Figures on these new lids are cast as one piece with the lid. Figures on tops of old lids are solid. Looking up into the lid, left, the figures on these new lids are hollow.

Metal, wood, and other materials

New 6-inch cast iron figure. Boy's head moves like a nodder. Distressed paint. Wide gap where two halves of piece meet; obvious grinding marks on base. No known old counterpart.

Mason's Blacking box. One of the most widely reproduced pieces of black memorabilia. New paper on new wood. Original paper is lithographed; new paper shows regular dot pattern of modern color printing and fluoresces under black light. Old boxes made from boards of solid wood; new boxes are frequently made of plywood.

New cast iron bottle opener made overseas. Original by Wilton Products in USA. Reproduction has rough mold seams. Tip of new alligator's tail is broad and round; old tail comes to a point. New pieces are "distressed" at factory to look old.

New 8-inch tall covered box. Original is ceramic; the reproduction is cast in resin.

Genuinely old 1940s clock with faked paper face dated 1946. The face was made on home computer and inserted into the old clock. The new paper glows under black light.

New pot metal wall match holder, 4 inches tall. Dull pewter finish. Back side marked with reversed letter "D" next to an "R."

Metal dart board. Old marked "Wyandotte, Made in USA." New marked "AAA Sign Co."

Black Memorabilia

New pot metal toothpick or match holder with imitation silver plating, 3½ inches tall. No old counterpart known.

New Topsy Turvy doll. Hand embroidered face, cloth printed with old style patterns. All hand sewn. New thread fluoresces under black light.

New 6-inch phonograph dancer, painted wood. A close copy of original black 1920s dancer sold by National Toy Co. The reproduction has been available since at least 1997 for $60. Originals sell for $200 to $350. Revolving record activates mechanism making figure "dance."

Close-up of new phonograph dancer. Note the ragged edges of brush strokes in the paint especially in the tie and vest. Paint on original is very smooth without ragged brush strokes. Eyes, nose, and mouth are little more than single brush strokes.

New 31-inch cut glass urn with "Brandy" engraved on the front. Electric blue glass overlay cut to clear crystal body. This is also available in other colors.

The glass collar that holds the spigot in the new urn shown above is glued into the side. It is shown here fluorescing brightly under black light. Old collars were fused when the glass was hot and were never glued.

New pickle castor frame with new Fenton cranberry opalescent glass insert. Although these inserts are marked Fenton, the marks are generally so faint they are virtually invisible. Many of the new inserts are being sold as old Victorian-era pieces.

A fantasy "mechanical" pickle castor frame. As the handle is pushed back, the lid rises. The first version of this reproduction was sold in the 1980s. Now, a second version is being imported from India. There is no original counterpart.

All the new bisque bathing beauties have this clown mark stamped in ink on the base. However, these stamped marks are easily removed and many new pieces are being offered as old.

New bisque bathing beauty made from original old mold. A number of new pieces from these original molds have "Germany" impressed in the backs. This piece is also marked with the new stamp mark shown at right.

New   **Old**

Copies of McCoy Pottery are getting better. The new Orchid pattern vase, left, is 10-1/4 inches tall. The original, right, is 10-3/4 inches tall. Both are marked "Hull U.S.A. 304-10-1/4."

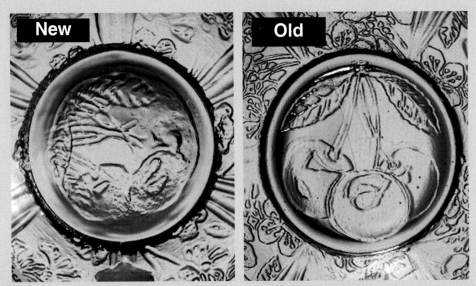

These two photos compare the bases on child-sized Cherry Blossom pattern cups. The bases are shown as they appear from the outside bottom. The three cherries and two leaves in the old cup, right, are very clear, distinct, and naturalistic. Cherries and leaves in the reproduction, left, are poorly molded with little detail.

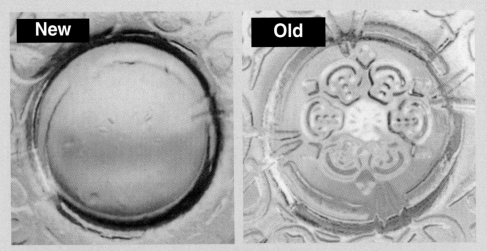

A comparison of bases on Florentine #2 footed tumblers. In the original tumbler, right, the pattern runs through the center of the foot. There is no pattern in the foot of the new tumbler, left.

This is a reproduction of an Oak Leaf pattern Tiffany leaded glass lamp. Both the shade and base have forged Tiffany markings. To suggest age, the lamp was coated with a brown spray.

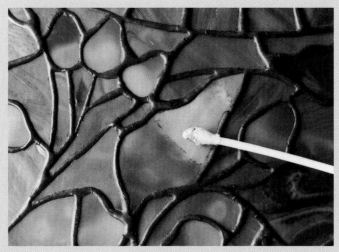

The brown spray applied to the Tiffany lamp shown above could not be washed off with soap and water. It was removed only by using a cotton swab and fingernail polish remover. This and any other unusual coatings should immediately raise suspicions.

A new opaque blue glass, or delphite, kitchen mortar with "Spices" on the side. These pieces are also available in jadite, green opaque glass. There are at least two sizes: four ounce and two ounce. No original delphite or jadite mortars are known.

A new opaque blue glass, or delphite, 12-inch bowl. It is very similar, but not quite an exact match, to two vintage patterns made by Anchor Hocking, Manhattan, and Park Avenue. Neither of those original patterns was made in opaque blue glass.

A new tin ABC plate, about 3 inches in diameter. This is virtually an exact copy of a Victorian original. The new plates are painted a dull brown to simulate a naturally aged patina. Original plates have a natural dark brown or black patina (see test below).

True patina is a chemical change within the material itself. Paint is an applied surface finish, not a patina. The painted "patina" on new ABC plates can be removed with fingernail polish remover. True patina will not be affected (never perform a test without the seller's permission).

New jadite, or green opaque glass, 4-inch shakers. This pair is decorated with black "Pepper" and "Salt" lettering.

New jadite 4-inch shakers with strawberry decals. The majority of original jadite shakers were large so-called "range-size," capable of holding 6 to 8 ounces. The new jadite shakers shown here and at the top of this page are a smaller table size, holding only 3 ounces each.

This new sterling silver matchsafe is a close copy of a Gorham original. The original is marked Gorham; the new piece has the mark shown below.

The new matchsafe above has this mark. Note the imitation hallmark in the center of a G and J inside a diamond. This GJ mark is appearing on a large group of new silver matchsafes with golfing and tennis themes.

A new bracelet carved from genuinely old inventory stock of authentic Bakelite. Stockpiles of old undecorated Bakelite stock from the United States are shipped overseas to be made into new jewelry.

Most carvings on recently decorated Bakelite are fairly crude compared to work on vintage pieces. New carving is frequently rough and has a gray appearance as seen in this new example.

A reproduction tile copied from an original by Rookwood Pottery. The new tile has a rubber stamped mark in black ink, "North Prairie Tileworks." Originals have an impressed Rookwood mark.

New 17-inch molded resin imitation of a whale jawbone. This piece is "signed" and "dated" by the artist.

An end view of the imitation whale jawbone shown above. The new casting captures the pitting formed by blood vessels found in genuine bone. The best way to catch these sophisticated fakes is with a black light.

These new posters are just two of the many different recent reproductions of Russian 19th century originals. Posters include the names of original printers and 19th century dates such as "1896." Originals were lithographed; the new copies show the dot pattern of modern color printing. The new poster above advertises Geelzi tobacco. The Russian Black Powder Company is featured in the new poster on the right.

A new figural watch fob fantasy; no old counterpart ever existed. Purportedly issued as an advertising piece for the City National Bank, Coffeyville, Kansas, which is stamped on the front, left.

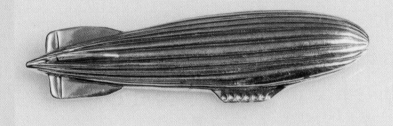

Two new sterling silver pins. Top, a 3-inch 1930s-era Zeppelin; below, a 1930s clipper-style airplane. Both pieces are marked ".925," meaning 925 parts silver. Virtually all silver marked .925 has been made since the mid-1970s. Similar 1930s vintage pins made in America would be marked "sterling," not .925.

New

New

It's often small details that separate old from new. The new butler decanter, above left, looks virtually identical at first glance to the original on the bottom. One of the key differences is in the bottle held in the butler's hand. The old bottle, below, had molded grooves in the side. The new bottle, above, is perfectly smooth.

Old

Old

This is a new ceramic oil lamp decorated in the Blue Willow pattern.

A "married" Westmoreland lamp made from recently assembled parts and pieces. This white glass base is not genuine Westmoreland. It was recently painted in a Westmoreland pattern. Carefully compare assembled lamps to know original shapes shown in reference books and company catalogs.

175

New ceramic food mold decorated with a Flow Blue-style decoration. No vintage food molds are known in Flow Blue.

A new 8-inch circus wagon made of wood and metal with colored paper on the sides. The paper is copied and reduced in size from a PT Barnum circus poster, probably scanned from a reference book. The new paper has been made on a digital printer with a home computer.

American Art Pottery

For many years, collectors thought art pottery was safe from the fakes and reproductions that plagued other fields of collectibles. This was generally true until the mid-1990s. First Roseville, then Rookwood, Hull, Grueby, and other potteries were all either faked, forged, or reproduced.

The mass-produced pottery reproductions like Roseville are relatively easy to document because they are so widespread. Do-it-yourself forged marks on Grueby or made-in-the-garage Rookwood pieces are so varied and limited in number, they can be difficult to track. In addition to the common factory-made reproductions, we have tried to include a cross-section of these one-of-a-kind fakes to show you the range of what's in the market today.

Roseville reproduction, Water Lily pattern, 7-inch vase.

New Newcomb or SEG look-alike vase, 6 inches.

Arts and Crafts style

Throughout the late 1990s, Arts and Crafts-styled green glazed Teco and Grueby pottery brought record prices. A 6¾-inch Teco vase brought $19,550 at Christie's 20th Century Auction in November 1999. Single-color Grueby was selling for $2,000 to $5,000; two-color pieces have brought more than $34,000.

The thick mottled green glaze and simple organic shapes that characterize Teco and Grueby originals are now recreated in a series of inexpensive reproductions by Haeger Pottery of Dundee, Ill. Some of the new pieces are direct copies of original shapes; others are based on the general Arts and Crafts style. New pieces retail for $25 to $45.

Collectors and dealers of Grueby and Teco won't have any problems spotting the new look-alikes. But if you've only seen these potteries in reference books or auction house press release photos, you might only recall the record prices and not be aware of how new and old differ.

The new ware is slip cast in molds; the mold halves

New

Old

New Haeger Pottery 7-inch vase, green mottled glaze. Stylized flower bud and stem in center. Design copied from original Grueby vase at right.

Original Grueby vase, ca. 1900, about 8 inches. Green glaze. Impressed mark on base, "Grueby Faience Co., Boston, U.S.A."

produce obvious seam lines. Original Grueby and Teco were hand- finished and are never found with an obvious mold seam.

The pattern on the outside of new pieces is visible as a mirror image on the inside; originals are smooth on the inside with no pattern visible. Bases on the majority of the new pieces are unglazed; bottoms of originals were almost always glazed on the bottom.

Most, but not all, of the new Haeger has a very small rubber-stamped black ink mark. On most pieces this was covered over by the factory applied felt pads. Virtually every authentic piece of Grueby has an impressed mark (although it is sometimes hard to see because of the thick glaze). Teco was also

Obvious casting seam across unglazed bottom of new vase. Such obvious casting seams are almost never found on original Arts and Crafts period pottery.

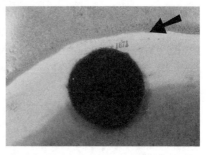

Small Haeger ink stamp is easily covered up. This 3/4-inch felt pad applied at the pottery concealed almost the entire mark.

New flower petal vase similar to Grueby and other Arts and Crafts organic shaped pottery. Green mottled glaze, 8-by-9 inches.

View inside new vase at left. The pattern on the outside of new pieces is visible on the inside wall. On authentic Arts and Crafts pottery the pattern is not seen on the inside.

179

American Art Pottery

almost always signed with an impressed mark.

A faked Grueby pottery mark stamped in ink started showing up in early 2000. The mark is applied in dark blue ink and covered with a new glaze.

The fake "Grueby Faience Co. Boston, U.S.A." mark is a copy of an old original mark. A similar original mark reads "Grueby

Fake Grueby Faience blue ink stamp.
Terry Stern photo

Pottery Boston, U.S.A." Both authentic lotus marks are *impressed* in the clay, not ink stamped. New Grueby look-alike pottery is a very likely target for faked ink stamped marks.

Authentic Grueby Faience lotus mark; always impressed, never ink stamped.

Authentic Grueby Pottery lotus mark; always impressed, never ink stamped.

New 12-inch Teco-like vase with green mottled glaze.

New tiles with Grueby style matte green glaze: tulip, left; orchid, right. The backs have a cast notch for hanging (below). This feature is not found on any Arts and Crafts period originals. Unglazed backs. New retail price, $24 each.

The generic Grueby/Teco look has also been copied to a number of tiles. At least one series of these new tiles is made in long vertical shapes especially designed for wall hanging. Despite a very convincing mottled green glaze, these new tiles can be identified by the notch molded into their backs for hanging. Their new retail price is $24 each. Three designs are available: tulip, orchid and daffodil.

Besides Teco and Grueby, Arts and Crafts potteries with incised or modeled decorations–such as Newcomb, Saturday

Left, impressed mark of new Ephraim Faience Pottery, ca. 1999. Right, new 8-inch Ephraim Faience Pottery vase. Incised oak trees around top shoulder, multicolored band on dark green body.

American Art Pottery

Evening Girls (SEG/Paul Revere Pottery), and others–are also being copied. A small studio in Wisconsin, Ephraim Faience Pottery, is now making incised pieces very similar to Newcomb and SEG/Revere originals.

When examining a suspected piece, keep in mind that all original Newcomb marks are impressed below the surface. A painted Newcomb mark would obviously be suspicious. Original SEG/Revere marks were commonly painted and generally more easily forged.

Bottoms on the new Ephraim pieces are painted the same color as the body decoration. The great majority of original bottoms on Newcomb, SEG/Revere, and other one-of-a-kind pieces usually were white, neutral-colored or otherwise plain, and generally do not match the decoration on the body.

Although the decorations on new Ephraim pieces are not exact copies of original vintage patterns, they are very close. The oak tree band vase on the opposite page and the water lily band vase shown at the beginning are very similar in appearance, though not in quality, to decorations on authentic Newcomb and SEG/Revere pieces.

New 8-by-11inch jardinière is very similar to Grueby original. Raised naturalistic leaves separated by slender flower buds is typical of original Grueby designs. Glaze on the new pieces–a dark matte green–is also a very close copy of the most famous original Grueby glaze, a "cucumber" matte green. The small flower buds on the new pieces are yellow. Original two-color Grueby jardinières the same size would have a current market value of $15,000 to $20,000. The reproductions are $300. These new pieces are made by Ephraim Faience Pottery. (See mark on previous page.)

Fulper Pottery

Original Fulper-marked pottery was made by Fulper Pottery of Flemington, New Jersey. This firm was started in the early 1800s but is best known for its Arts and Crafts-styled art pottery produced between 1909 and 1930. In 1930, former Fulper superintendent J. Martin Stangl bought Fulper Pottery and shifted the emphasis from art pottery to other wares.

The Fulper name was revived in 1984 by four granddaughters of William Hill Fulper II, who started Fulper Glazes, Inc. The new Fulper began making products very similar to 1909 to 1930s originals with glazes said to be made from original formulas. Among the new products are lamps and tiles made famous by the original Fulper Pottery.

The new wares can be separated by the embossed mark of Fulper Tile set in two square-cornered boxes. Marks of the original Fulper never include the word "Tile" and have rounded ends.

New artichoke pattern lamp by Fulper Glazes, Inc. (left). New multicolor tile (right).

New mark of Fulper Glazes, Inc. with right angled corners and word "Tile."

Original Fulper Pottery marks enclosed by rounded border.

Hull Pottery

Reproductions of Hull Pottery are being seen in Orchid and Bow-Knot. So far, both patterns are made here in the United States. New pieces have marks very similar to original markings.

The large new Orchid vase is probably the most difficult to detect. Colors are like the original with a light blue base, ivory middle and pale pink top. Original Hull shape 304 Orchid vases in this size are currently selling for $250 to $325. The reproduction wholesales for $45.

The new vase is about ½-inch shorter than the original. New vases measure 10¼ inches high; original is 10¾ inches high. Circumference around the widest part (the lower bulge) of the old vase is 22 5/8 inches; the same spot on the new vase is 21 7/8 inches.

The only significant quality problem with the new Orchid vase is pitting. There is the occasional burst bubble or pit in original glaze, but nothing like the widespread repeated patches of pits in the new. Average size of the new pits is about the size of a pinhead; some larger, others smaller.

Reproduction Hull Pottery vase in Orchid pattern, shape #304 shown at left. Original on right. New vase is 10¼ inches tall; original is 10¾ inches tall. New vase marked like original.

Mark on new Hull Orchid vase from opposite page. Note the script style of lettering, which is particularly evident in the word Hull.

Mark on original Hull Orchid vase. Note that the lettering is a block style, not script like the reproduction mark on left.

Mark on new cornucopia below, "U.S.A. Hull Art B-5-7½", the same as the original. Image blurred due to thick glaze.

Reproduction Hull Bow-Knot 7½-inch cornucopia. Original Bow-Knot was only made in two color styles: pink top rims with blue-green bases or blue top rims with blue-green bases. This piece has gray top rim with green base. Reproduction with molded raised lettering.

Rookwood

There are two types of new Rookwood circulating in today's market. The first group consists of unauthorized fakes and copies having no connection to the original company. These pieces are usually individually made to intentionally deceive or are made in limited numbers in imitation of original patterns and shapes. The other pieces are from the "new" Rookwood Pottery operating again in Cincinnati, Ohio, with molds rescued from the original Rookwood company.

The New Rookwood Pottery

The original Rookwood Pottery was founded in Cincinnati, Ohio, in 1880. For 50 years, its products were considered some of the world's finest art pottery ever made. Then the Great Depression and shortages of material in World War II led to the company's failing. During the 1950s, the company passed through various owners and was moved to Starkville, Mississippi. The business completely shut down in 1967 under the ownership of Herschede Hall Clock Co.

The molds and equipment were unused through 1982. At that time, a group of investors began preparing to move what remained of the company to Korea, where production would be

New 4¼-inch Rookwood honey bear, shiny black glaze. Retail, $37.

New Rookwood 4½-inch paperweight, gun-metal blue glaze.

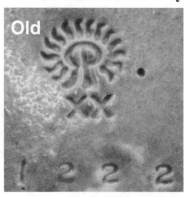

New Rookwood has the impressed "RP" and flames mark with the year of production *engraved* in *Arabic* numerals, not Roman numerals.

Original impressed RP and flames mark. The year of production is in *Roman* numerals. The year shown is 1920.

resumed. The move would have included the molds, company records, medals Rookwood was awarded, and all other physical assets.

Word of the move reached Arthur Townley, a Michigan dentist. Townley went to Starkville and made a deal to buy Rookwood and prevent it from going overseas. The remains of the original company were in 31 crates stored on a cotton plantation. Their contents included: approximately 2,000 molds, 13 medals won by Rookwood, original shape books with freehand drawings, about 1,200 master blocks (from which were taken master molds), and around 5,000 glaze and clay formulas.

Perhaps most valuable of all are the Rookwood name and associated trademarks. Along with the physical assets, Townley's purchase also included the rights to the reverse R and P mark, the name "Rookwood," and the RP mark with flames.

Townley and his wife Rita began making pieces from original molds in the mid-1980s. The Townley's new Rookwood has the same RP flame mark as the original but there are several major differences. First, all the new pieces are dated in *Arabic* numbers, not Roman numerals. The dates are *ground into the glaze* with a diamond drill, not cast into the ceramic material. New Rookwood is all stark white *porcelain,* not the softer Ohio clay used in the original pottery. The glazes are also different in color and finish from glazes used on originals.

The Townleys limit production to 500 pieces of each mold number. Currently in production are about 30 different pieces, including 14 figural paperweights, various vases, a dealer sign, tiles, and bookends. Prices for the paperweights average about $30 retail; the larger vases sell for $125 to $150. Total production is limited to about 1,000 pieces per year. All new pieces are glazed only; no hand decorating is applied.

New Rookwood is sold through independent retailers throughout the United States. The majority of sales, though, are made in Cincinnati to pottery collectors and tourists.

Fakes, forgeries, copies

The rabbit tile below is typical of new pieces copied directly from Rookwood originals. The copy is multicolored under a high gloss glaze, 5¾ inches square, and retails for $50.

The only mark on the copy is "North Prairie Tileworks" rubber stamped in black on the unglazed back. This mark is not permanent and could be removed. If the tile were mounted in a frame or if the tile were backed with cork or felt, the new mark also might go unobserved.

Riley Humler, gallery director of Cincinnati Art Galleries, a leading auction firm of American art pottery and Rookwood specialist, said the original rabbit tile is scarce and rarely seen.

"The last one we sold was in 1996," Humler said. "It was a trivet form, in a single matte-color made in 1918 and brought $375. A multicolor original would easily be worth $400 to $600."

Humler said the vast majority of original Rookwood tiles

Rubber stamped mark on back of new tile "North Prairie Tileworks."

Reproduction Rookwood tile available for $50 retail. Multicolor, high gloss glaze, 5¾-inch square.

have permanent impressed marks. The exact mark found on tiles depends on when the tile was made. Before the tile division was combined with the overall operation, tiles were marked "Rookwood Faience," plus the date and various shape and production codes. Later production would be marked with the reversed R and P with flames mark, along with the date and various production codes.

Individually made fakes like the piece below are hard to categorize due to their one-of-a-kind nature. As a general rule, the RP mark must always be accompanied by a model number. Another good indication of an authentic mark is to look for the small "hooks" that appear on the ends of authentic flames surrounding the RP. Most faked marks don't include this small detail. Original Roman numeral year dates are about one-third the size of the RP and flames. Roman numerals on the fakes are frequently much larger or much smaller than original year dates.

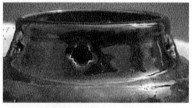

Pierced (reticulated) rim on fake 3-inch diameter vase at left.
Photos of fakes courtesy Connie Swaim.

Fake Rookwood vase. Dark green mottled glaze with lighter green specks.

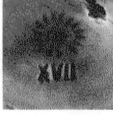

New

Old

Mark on fake Rookwood above. Roman numerals too large, no hook to tips of flames, no model number.

Authentic mark. Note hooks on flame tips. Mark includes model number, 1222.

Roseville

New Zephyr Lily ewer, marked Roseville 24-15. Wholesale price, $19.

The original Roseville Pottery Co. was founded in 1892 in Roseville, Ohio. In 1898, the pottery relocated to Zanesville, Ohio, where all the art pottery was made. The business closed in 1954.

The first commercially made reproductions of Roseville Pottery began appearing in late 1996. These reproductions are made in China. They have virtually the same shapes, patterns, colors, and molded marks as original Roseville.

New Chinese Roseville copies originals from two style periods. The vast majority of reproductions are copied from Late Period patterns, those originally made 1935 to 1954. The balance of reproductions copy original Middle Period patterns made from about 1910 to 1934. Reproductions sell for $5 to $25 each, depending on size.

Late Period reproductions fall into two groups: group A is marked exactly the same as originals; group B is marked nearly the same as originals. All original Late Period pieces were marked on the base in raised letters, "Roseville U.S.A.," followed by a shape code and size number. The only exceptions are a very few

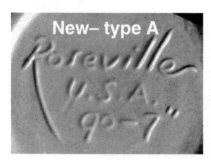
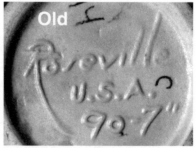

Left, type A mark on new Magnolia vase includes raised "Roseville, USA" with shape code "90" and size number "7." New mark identical to original mark, right, found on authentic 7-inch Magnolia vases.

Inside view

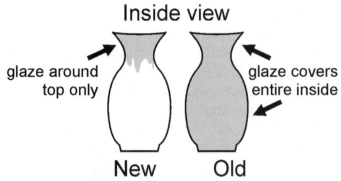

glaze around
top only

glaze covers
entire inside

New   **Old**

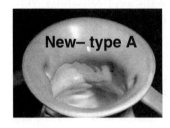

New– type A

The first reproductions with type A marks can be detected by the glaze. These first reproductions are not fully glazed on the inside. The glaze stops a couple of inches below the top rim. Interiors of all originals are fully glazed. Interiors of type B reproductions are also glazed but they can be detected by the marks.

creamers, sugars, flower frogs, candle holders, and other small pieces where part of the mark is omitted for lack of space.

Group A reproductions are marked exactly like originals with the raised "Roseville, U.S.A." and shape and size numbers. To detect these fakes, you need to reach down inside the suspected piece with your fingers. The group A reproductions are glazed on the inside only around the top few inches of the piece (see above illustration). The remaining inside surface is unglazed in a biscuit finish. All original Roseville is glazed completely on the inside because it was sold as practical functional flower hold-

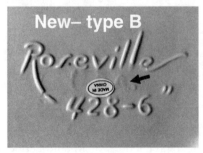

Left, new type B mark with "USA" very faint. Except for a handful of very small original shapes, "USA" is the same height as all other raised lettering in authentic Late Period Roseville raised marks.

ers that held water.

Reproduction importers countered within a few months by introducing group B with the insides of pieces completely glazed. Although the glaze clue was lost, another change in group B pieces proved an important help to collectors.

According to the McKinley Tariff Act of 1890, all objects sold in the United States must be marked with the country of origin. Group A reproductions met this requirement with a re-movable "Made in China" paper label. However, U.S. Customs ruled that "U.S.A." in the mark implied the reproductions were made in the United States. Chinese manufacturers were ordered to remove it, and marks on group B reproductions no longer in-clude the raised "U.S.A."

All letters of original Late Period raised marks–"Roseville, U.S.A.," shape code, and size number–are an equal height above the surface. Some Group B marks are still found with a very faint or very unevenly formed "U.S.A." If you find "U.S.A." in weak, shallow letters but with Roseville and shape numbers sharp and clear, it is from a new mold where the "U.S.A." has not been completely removed. The absence of the "U.S.A." is now an im-portant clue to the detection of the group B reproductions.

Chinese reproductions of the Middle Period can also be iden-tified by looking at the mark. Original Middle Period patterns–Luffa and Jonquil for example–are virtually never found with a permanent mark. The vast majority were marked with paper

New Jonquil 8-inch vase, marked "Roseville" in raised script.

This new raised script mark appears on reproductions of Middle Period patterns such as Luffa and Jonquil. No original Middle Period patterns ever had such a raised script mark.

labels only. When an authentic Middle Period piece is found with a permanent mark, it is the single word "Roseville" only, impressed into the clay (not raised).

The Chinese reproductions of Luffa and Jonquil are permanently marked with the single word "Roseville" in *raised* letters. This is the exact opposite of the authentic mark found on originals of the same pattern.

Roseville copies have also been made on a more limited scale in the United States. American reproductions include a Rosecraft (nude) Panel wall vase, La Rose vase, and various early pitchers in Tulip, Wild Rose, and Landscape. Many of the American-made fakes have "Rv" marks stamped in ink. Fake-ink stamped marks of "Roseville Rozane" have also been found in blue ink under new glaze.

Roseville reproductions are not limited to pottery. A reverse painted glass "dealers sign" has been showing up since about 1997. It is 15 7/8-by-8 inches with gold lettering and black background, and reads, "Roseville Pottery Sold Here."

Most new Roseville has poor detail and bad paint but some pieces are the equal of originals. Quality is not always apparent, though, especially when viewing an online image.

Study original marks and learn how they were applied and on what patterns they should appear. If bidding online or buying over the phone, be sure to ask very specific questions about how the piece is marked and glazed. Insist that a written receipt include the approximate year of production. "Roseville vase" on a receipt is not a statement of age or authenticity.

New Roseville is available in more than 100 shapes copied from old original shapes. Don't assume any particular shape or pattern is safe from being reproduced. **New**

New   **Old**

American Art Pottery

New Rosecraft Panel nude wall vases began appearing in 1997. The new pieces have a very crude "Rv" ink stamp in light blue. Original ink stamp marks are deep navy blue, almost black. Reproductions have poor mold detail and blotchy glaze.

New La Rose 9-inch handled vase, original catalog shape #242. Fake "Rv" mark on the base is very pale blue ink. Mark is thin and watery overall. Pottery is very heavy, little detail in molded garlands on sides.

One of the most unusual Roseville reproductions is this 16-inch vase with Art Nouveau-styled nude. It is marked on the base with hand-incised script "Roseville USA." White background with gold trim decoration.

Van Briggle Pottery

Van Briggle Pottery was founded by Artus Van Briggle in 1901 in Colorado Springs, Colorado. Before moving to Colorado for health reasons in 1899, Van Briggle was a major decorator for Rookwood Pottery in Ohio.

After Artus died in 1904, the business was taken over by his wife Anna and was renamed the Van Briggle Co. The business was reorganized again in 1910 as Van Briggle Pottery and Tile Co. Anna's involvement ended about 1912. Various managers and owners ran the business through the 1920s. In 1931, the name was changed back to Van Briggle Art Pottery, which remains in production today. Current products, although made in original shapes, are generally made in different colors and don't present a major problem to collectors.

Unauthorized fakes and reproductions, however, of original pre-1931 Van Briggle Pottery have been an increasing problem since the late 1990s. These new pieces are intentionally made to deceive and include what appear to be original company and finisher's marks. These false marks appear on three types of wares: reproductions of original Van Briggle shapes; new fantasy shapes never made by Van Briggle; and, some genuinely old pottery by other manufacturers to which forgers have added a Van Briggle mark.

Despite the various business names, the words and symbols that appear on genuine Van Briggle Pottery have been fairly consistent over the years. Authentic marks can be divided into two broad categories: those from 1901 to 1920; and those after 1920. The vast majority of authentic marks from both periods include

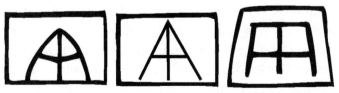

The AA monogram, which stands for Artus and Anna, appears on virtually all Van Briggle pottery. It is hand-inscribed and can appear in a number of different styles; no one style is right or wrong. Several typical original versions are shown here. This mark also appears in forged marks.

American Art Pottery

Fake 6-inch bowl with American Indian designs. Fantasy piece, no original ever made. Reddish brown glaze, no highlight color. Mark shown at right.

Typical fake mark hand-inscribed in wet clay on fake piece at left.

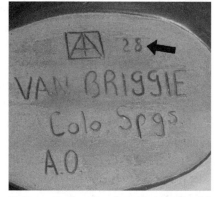

Fake 9-inch vase. Brownish red glaze, no highlight color. Mark shown at right.

Fake mark showing finisher number 28 and finisher initials "AO." Two different finisher marks never appear on the bottom of an original.

a monogram consisting of two letter As and "Van Briggle." Pre-1920 marks usually included a date and often had a design or glaze number. After 1920, pieces were rarely dated and Colorado Springs was added, usually abbreviated as "Colo Spgs." There is considerable variation among authentic marks because marks were inscribed by hand, rather than molded or stamped.

Since original hand-inscribed marks vary so much, it is somewhat difficult to detect the fakes by marks alone. Most of the fakes with forged marks so far have been shapes never originally made by Van Briggle. Unfortunately, unless you are very

This fake 6-inch jar is about 4 inches across with a reddish brown glaze. The lid has a sponge hole to suggest it is a humidor. Marked with "AA" monogram and "Colo Spgs." No authentic piece like this was ever made by Van Briggle. It is similar to a limited edition (below) series of busts of famous American Indians Van Briggle Pottery issued in the 1980s. Those pieces were 8 to 10 inches tall; no jars were made.

New

familiar with the large number of original shapes, you'll probably have trouble recognizing fantasy shapes.

At this time, there is no single test or clue to catch the fakes. Other than finding two finisher monograms on the same piece or the obvious mistake in the AO monogram (see opposite page), the forged marks are virtually identical to original marks. Here are some suggestions to help you catch most of the fakes:

• Almost all original Van Briggle Pottery had a highlight or accent color applied over the main body color, i.e. dark blue over light blue, dark blue over maroon, etc. So far, all of the fakes with forged marks have been solid, single colors with no highlight colors.

• Experienced Van Briggle buyers say that colors of fakes do not match colors of original glazes. However, colors are subjective and may change. What may be obvious

Chief Sitting Bull 10-inch bust, not a jar. Issued in 1984 by Van Briggle Pottery.

American Art Pottery

New   Old

Comparison of forged "AO" finisher's mark (left), and original on right. Note that original "O" has a distinct curl at the top.

Forged mark with finisher initials "AO." The forged initial "O" does not match the "O" found in original marks. (See illustration, above right.)

The "KV" finisher monogram is found only in fake marks. No old marks have ever been found with this monogram.

to an experienced eye may not be noticed by a general or beginning buyer.

• The most common original shape reproduced seems to be the 8-inch Columbine vase (original shown at right). Three were seen at a single Ohio flea market. The reproduction has good detail and a convincing bottom mark. All the fake Columbine pieces reported have a forged finisher's mark of the letter K joined with the letter V (see illustration above). There is no record of any vintage KV mark.

• Beware of any unusually rough or crude bottom marks. Be especially suspicious of flat sided "trench-like" lines in marks. Such marks may have been engraved with rotary tools after the clay has been fired. Also be wary of any marks with the clay raised along the lines of the mark.

Original 8-inch Columbine vase.

Photographs of fakes courtesy William Schulze.

Weller

At this writing, Weller Pottery is the only American art pottery without mass-produced reproductions. Weller reproductions that have surfaced so far have tended to be more one-of-a-kind pieces made in limited quantities.

This faked 7-inch vase is typical of those types of fakes made in limited numbers. It has a Weller Pottery script mark molded in the bottom with forged painted monogram of Weller artist Frank De Donatis. An unsuspecting buyer paid $500 for this fake. It was sold in Zanesville, Ohio. The forger was apparently trying to copy a Bonito line shape originally made from 1927 to 1933. De

Donatis' monogram does appear on many old Bonito pieces.

Compared to originals, almost everything about the fake is wrong. First, virtually all original Bonito is matte finish, not high gloss. Most Bonito was made from 1927 to 1933 and was marked "Weller Pottery" by hand, not molded. The molded Weller Pottery script mark, like that used on the fake, wasn't introduced until 1933.

These types of fakes are harder to catch than the mass-produced fakes imported from overseas. Since they appear in such small numbers, they usually don't arouse suspicion and are seldom reported in collector publications. A healthy scepticism is often the best protection. Carefully inspect the mark, glaze, decoration, and shape.

Bronze

Statues, Figures, Accessories

Reproduction *Mountain Man*, with Frederic Remington signature. Cast zinc with bronze colored finish, 14-inch black marble base.

"Bronzes" by almost every important 19th and early 20th century sculptor are widely available as reproductions complete with signatures. Although these pieces are offered and represented as "bronze," almost all are made of other metals such as iron, zinc, pot metal and common brass. The vast majority are poor quality, low-priced, mass-produced objects made overseas for antique reproduction wholesalers and decorators.

Sophisticated one-of-a-kind forgeries that take months to

New sculpture commonly sold as "bronze." Left, cast iron Art Nouveau styled 6-inch tray, $12.50; right, 4-inch cast iron dog, artist signed, $12.50.

make can fool trained specialists and those are beyond this book. But knowing just a few basics will protect you from virtually all the mass produced copies commonly found in today's market.

What is bronze? Bronze traditionally used in fine art sculpture is generally an alloy of around 90% copper and about 10% tin. Small percentages of zinc and lead may also be added to improve strength or handling in the casting process. The exact metallic content, however, is less important than the combination of skills related to creating a final work– the artist's model, the mold maker's ability to duplicate the model, the pouring of melted metal, and the quality of patina. Patina is the surface coloring applied to the finished bronze, generally an acid treatment applied with heat. Patinas duplicate the natural oxidation that occurs on bronze over many years of exposure to air.

Here are some of the best guidelines to use when evaluating

New 2½-inch mountain goat and 2-inch zebra marked Tiffany Studios New York (see mark page 206). Painted dark brown "patina" over brass.

Bronze

Statue and base shown separated. Note the threaded rod extending from the bottom of the statue.

The mass-produced reproductions use only a few styles of bases.

The "marble" bases on most reproductions are really plastic. A sharp blade will peel shavings like these off plastic bases. This was done around the bolt hole in the bottom of the base.

a suspect sculpture.

Bases

Original bronze sculpture of the 19th and early 20 century was rarely permanently attached to separate non-bronze bases. When original bronzes were purchased, customers chose their own bases to match their particular decorating needs.

By contrast, virtually all the reproduction metal sculptures are permanently attached to bases. This fact is generally concealed under a rubber-like pad. Removing the pad shows how the statue and base are joined. The vast majority of new bases are actually plastic. You can test a base (in a hidden spot) with

Pad cut away on new base showing hardware connecting new statue to base.

202

Metal tags with titles and artists' names are almost a guarantee that the statue is a reproduction. Such tags almost never appear on vintage original bronze sculptures.

Genuine 8-inch marble base permanently attached to new "bronze" statue. Although the base is genuine marble, virtually no old genuine good quality bronze statue is found permanently attached to its base.

any sharp blade. Plastic will peel off in shavings as shown on the previous page. Be suspicious if you see the same base on different sculptures offered by the same seller. New bases are made in only a limited number of shapes, bases of the same style are often used for many different sculptures.

A genuine marble base, however, is no guarantee of age or quality. Some reproductions do have inexpensive dyed marble bases, but these too are permanently attached bases.

New cast metal base on new statue. Modern Phillips head screws have been used to reinforce the connection between the base and the statue.

Bronze

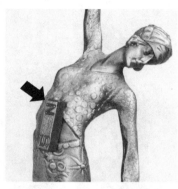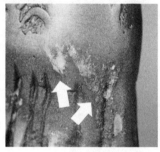

New 16-inch flapper girl, wholesale $35. Bronze-plated finish over iron. A magnet is the easiest way to catch these fakes (upper right). Small patches of red rust (lower right) are fairly common on new sculptures made of cast iron.

Some new bases are made of the same metal as the sculpture they support. Like other new bases, the majority of new metal bases are also permanently attached, which indicates their recent manufacture. Many new metal bases are also fastened with Phillips head screws, which would never have been used on vintage bronze sculpture.

Another easy clue to a recent product is a metal tag with the sculpture's title and the artist's name applied to the base. Virtually no originals have these tags. Some vintage sculpture does have similar tags on presentation pieces, but those clearly state who is presenting the sculpture, the occasion, date, etc., not just title and artist.

Metal content

Given the low wholesale prices, it shouldn't be surprising to find that most new "bronze" sculptures in the antiques market are really cast iron. How can you tell? It's easy; use any small magnet. Regardless of the color of the surface, if the magnet sticks, the piece is made of iron.

Look closely, and you'll soon find many new pieces have small patches of red rust. Such patches are especially common down in crevices where moisture was apparently slow to evaporate. This is why all the iron statues from the wholesalers come packaged with little bags of desiccant (silica gel) to absorb moisture.

This is one of the reasons why most new pieces have permanently attached bases, to prevent you from examining the metal. If you could easily look up inside most new bases, it would be easy to see the metal was not true bronze but something else.

Patina

True patina is a chemical change, or oxidation, in unfinished bronze exposed to air. Rather than wait for natural patinas to develop, artists found they could produce patinas in the studio by applying acid with heat. Virtually all vintage bronze sculptures were originally made with skillfully applied acid-based patinas. Original patinas can be a wide range of colors from deep black to gold to green. These original patinas can usually only be removed by abrasives like steel wool or sand paper; paint remover very rarely can remove an acid-based patina applied under heat.

By contrast, the "patina" on virtually all mass-produced reproduction bronzes is simple paint or stain. The most obvious clues are runs and drips in the painted patinas. True acid-based patinas never have runs or drips. No true patina flakes or chips, but paint peels relatively easily on metal. New bronzes with painted patinas commonly have flakes and chips in the surface finish.

Many new painted or stained patinas are so thin they are easily removed with ordinary fingernail polish remover on a cotton swab; however, use this test with care. Many authentic patinas are protected by wax. Attempts to test the paint could possibly dull authentic patinas.

On virtually all originals, metalwork was marked before the

Bronze

 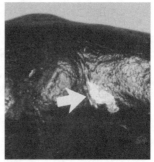

The painted "patina" on the majority of new bronzes (left) can be removed with fingernail polish remover (acetone). Chips and flakes (right) in new painted "patina" are common.

patina was applied. This means that the same patina or finish on the overall surface should also be found in the letters of the mark below the surface. Some forgers who have made a fake Tiffany stamp will try to mark a non-Tiffany item. If the letters in the mark show up as shiny metal, the stamp has been applied *after* the surface finish. This also applies to forged model numbers.

Never test a patina by scratching a suspected surface. Scratches do not reveal any useful information and will permanently scar an authentic bronze.

Details

There are significant differences between old and new in details of casting. This is particularly true in hands, hair, and eyes in human subjects, and paws/hooves, fur and eyes in animals. Human hands of reproductions are frequently unrealistic ball-shaped, club- or flipper-like shapes with no clearly defined fingers. Hands that hold or grasp something are almost always poorly made, often with drilled holes.

Be alert for crude welds and fiberglass fillers used to fill gaps and other flaws common in new sculptures. Many new sculptures have also acquired Asian facial features, especially eyes. It

Beware of sudden or dramatic color changes in surface color or "patina." This is a clue to a modern reproduction.

Hole drilled in hand.   Filler used to cover gap in casting.

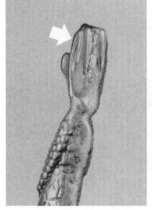

New flipper-like hand lacks   Patina missing in spots; note Asian
realistic detail   styled eyes.

is also common for prominent areas of new sculpture, like the face, to be missing patina.

Signatures

About 90 percent of reproduction sculptures have a signature of an important sculptor or foundry of the 19th and 20th century. That's why you are better advised to base your tests of age on construction methods rather than marks and signatures.

One of the most commonly found faked marks is some variation of Tiffany, especially "TIFFANY STUDIOS NEW YORK." This mark frequently appears in a depressed rectangular area with *raised* letters (as shown on the next page). This mark was cast (molded) at the same time the new sculpture was made.

The vast majority of authentic metal items made by Tiffany, such as small bronzes, candlesticks, desk sets, etc., made

Bronze

The majority of new metal statues include an artist signature. Most new signatures, like this Frederic Remington, are of well-known artists.

Other new sculptures have signatures of unknown artists or deliberately unreadable signatures like the one above.

Chinese characters, actually a production code, on the base of a new "bronze." The characters were hidden under the rubber pad on the base.

Tiffany Studios New York mark on animal figures shown at the beginning of this chapter. This mark is cast (molded) in raised lettering on recessed panel. No model number.

Authentic "Tiffany Studios New York" mark is die-stamped and includes die-stamped model number.

between 1900 and 1919, are in fact marked "TIFFANY STUDIOS NEW YORK." But unlike the fake marks, original marks are die-stamped or impressed *below the surface*. The location of original die-stamped marks can vary since they were individually applied. But original marks never appear in depressed rectangular areas found on the fakes.

Another major feature of virtually all authentic Tiffany metalwork is the presence of a *model number*. This three- or four-digit number is stamped or impressed *below* the surface. Model numbers on a piece you examine should match the model numbers on a similar piece listed or shown in original Tiffany catalogs and price sheets. Each shape had its own number. Each piece in a metal desk set–for example, inkwell, blotter holder, stamp box, etc.–should be marked with different model numbers.

Although there are a handful of confusing original Tiffany model numbers used on more than one shape, they are the exception to the rule. Model numbers, which can also be forged, are not by themselves a guarantee of authenticity but another factor to add to your examination check list. (Also see Tiffany belt buckles at the end of this chapter.)

Another common signature on reproductions is Frederic Remington. Since the original copyright protection expired in the 1960s, the number of Remington reproductions in the market has exploded.

So how do you authenticate a Remington bronze? The best

New Art Nouveau style 7-inch bowl (left) marked Tiffany in cast (molded) block letters one-quarter inch tall (above). Bowl made of cast brass with painted patina.

Bronze

Widely available reproduction sizes | Original sizes

7" 12" 23" 34" 54" | 23" 32"

Only two sizes of Remington's original Bronco Buster were produced: one about 23 inches, the other, about 32 inches. Reproductions appear in a wide range of sizes from under 8 inches to more than 8 feet.

way to start is with a healthy dose of realism. The whereabouts of virtually all original Remington bronzes is well documented. Practically all original Remingtons sold today are offered through major auction galleries or well-known art dealers. The least expensive original will probably sell for $75,000. Chances of you finding an original at the local flea market or having one walk into your shop are extremely remote. Further, many originals were made in such limited numbers that any subjects in those titles are suspect. Only one original of *The Buffalo Signal* and *The Buffalo Horse,* for example, were made.

New Remington 22-inch tall sculpture. Cast zinc, bronze surface color, signed Frederic Remington. Made in China.

Less than 15 *Coming through the Rye* were made originally.

Most Remington reproductions can be detected by simply following the guidelines discussed in previous pages. Here are three more specific tips to help you eliminate other Remington lookalikes:

1) Authentic Remington bronzes are permanently marked with the foundry name. The majority of reproductions do not have foundry marks. All of Remington's originals were produced by only two firms: Roman Bronze Works and Henry-Bonnard Bronze Co. Any other name is automatically a forgery. Henry-Bonnard produced only sand castings for Remington; Roman

Bronze Works made only lost wax castings. Any lost wax cast piece with a Henry-Bonnard foundry mark is automatically a forgery.

2) Original Remingtons are permanently marked with a number indicating where in the production sequence they were produced. Many reproductions are marked in a limited edition fashion with a purported casting number followed by the edition number such as "12/250" or "55 of 500."

3) Consider the size. Most original titles were made in only one or two sizes. Reproductions appear in many sizes, most of which are vastly different than original sizes.

Tiffany belt buckles

Wells Fargo and Company buckle, marked Tiffany New York on back.

"Bronze" belt buckles marked Tiffany can be traced back to the mid-1960s. At that time, buckles began surfacing with highly collectible names such as Winchester, Coca-Cola, Wells Fargo, and historical figures and celebrities such as Abraham Lincoln and Lillie Langtry. Although no one had seen similar pieces before 1965 and some questioned the age, buckles were soon selling for up to $400 and more. The question of age seemed

Bronze

Close-up of fake Tiffany New York mark on back of buckles. Wording of marks vary slightly.

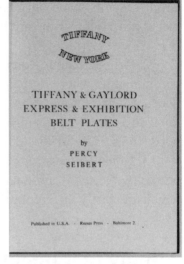

Title page of book published to "document" fake buckles.

Back side of typical Tiffany fake buckle. Actual size of this and most other fake Tiffany-marked buckles is about 4 by 3 inches.

to be settled in 1970 when a book exclusively on the belt buckles titled *Tiffany & Gaylord Express & Exhibition Belt Plates* began appearing at book sellers.

This book detailed a collaboration between Tiffany's of New York and Emerson Gaylord, a hardware manufacturer in Chicopee Falls, Massachusetts. The book included specific company records with order dates, production quantities, and other detailed information. Buckle sellers pointed out the book's 1950 copyright date as proof the buckles were documented years earlier. The question of age seemed to be resolved.

But that was only the beginning.

In 1973, J. Duncan Campbell, an expert in metal insignias who was an advisor to the Smithsonian, published *New Belt Buckles of the Old West*, a book exposing the Tiffany buckles as frauds. Not only did Campbell prove the buckles were recently made,

New buckle marked Tiffany. "Coca-Cola Marathon Dancing Trophy" on front. Reverse has lettering "Awarded for 24 Hours of non-stop Dancing."

he also showed how the *Belt Plates* book was also faked apparently to support the sale of the fraudulent buckles.

Although these buckles first appeared almost 25 years ago, they have never been widely exposed as fakes. A Lincoln buckle, for example, was recently offered by a prominent West Coast auction firm that pictured the buckle in a catalog with a presale estimate of $300 to $400.

There are at least 75 different styles of these buckles with designs ranging from Mickey Mouse to the Ku Klux Klan. All are fakes; no originals of any of these buckles were ever made by Tiffany. Original wholesale prices of these buckles were $5 to $10.

All the new buckles are cast in brass. Most buckles have been treated with chemicals or other artificial means to create an impression of age.

Western Union Telegraph Company fake buckle marked Tiffany. One of the few fakes based on an original 19th century buckle. However, the original was issued by the U.S. Army Topographical Engineers not Western Union.

Furniture

The hand-carved decoration on this armoire suggests it is an authentic antique, but it's a reproduction. In this chapter, we discuss construction details you can use to identify furniture reproductions, especially those from Asia.

By far the largest source of reproduction antique furniture in today's market comes from Asia, particularly Indonesia. This new furniture copies virtually all old styles from Chippendale to Arts and Crafts, Boston Colonial to New York East Lake. It can be found in all shapes and forms from simple chairs to fireplace mantels, ornate pedestals to mirrors, hall stands to dining tables.

In this section, we'll begin our discussion with the Indonesian imports then look at other typical furniture reproductions including painted furniture and Arts and Crafts styled furniture.

Indonesian imports

Child labor is common in typical Indonesian furniture factories.

New Indonesian furniture is made of several species of mahogany never used in old furniture.

Indonesia has the two essential ingredients for manufacturing reproduction furniture: cheap labor and cheap wood. Furniture manufacturers use the low-cost labor to attempt to duplicate the hand carved details found on original antique furniture like elaborate carving, detailed ornaments, and intricate forms.

There are three fairly obvious construction clues you can use to identify the Indonesian reproductions that require no prior furniture experience. These three basic telltale signs are: a single type (species) of wood is used throughout the piece; many wood-to-wood joints are hot-glued only; and, widespread use of common nails.

Wood

Indonesian imports are frequently advertised as "genuine ma-

New table made in Indonesia. Heavily carved details similar in appearance to Victorian original.

Furniture

New Indonesian figural carved dolphin table base (above). New Indonesian cupboard (right).

hogany" in auction notices or "estate sale" listings with the implication that such pieces are old. Look in reference books on antique furniture, and you'll see some of the finest 18th and 19th century pieces are mahogany.

But "mahogany" can be deceptive.

Why? Because there are few legal restrictions today on how wood is marketed and advertised. As a result, trade names have been developed to help promote little known wood or to make common woods sound more valuable.

The wood in Indonesian reproduction furniture, for example,

Close-up view of mahogany in the Indonesian reproductions. Deep dark brown or black pits. Marketed as mahogany or Philippine mahogany.

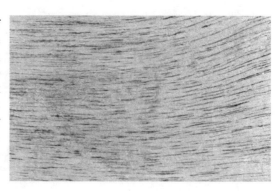

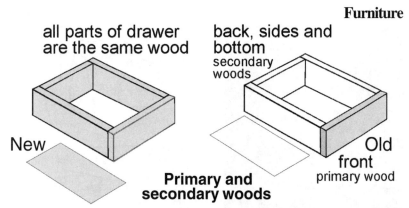

all parts of drawer are the same wood

back, sides and bottom
secondary woods

New

Old front
primary wood

Primary and secondary woods

All parts of new Indonesian furniture are made of the same species of wood. Old furniture is made of several species of wood. Exposed wood, or *primary wood*, is used on drawer fronts, table tops, etc. Pieces hidden from view, such as glue blocks, drawer bottoms, etc., are made of less expensive types of wood or *secondary wood.*

is from the groups *Shorea, Parashorea,* and *Pentacme,* which grow in the Eastern Hemisphere and are not true mahogany at all. All three

Back view of typical old drawer. The pieces of the drawer hidden from view–side #1, back #2, and bottom #3–are made of common, less expensive woods than the exposed drawer front. This example shows three secondary woods.

woods, however, can be and are legally advertised and sold as "mahogany." Two other generic trade names for these woods are *Philippine mahogany* and *Lauan mahogany.* Products made of these woods, including the new Indonesian furniture, can legally be described as mahogany.

But mahogany used in fine antique furniture–and even good quality reproductions–is from entirely different botanical groups. The traditional mahoganies used in period furniture are from *Swietenia,* from Central and South America, Cuba, Honduras, and the West Indies, and *Khaya* from Africa.

Thankfully, it is not necessary to be able to identify these woods

Furniture

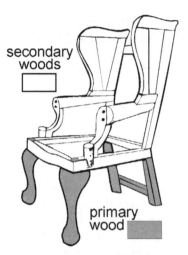

New wing chair from Indonesia. Upholstery removed. Entire frame, including hidden supports and glue block, is made from a single species of wood.

Frame of typical old wing chair made from two or more types of wood. Wood not hidden by upholstery is primary wood. Wood covered with upholstery is made of secondary wood.

to detect the new furniture. Simply knowing how vintage furniture was made will help you catch most new pieces.

Genuine mahogany, like other cabinet woods, has always been expensive and used in furniture only as *primary woods*. Primary woods are used on the most visible surfaces of furniture–such as drawer fronts, table tops, etc. The common woods used in parts hidden from view–such as the bottoms of drawers, glue blocks, and other structural supports–are called *secondary woods*. This means you should normally and logically find more than one type of wood in virtually all old furniture attributed to cabinet makers, workshops, and factories (excepting homemade "country" furniture). It would have been financial suicide for furniture makers of the 18th or 19th century to use expensive Honduran mahogany for a glue block that no one would ever see.

In marked contrast, entire pieces of Indonesian furniture are made of a single species of wood, the so-called Philippine mahogany. The same type of wood is used for all surfaces, whether hidden (secondary) or visible (primary). The front, bottom, back, and side of a new Indonesian drawer, for example, are all made of

Glue blocks

Furniture

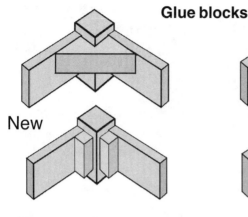

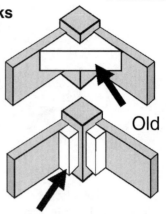

New

Old

Hidden Indonesian glue blocks are made from the same species of wood as visible surfaces.

Hidden glue blocks in typical old furniture are made of less expensive secondary wood.

mahogany. With antique drawers, only the exposed drawer front would be a fine wood; all the hidden parts–sides, bottom, and back–would be of common inexpensive woods.

Glued joints

Typical joints in old furniture are reinforced with dowels, splines, or special joints such as mortise and tenon, rabbet, etc. Many wood-to-wood joints in the Indonesian furniture are simply hot-glued without even nails for support. As the new furniture dries, the glued joints split, leaving large obvious gaps. You can test a suspected joint by passing a slip of paper through it. Production grade hot glues generally dry white and can usually be seen without difficulty. These same glues also usually fluoresce under long-wave black light; older glues rarely fluoresce.

Typical gap in glued joint in new Indonesian furniture. Passing a piece of paper through the gap proves the joint is not fastened with nails, dowels, or tenons within the joint.

Furniture

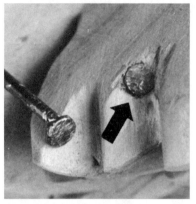 

Common nails with large, round heads, rather than finishing nails, are frequently found in new Indonesian furniture (above, filler removed).

Large fill area (arrow) concealing round head nail. These ¼-inch diameter fill areas are an important clue to new Indonesian furniture.

Common nails

Common nails have flat, disc-shaped heads. They are normally used where strength is more important than appearance. Such nails were never used in exposed surfaces of furniture of any reasonable quality, new or old, because it is difficult to hide the head. Common nails are frequently used in exposed surfaces of many pieces of new Indonesian furniture. These nails can be located by ¼-inch diameter areas of filler material (see photos above). These filled areas can be detected under dark or light finishes if you look closely.

The nail most commonly used in furniture is the finishing nail whose small heads are driven below the surface of the wood. The hole above the head is filled in and the nail is almost invisible. Flat-shank finishing nails with flat T-shaped heads were used from about 1800 to the 1880s; modern round-shank finishing nails have been used since the 1890s.

Other considerations

Indonesian reproductions also include child- and doll-sized furniture and copies of Black Forest three-dimensional pieces. Virtually all styles of collectible furniture are being reproduced.

The quality and value of furniture is based on how it is put together, rather than the wood it is made of. Don't be influenced by advertising descriptions or names on tags. Politely insist on *thoroughly* inspecting any furniture you're thinking of buying. This means pulling drawers out of chests and asking that dust covers be removed or lifted from upholstered pieces. Of course, always ask the seller's permission before you move, tip, or remove parts of a piece of furniture.

Here are some typical wholesale prices for new Indonesian mahogany furniture: dining chairs–unfinished, $50/finished, $75; Victorian parlor chairs–$75 to $150; Victorian writing desk– $125 to $450; hall tables–various styles, $75 to $450; dining tables–various styles, $100-$350.

New Indonesian mahogany fireplace mantel (left). New mahogany pedestal, right.

Indonesian reproduction of Black Forest bench.

Painted furniture (colonial, folk, country styles)

For years, the majority of reproduction American antique furniture was made of traditional stained hardwoods. Recent trends, however, have been towards ever-increasing amounts of mass-produced furniture painted in colonial, folk, and country styles. The vast majority of these painted reproductions are imported from India, Indonesia, and Mexico. The low wages paid in those countries allow manufacturers to apply extensive

Furniture

handpainting that can be confused with handwork found on antique painted furniture. In this section, we'll look at how to separate new from old painted furniture based on paint, construction details, and determining if wear is natural or artificial. The focus will be on the country and folk-style painted furniture originally made at home or in very small rural furniture shops up until the last

New chest of drawers with handpainted nautical scene. Made in India.

quarter of the 19th century. The formally painted furniture from master cabinet makers in large cities is not included.

Paint

Original furniture was painted for very practical reasons. Paint protected and sealed the wood's surface and covered up flaws such as knots and streaks in the grain. Paint also hid the fact that several types of wood were used.

These practical-minded furniture makers—small shop owners or rural craftsmen—did not waste time painting or decorating areas that were not visible. You should not find original paint on the insides of drawers, for instance, or the bottoms of tables. Why waste your time, effort, or paint? Painting these hidden areas may make sense though, if you're mass-producing an "antique." About half of all the painted reproductions have paint in hidden areas.

This apparently old, battered, and weathered painted chest of drawers is new. The wood is all mahogany, made in Indonesia.

Typical new crazed paint. Dark lines are paint that shows through cracks in topcoat of paint.

Typical old crazing in antique surface. Dark lines are cracks filled in with dirt.

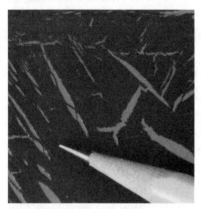

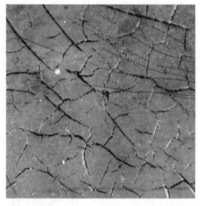

Typical new crazing. Lighter colored paint shows through dark crackled topcoat.

Typical old crazed paint. Black lines are cracks filled in with dirt.

Virtually all reproduction painted furniture has a heavily crazed surface. This finish is created by applying a crackle paint topcoat to a base coat of a contrasting color. As the topcoat crackles, or splits, the base coat below shows through as dark lines. Such crazing or crackling may or may not be present in original painted surfaces. But crazing by itself is *never* a guarantee of age.

There are two types of surface crazing that may occur in old original painted surfaces: crazing of varnish or glaze applied to protect the paint, and crazing within the paint itself. Varnish gets brittle as it ages. As the wood expands and contracts, the hardened

223

Furniture

varnish can split, bubble, and develop fine networks of lines.

True crazing in paint is more properly called "alligatoring." In this condition, the paint surface develops cracks as it ages. Over time, these cracks fill in with dirt and appear as dark lines or veins. Whereas most dark lines in genuinely old paint are actually dirt, dark lines in new "antiqued" paint are simply a contrasting color of paint. In some original surfaces, you may see two layers of crazing– one in the varnish and another in the paint. So far, we have not seen any crazed varnish in the painted reproductions, only the crazed paint.

The surface of original painted furniture is rarely *all* alligatored or crazed. Such conditions in original paint are usually the result of three factors: *environmental effects* such as heat, humidity, ultraviolet (sunlight) exposure; *accidents* like spills, water, fire or smoke damage; and, *defects* in the paint or wood, or problems in initial drying and curing. By contrast, the *entire* surface of virtually all the painted reproductions is crazed.

Here are some guidelines to help you judge the age of paint. First, old paint is generally very, very hard. It is brittle and breaks or shatters into irregularly shaped chips or powders when scraped with a knife. Old paint is almost impossible to dent with a fingernail. New paint comes off in curls with a knife and dents with a fingernail. Newly painted pieces very often have a strong new paint odor, especially in confined spaces like drawers. Don't be afraid to put your nose to the surface and take a whiff. All crazing on the same piece should have roughly the same appearance.

Original paint used on country and folk pieces varied widely from oil bases to milk. Virtually without exception, all the new painted furniture is decorated with water-based acrylic paint. Acrylics weren't invented until the 1940s and not generally available until the early 1950s.

Paint wear

The absence of normal wear, or the presence of artificial wear, are among the most important clues to age. Authentic paint wear is *always* logical and consistent with the original function of the piece examined. In other words, does the paint wear match how the piece was supposedly used? Put your hand on a drawer

New painted
wood cabinet with illogical paint
wear on the doors.

pull, open a cupboard door, sit in a chair. Do natural motions of using a piece match the pattern of paint wear?

Look, for example, at the new painted cabinet at left. Note that the paint is completely "worn" from the edges (arrow) of the door. This is illogical; what caused paint to wear here? These worn areas are actually protected from normal everyday use such as opening and closing the door. Natural paint wear can always be explained and appears on surfaces that logically are exposed to obvious patterns of use.

You also need to pay attention as to how paint wear relates to the underlying wood surface. Gouges and dents in a painted surface should generally expose bare wood. If there is paint in or over a dent or gouge, that means the paint has been applied *after* the gouges and dents were made. This could mean a genuinely

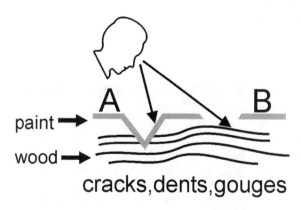

cracks,dents,gouges

If paint is down inside cracks (A) or covers holes and dents, the paint has been applied *after* the cracks and dents have been made. Genuinely old dents and gouges *go through* the original paint and expose the wood below (B).

Furniture

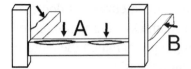 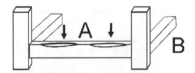

Front rungs of chairs should show the heaviest wear because that is where feet naturally fall. Side rungs may show some natural wear but should not show as much wear as front rungs. If all rungs–front, back, and sides–show about equal wear, chances are the wear has been artificially created.

old piece has been repainted, but is much more likely to indicate a new piece has been "distressed"–hit with chains, hammers, etc.–before new paint was applied. Likewise, be suspicious of paint in cracks. Cracks that develop through an original finish will not have any paint in them; dirt maybe, but no paint. If paint is down inside a crack, it means the paint was applied after the crack occurred. Again, this might mean an old piece has been repainted, but far more often, paint inside a crack means an "antiqued" reproduction.

Be particularly suspicious of any surface wear that appears in a regular pattern. The photo below shows a wood surface where the soft grain has been removed with a power wire brush. The wire brush has left a series of fine parallel valleys and ridges that was painted over. Parallel lines, concentric circles and most other repeating or regular patterns are almost always the result of artificial wear produced by modern power tools. Natural wear, produced one scratch or dent at a time, occurs over many years and should generally appear in random widths, directions and depths.

Soft grain in wood removed by wire brush before the surface was painted. Genuine wear does not occur in a repeated regular patterns like this series of parallel ridges and lines.

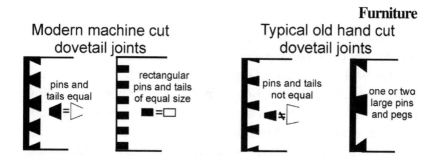

Modern machine cut dovetail joints — pins and tails equal — rectangular pins and tails of equal size

Typical old hand cut dovetail joints — pins and tails not equal — one or two large pins and pegs

Construction

Certain construction techniques and fasteners virtually eliminate the possibility of a piece being old. Finding staples and Phillips head screws under the finish coat of paint, for example, is an obvious sign of new manufacture. Fiberboard (Masonite) is another modern material commonly found in new pieces as drawer bottoms and the backs of cupboards and chests of drawers. Machine-cut dovetail joints are another sign of modern construction (see illustrations above). Country and folk painted furniture should show hand-cut dovetails, not machine-cut dovetails.

Another good test is to look at boards used in large surface

New   Old

boards of equal widths
evenly divide the surface

large single boards or unequal
widths with irregular spacing

Typical arrangement of new and old boards used in large surface areas such as table tops, trunks, sides of chests of drawers, etc.

Furniture

areas such as table tops, solid backs of large cupboards, trunks and the sides of chests of drawers (see illustration on previous page). Boards used in new painted furniture tend to be the same width and divide the surface equally. Boards in old country style construction, pre-1875, are generally much wider and tend to be irregular in width.

The wood used in most authentic American country style painted furniture is white pine but can be almost any native American species. The majority of new painted furniture is made of foreign species of which the most common is the so-called Philippine "mahogany" (discussed earlier). Although pine construction is not conclusive proof of age, the use of mahogany in painted country styled furniture is a virtual guarantee of a reproduction. No species of mahogany was ever used in original American country painted furniture.

Repaints, repairs

Genuinely old pieces are frequently repaired and repainted to increase the selling price. You can generally catch most of these alterations with a simple checklist of questions:

• Does the entire surface *feel* the same to the touch? If the painted surface is all original, the finish should feel the same all over. If one area or one color feels different, investigate further.

• If there is crazing, does all the crazing look the same? Mismatched crazing is a warning sign that different materials from the original have been used.

• Does the surface look the same under black light? New materials rarely fluoresce the same as old materials. Any differences would indicate a disturbance in the original surface. Be particularly cautious of dates and names which are probably the most common enhancements made to genuinely old pieces.

Arts and Crafts

The name "Stickley" has appeared on American furniture for more than 100 years. Since about 1990, the present furniture company using the name of Stickley has been making copies of original Stickley Arts and Craft designs.

Five Stickley brothers–Gustav, Leopold, John George (J.G.),

New Stickley spindle chair is virtually identical to old chair.

Original Gustav Stickley spindle chair as shown in 1905 catalog.

Albert and Charles–began a furniture company in New York in the mid-1880s (see chart next page). Gustav, Leopold, and J.G. were a leading force in spreading the Arts and Crafts style in America. Gustav was the most dedicated to the ideals of the Arts and Crafts movement and published a magazine in addition to making furniture and related Arts and Crafts products under his own name.

As public taste changed over the years, however, Gustav failed to update his designs and his business failed commercially. Leopold and J.G. adapted their furniture to changing styles, and were more of a commercial success.

The number of furniture businesses that involved the Stickley name can easily confuse buyers who are not familiar with the various marks. You may read an auction report of a "Stickley chest of drawers" selling for thousands of dollars and incorrectly conclude that all chests of drawers with any Stickley mark are in that price range (generally, Gustav Stickley pieces are the most valuable). Or you may confuse a recent Stickley mark with an earlier mark and think a piece is much older than it really is. The

Stickley furniture companies through the years

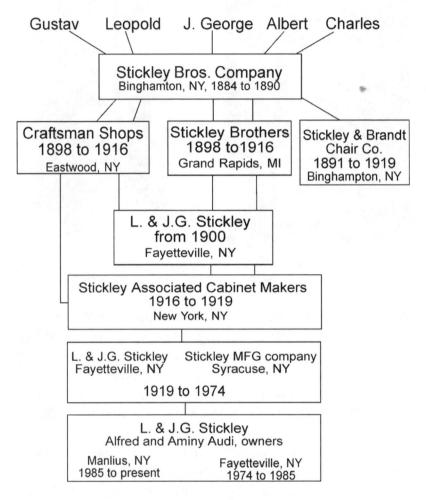

Gustav   Leopold   J. George   Albert   Charles

Stickley Bros. Company
Binghamton, NY, 1884 to 1890

| **Craftsman Shops** 1898 to 1916 Eastwood, NY | **Stickley Brothers** 1898 to 1916 Grand Rapids, MI | **Stickley & Brandt** Chair Co. 1891 to 1919 Binghampton, NY |

L. & J.G. Stickley
from 1900
Fayetteville, NY

Stickley Associated Cabinet Makers
1916 to 1919
New York, NY

L. & J.G. Stickley   Stickley MFG company
Fayetteville, NY   Syracuse, NY

1919 to 1974

L. & J.G. Stickley
Alfred and Aminy Audi, owners

Manlius, NY   Fayetteville, NY
1985 to present   1974 to 1985

marks of the more important Stickley businesses are shown on the opposite page.

To the inexperienced eye, new Stickley furniture is virtually identical to earlier vintage pieces. All pieces are handmade of high-quality wood, such as quarter-sawn white oak and are constructed with complex joints, such as keyed tenons and blind dovetails.

Look for the appropriate types of normal wear to help you date Arts and Crafts style furniture. Don't rely on marks as your only test of age. Marks are easily removed or added.

Gustav Stickley
1901-1916

L. & J.G. Stickley
1905

L. & J.G. Stickley
ca. 1906-1912

L. & J. G. Stickley
1912-1917

Stickley Associated
Cabinetmakers
ca. 1916-1919

Stickley Marks

Marks not shown in scale; marks vary in size. Other marks and variations on the marks shown also exist. Marks may appear stamped in ink, burned in, or on a paper, leather or metal tag. More than one mark may appear on the same piece.

1926-1977

ca. 1927-1935

1950-PRESENT

Stickley

1985-PRESENT

1989-present

New metal tag and burned mark in current use. Note that the mark in the tag is the same as the 1916 tag above. The only change is the name of the town. Original tag reads "Syracuse and Fayetteville"; current tag reads "Manlius."

Roycroft furniture

Elbert Hubbard (1856 to 1915) was a leader in the Arts and Crafts movement and founded the Roycroft Community in East Aurora, New York.

New stool with Roycroft mark.

Although the Roycroft Community was based on a philosophy of life, it was also a business. More than 500 workers produced a wide range of products, including metal goods, furniture, textiles, ceramics, and various printed goods. The Roycroft Community was weakened by the Depression of the early 1930s and closed in 1938.

Many Roycroft products were marked with a distinctive trademark, the letter "R" enclosed in a circle (see marks opposite page). Variations in this mark can generally be used to establish an approximate date of production.

New cabinet with Roycroft mark, 40 inches tall.

Rolled ends on the tail and top of the "R" indicate a production date from about 1906 to 1910. The ends were smoothed and straightened in the "R" from about 1910 to 1915. After Hubbard's death in 1915, the word "Roycroft" was added below the trademark, and this version was used until 1938.

Until the 1990s, Roycroft marks were relatively good indications of age. Now, copies and revisions of old marks are available on new furniture. This situation is caused by separate legal claims to the various original marks.

As of this time, copies of original marks are registered only in the state of New York, which permits marks to be registered for specific materials. One person, for example, registered the

rounded curls
on R
ca. 1906-1910

rounded curls
removed from R
ca. 1910-1915

Roycroft added
ca. 1915-1938

R O Y C R O F T

original "R" in circle mark for use on metals. The new company, Roy-croft Shops, Inc. (RSI), has also registered the original "R" in circle mark in New York state for use on a wide range of materials.

RSI has in turn licensed use of the old mark to L. & J.G. Stickley, Inc. furniture company (see previous section), which uses the mark on reproduction furniture. New pieces include a chafing dish cabinet, cellaret, magazine holder, writing desk, and small stool. The Roycroft trademark is routed into the surface to a depth of about 1/8 inch. These pieces also carry two new Stickley shop marks; one, a metal plate attached by nails, the other an oval trademark burned in with a hot iron (see Stickley marks on previous pages). If a buyer is not aware of the new Stickley marks, or if the marks are tampered with, the new Roycroft can be confusing when it's offered for sale in the secondary market.

Another new mark resembling originals consists of *two* "R"s back-to-back in a circle. This mark is owned and licensed by Roycrofters At Large, an organization dedicated to the preservation of the original Roycroft site in East Aurora, New York. The two "R"s is the mark of Roycroft Renaissance, a licensed trade name belonging to Roycrofters At Large. This mark has been used on a wide variety of materials since about 1984.

from ca. 1984

Newly created mark used by Roycroft Renaissance since 1984 has two Rs.

Digital Fakes
and Forgeries

Inkjet and Laser Prints

Full-color portrait of Theodore Roosevelt with advertisement for Simpson's
Golf Clubs under thick, clear glass paperweight. Simpson is an authentic
turn-of-the-century club manufacturer. This pose is from a well-known period
painting by artist John S. Sargent and frequently appears on authentic TR
pieces.

Digital fakes

New glass paperweight and political collectibles reference book are all the raw ingredients needed for a digital forgery.

In many cases, factory-produced reproductions are made in such large numbers that their sudden appearance alone is often enough to make buyers suspicious. Most are relatively easy to detect after they are publicized. Once buyers are informed of specific differences between new and old–such as marks, signatures, mold seams, dimensions, etc.–catching mass-produced fakes often becomes simply a matter of communication.

A more serious, growing problem has become detecting one-of-kind fakes and fantasies based on digital (computer-based) images. As the price of good quality color printers, scanners and imaging software continues to fall, the number of do-it-yourself fakers and forgers continues to rise. In the past, collectors could keep up on the latest reproductions by monitoring the catalogs

Book image is scanned into the computer and
new fantasy lettering is added.

Digital fakes

Fake 1904 Worlds Fair Coca-Cola paperweight. Color digital image on paper under glass. Image scanned from reference book on Coke; Worlds Fair lettering added in computer.

and showrooms of four or five importers. Now, anyone with a home computer is a potential source of custom-made fakes and reproductions.

Such homemade fakes are particularly dangerous. First, they dribble into the market in such small numbers no one becomes suspicious. Second, they exist in countless variations and are hard to categorize and warn against. Third, while most buyers know that signs, posters, prints, postcards, and catalogs are widely

Genuinely old 1920s wooden recipe box with digital fake label applied. The normal wear on the box makes the entire piece look authentic. New paper label can easily be aged by rubbing with steel wool or sandpaper. The facial images were scanned from an illustration of a genuinely old game found in a reference book on black memorabilia. The lettering was added in the computer.

Genuinely old perfume bottle with a faked digital label, left. The fake was created by scanning the genuinely old, but low value "Stearns" perfume label, center. The Stearn name was removed and "California Perfume Co.," a more sought after and expensive name, was added, right.

reproduced, very few are aware that paperweight inserts, labels for crates, barrels, bottles and boxes, company stationery, clock and watch faces, toys, political and campaign memorabilia, and a virtually endless list of other three-dimensional items can be faked with digital images.

The most convincing digital fakes are usually combined, or "married," to a genuinely old object. Starting with an inexpensive original item from a common manufacturer with no

Low value original image removed from this old match safe. New digital Coca-Cola image added to enhance value.

New digital Keen Kutter face added to old alarm clock.

Digital fakes

New digital paper prints applied to wood imitate Victorian lithographed paper over wood toys. Digital prints are also used to repair genuinely old toys that are damaged.

collectible value, the faker adds a new digital image of a widely sought after name or trademark with a very high collectible value. Originally having labels from unknown makers, these types of items can be picked up for just a few dollars at flea markets and garage sales. The original labels are removed or covered over, fake digital labels applied, and the items are resold with now highly collectible names.

Besides using genuinely old objects, skilled digital forgers carefully combine genuine graphic elements to enhance the appearance of authenticity and to increase demand. The Coca-Cola image under the glass paperweight, for example, was actually used by the Coca-Cola company in 1901 as the top of a calendar. It was scanned from a reference book on Coca-Cola and the original lettering above the woman's head removed. The original calendar currently lists for around $4,000 in price guides. How much would the "rare and unlisted" Worlds Fair paperweight be worth?

Faked digital print. Winchester Rifles advertising added to image copied from original Currier & Ives print taken from reference book. Framed with brass chain. These fakes have brought $200 to $500.

Digital printers can produce images on a wide variety of surfaces. This Maxfield Parrish reproduction, for example, is printed on canvas to create the appearance of an oil painting.

The perfume bottle shows another common way to combine old and new. First, the genuinely old original label was scanned. Then, the original low-value company name was removed and California Perfume Co. added. The new high-value label was then applied to the old bottle. Note the original paper band around the bottle neck. California Perfume was the forerunner of Avon and, if original, this bottle would be worth $125 to $175.

The Roosevelt paperweight at the beginning of the chapter and the recipe box are other examples of fantasy digital images "authenticated" in reference books. The Roosevelt image is a well-known painting by John Sargent that appears on many vintage Roosevelt campaign items. Simpson is a real golf club manufacturer. Although neither the Sargent image or Simpson Golf Club name ever originally appeared together, both names could be "documented" in reference books.

Once a digital image is captured, it can easily be repeated in slightly different versions. It's only a minute or two of typing to change the advertising message of the Roosevelt paperweight, for example, to Winchester Rifles, Libbey Glass, or any other message. Forgers can produce images as they are needed, one or

Digital fakes

Digital printing heads are quite small and must make repeated passes to build an image. Completed digital images frequently show "banding," as seen at right, about five times actual size.

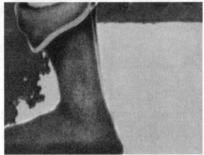

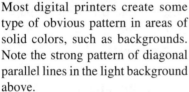

Most digital printers create some type of obvious pattern in areas of solid colors, such as backgrounds. Note the strong pattern of diagonal parallel lines in the light background above.

Original image shows no diagonal lines in background. Any obvious pattern is a warning sign of a digital image. Digital patterns vary. Some are lines, others are blocks, grids, or swirls. Images about twice actual size.

two at a time, slipping items into the market without raising suspicion. Unlike traditional printing, which requires large investments in minimum press runs, digital images can be printed for as little as $1 an image.

Another use that's developed for digital images is the creation and repair of paper-covered wood toys such as 19th century doll houses, fire stations, animals, and soldiers, plus 20th century collectibles like Fisher-Price. Repairs are made by simply scanning the undamaged side of a genuine toy, reversing the image in the computer, and printing out the new image ready for pasting. New toys are created by either directly copying

Virtually all color printers driven by digital signals print letters and backgrounds at the same time. This almost always produces letters with a fuzzy "halo" around the edges. Solid-colored letters on colored backgrounds in original lithographs, silk screens, and traditional press work are practically always a solid mass with clear borders.

Lettering is a good test of printing. The lettering above is as seen on typical digital color image. Note jagged-edged letters with dot-like blurry bodies, seen with 10X loupe.

Lettering on typical early 20th century color image from printing press. Note letters have well-defined outlines and solid-colored bodies, seen with 10X loupe.

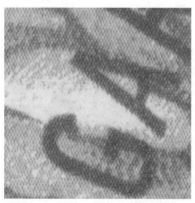

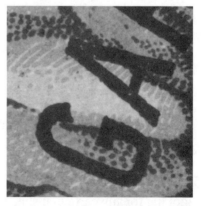

Typical jagged pattern produced in background and letters by inkjet printer, as seen with 10X loupe.

Stone lithograph. Background composed of random-sized and spaced patches of ink. Solid-bodied letters with smooth edges, as seen with 10X loupe.

Digital fakes

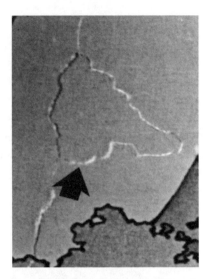

Don't overlook the obvious. Many reproduced images, digital or traditional, often include damages, flaws, and tears contained in the original image. The reproduced images above show how a tear was copied (left) and a crease copied in the image (right). These damages are printed into the reproductions.

originals or making new creations from images scanned from books or catalogs.

Examinations of suspected digital images should begin with text or lettering using a good quality 10X loupe. Lettering and text in traditional color printing almost always appear as solid colors with well-defined outlines. Lettering and text produced by the majority of digital printers is virtually always composed of fuzzy or jagged dots with a hazy, blurred outline. Even if the body of digital letters appears to be solid, there is almost always a halo of mixed colors around the edges of the digital letters.

Another common problem with digital images is the frequent appearance of unpredictable patterns created by the scanning process. Some of the more frequent patterns are fine, parallel lines and grid-like structures. But keep in mind that you aren't looking for any particular shape, just any unusual patterns. Strange patterns most often occur in broad areas of solid colors, especially areas where contrasting colors meet. Many digital images produced on inkjet printers also display an effect called "banding," appearing as parallel horizontal rows.

Digital fakes

The highest quality digital images are produced by thermal and dye-sublimation printers. These machines use various versions of solid wax to produce superb images of photo-like quality. In addition to the other detection techniques described previously, thermal and dye-sublimation prints are generally very slick and even waxy feeling; printed areas may have a slightly tacky surface.

Perhaps the easiest way to catch about 99 percent of the fake digital images is with a black light. Although some digital printers can produce images on any plain paper, most digital images are produced on specialized paper made expressly for digital printing. All of those new papers fluoresce bright white under black light. Even if a new piece of paper is glued to an object, the exposed edge of a label, clock face, or photo is all the surface you need to conduct an accurate test.

The best defense against the increasing number of digital images is simply to be aware they exist. Maintain a healthy skepticism about all printed images, not just the flat-framed pieces that hang on the wall. And don't limit your suspicions to images on paper. Digital printers can deposit images on a wide range of material, including linen and canvas.

Remember, there are also plenty of reproductions in the market made by traditional printing techniques. Study and know how original images of interest to you were produced and learn to recognize that process.

Fairly convincing fakes can be made on relatively simple software that comes with most scanners. But even special software with advanced controls, like pattern filters, color shifts, retouching, advanced lettering and other features, costs only $300 to $600.

The term "digital printer" in this chapter has been used to mean any printing device controlled by digital/computer commands. A "digital fake" refers to an image edited and manipulated by computer software and whose output was controlled by computer commands.

Lamps and Lighting

This chapter is divided into a number of sections, including Aladdin, figurals, scenic metal overlays, glass kerosene, reverse painted, Tiffany, and motion lamps. Additional single lamps are shown in other chapters such as Nippon and Cameo Glass. Refer to the index for complete listings.

Aladdin

Among the Aladdin lamps reproduced are both the short and tall Lincoln Drape varieties shown below. The cheap overseas reproductions are glued together between the font and base. The glue fluoresces under long wave black light. (See the following pages on glass kerosene lamps for more information about glass lamps.)

Both tall and short versions of Aladdin Lincoln Drape lamps are reproduced. These and other Aladdins are glued together rather than fused together when hot.

Figural metal lamps

There are many reproductions of figural lamps, especially in Art Nouveau and Art Deco styles. Many new lamps are direct copies of well-known originals. The lamps on this page, for example, are in almost every book on Art Nouveau lighting or decorative lamps. Names of original designers–like Gallé, Gurschner, Behrens, and others–are prominently mentioned in wholesale catalogs featuring the new lamps. "Art Nouveau," "Art Deco," and other related terms are also used in catalogs to describe the new lamps.

New 25-inch hooded woman lamp base in iron copies original bronze base by Art Nouveau designer Peter Behrens, Berlin, Germany.

Many of the new shades are very similar in shape to old originals. But there the similarity ends. Where originals would be made of a variety of glass, a great percentage of all the new shades are made from a distinctive mottled glass. Look for large, white spatters in backgrounds of various colors including purple, amber, green, blue, and the most widely used new colors–amber and yellow. All of the new mottled glass shades have frosted finishes with ground rims.

New 22-inch copy of original bronze lamp by Austrian designer Gustav Gurschner.

Some of the more convincing new lamps are those resembling French wrought iron. Although some of the new pieces are in fact iron and not pot metal, the new parts are *hollow* and cast in molds. Originals are almost always

245

Lamps and Lighting

All the new shades on the new figural lamps shown in this section are made of the same mottled glass. Random blobs and spatters of white glass appear in backgrounds of various colors, including purple, amber, yellow, green, and blue. All have frosted finishes.

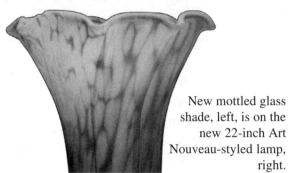

New mottled glass shade, left, is on the new 22-inch Art Nouveau-styled lamp, right.

solid bars or rods welded or forged together. Yes, new pieces do have some tiny vines attached by spot welds, but the main supports and bases are hollow, not solid throughout.

Be sure to carefully inspect the finish. Like most other metal reproductions, there are obvious mold seams and grinding marks never found on originals and some parts are unfinished or the finish doesn't match the rest of the lamp.

And last, look at how the lamp is wired. Virtually all period originals have concealed wiring that blends into the design. Wiring in most reproductions is dictated mostly by the need to keep production costs low, not by good design. That's why exposed wiring and wires running in awkward locations are generally a sure sign of a reproduction.

New Art Nouveau-styled snail with iridescent art glass shade, 10 by 6 inches. Base glass in shade is mottled and streaked with white spots like other new glass shades.

New 14-inch lamp, mottled glass blown into brass frame with antique finish. Figural women form handles on each side.

New 14-inch "wrought iron" lamp. The base and vertical supports are cast as one continuous hollow piece. Mottled glass shade.

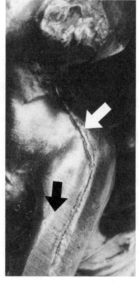

Almost all the new lamps have obvious casting seams (white arrow) and grinding marks (black arrow).

Cords frequently enter new lamps in exposed, unsightly locations.

Many new lamps have exposed hardware with bare metal. This metal nut is shiny bright steel with no finish, although the surrounding surface has a dull antique brass finish.

Bridge lamp parts

Bridge lamps are named for an arm or "bridge" that holds the bulb and shade out and away from the lamp base. Figural bridges can double or quadruple the price over lamps with non-figural bridges. New, low-quality bridges are now being imported from China. Watch for finning, rough edges, and pitting in the surface. It's common to see new figural bridges "married" to genuinely old lamps that originally had plain, inexpensive bridges. Prices for new bridges shown, $12 to $15 each.

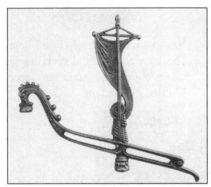 

New 12-inch Viking ship (left), dolphin sail, figural dragon head on end. New 12-inch tropical bird (right).

New 11-inch Angel bridge, right, detail below.

Look in open areas for thin flashes of metal or "finning" caused by metal leaking through poorly fitting molds.

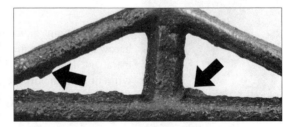

Glass kerosene lamps

New glass kerosene lamps have been coming on the market in increasing numbers. Reproductions include everything from simple clear glass finger-lamps to multicolored banquet lamps. New lamps continue to be made overseas, as well as in America, in both pressed and blown forms.

Regardless of pattern, there are several basic ways to identify these new lamps: how fonts and bases are joined; how burner collars are mounted; and, other hardware.

Font-to-base joints

Original glass kerosene lamps were made in two pieces, the font and the base. All originals were fused together while the glass was hot and cannot be separated. New lamps are also made in two parts, a font and base, but 99.9 percent of all new lamps are *glued* together.

Pure acetone has no effect on the glue; neither do most other solvents and paint removers. The lamps can only be separated by boiling them in water for about five minutes. Fortunately, it is not necessary to separate the lamps to prove they are new. The glue fluoresces under long wave black light. All the kerosene lamps with bases and fonts shown in this section are glued.

New cobalt blue Bull's-Eye lamp as it comes from reproduction wholesaler (left). Font glued to base, burner collar glued to font. Placing in hot water dissolves the glue, and the lamp separates (above).

Lamps and Lighting

Close-up view of glue between font and base of typical new glass kerosene lamp. Glue is best seen with black light.

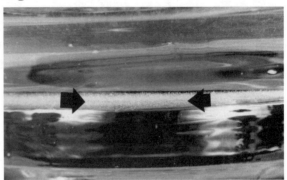

Burner collars

Another important clue to age is the burner collar, the point where the metal burner attaches to the lamp. In the vast majority of lamps, a brass collar is mounted to the glass and the burner screws into the brass collar. With only rare exceptions, all old brass collars are mounted with plaster. Virtually all new burner collars are glued to the glass, not mounted in plaster.

To inspect the collar, you need to remove the burner. Once the burner is removed in new lamps, you'll see a ridge of glass directly under the collar (top photo, left). With old collars, you'll see the old plaster under the collar once the burner is removed (top photo, right).

It is not always necessary to remove the burner. A black

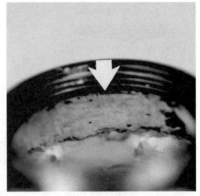

New burner collars are glued directly to the glass (left). Notice how the glass neck is exposed. Burner collars in old lamps are plastered in (right), not glued. There is no gap between the metal collar and glass; it is filled with plaster.

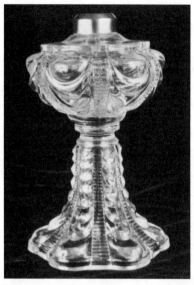

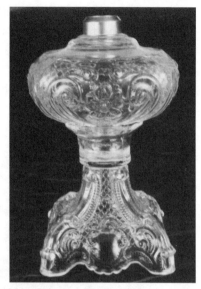

New clear Waterfall pattern lamp, commonly called Coolidge Drape.

New Princess Feather lamp is made in both tall and short versions in a variety of colors.

New 8-inch clear Button & Swirl lamp (left); new finger lamp in clear Petal and Rib pattern (right). The finger lamp has an applied handle just like the old, so check other details. It has a glued burner collar.

light usually will fluoresce the glue around the outside of new burner collars. Metal collars on new filler necks, where the oil is added to the lamp, are also glued. Original metal collars on filler necks were set in plaster.

Hardware

The connecting hardware on this new Cathedral lamp looks

complicated, but it is just another glued joint. A metal plate is glued to the bottom of the glass font; a bolt passes through this plate into the glass base where it is fastened with a nut.

Nearly all old connectors are fastened with plaster. The old bolts are packed in plaster so they don't move; the new bolts are loose within the metal plate and are free to move.

Most new metal connectors (left) are only glued to the glass font. This leaves bolts in new connecting hardware loose because the bolts have no support within the connector. Old metal connections (right) are filled with plaster. Old bolts set in solid plaster do not move.

New Cathedral lamp, 12½ inches. New connector shown in photo above. Fonts and bases available in various contrasting color combinations.

New 10-inch Sweetheart or Beaded Heart lamp, available in many colors.

New 7-inch clear Shield and Star.

14-rayed base on finger lamp at left.

New colored glass finger lamp. Good quality blown colored glass font with applied clear glass handle. Available in cranberry, cobalt, and other colors. Made by Fenton for a private lamp company in the mid-1990s, but not marked. Unlike most reproduction lamps, the solid brass mounting collar of this lamp is plastered rather than glued. These lamps can be identified by the 14-rayed base (see illustration above right) created by the pattern mold. Font 3 5/8-inch diameter.

Reverse-painted shades

New reverse-painted 18-inch shade with parrots copies 1920s-era Handel Company original. Wholesale price, $149.

Glass lamp shades with painted decorations on the inside of the shade–called reverse-painted–were originally produced in America around the turn of the century.

Authentic lamps by major companies, such as Handel and Pairpoint, average $2,000 to $6,000, with rare pieces bringing $30,000 to $50,000. Lamps by other makers such as Jefferson and Moe Bridges, etc., average $1,000 to $3,000.

Many of the most popular original designs are now being made in China. The new shades, like the originals, are individually painted by hand. And since many are direct copies of originals, many new shades appear to match the original shapes and designs pictured in reference books.

In general, new reverse-painted shades are cold-painted. New paint frequently flakes off and can be chipped with a fingernail. Original paints were fired on the glass and are virtually indestructible.

New 18-inch shade, flowers and butterflies. Closely resembles original Pairpoint shape.

Because new paint can be chipped, the inside, or reverse side, of virtually all new shades have a protective coat of paint, usually white, that covers the entire

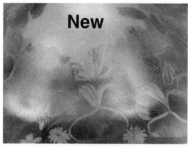

View of new shade from inside. Design barely visible under white paint applied to the entire inside surface.

View of another new shade from inside Details clouded by white background paint applied on top of pattern over entire inside surface.

Cracking and flaking of unfired paint in new shade. Old shades have fired, permanent paint.

design. This makes details on the inside of new shades muddy and cloudy. Old shades do not have this protective paint. Backgrounds of old shades were carefully painted up to but not over the design. Designs in old shades are as clear and sharp on the inside as they are on the outside of the shade.

The majority of old shades do not have a lip or raised rim of glass around the top opening in the shade. Most new shades with a top opening have substantial rims.

Pairpoint Puffy Lamps

The Pairpoint Corporation of New Bedford, Massachusetts, made a special type of reverse-painted shade called a "Puffy."

Typical original reverse-painted shade as seen from inside. Main pattern details sharp and distinct. Original paint is fired on and does not have to be covered by a protective coating like the new shades.

255

Lamps and Lighting

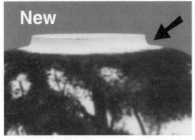

Nearly all new reverse-painted dome shades have a *raised lip* around the top opening, left. Height varies: ¼ inch to more than ½ inch. Original shades, right, do not have a raised lip at top of dome. Most old reverse-painted dome shades have metal fitting rings attached flush to the opening in the shade.

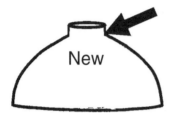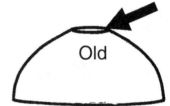

Typical 18-inch dome shades. New shades frequently have a raised rim or lip around the top opening in the shade. Top openings in old shades are flush with the surrounding surface.

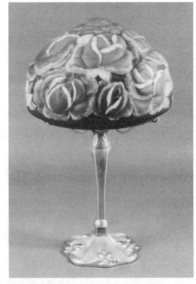

New Pairpoint Puffy 12-inch shade, hummingbird and roses. Copy of original 14-inch shape.

New Pairpoint Puffy lamp copies original Rose Bouquet. Original lamps sells for $15,000-plus.

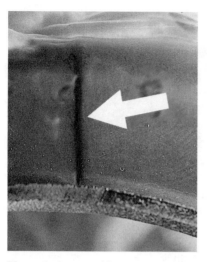 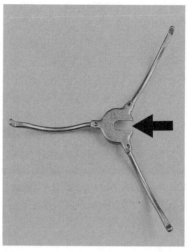

Very obvious mold seams appear on most reproduction Puffy shades. Shown here about 1½ times actual size. Original Pairpoint Puffy shades do not have mold seams.

This type of spider is supplied with the new shades. It is notched (arrow); original spiders have a hole in the center.

Made from around 1907 to the beginning of the Depression, about half of all Pairpoint reverse-painted lamps were the so-called "Puffy" shades. That is to say, the surface of the shades was "puffed" out or raised in three-dimensional designs.

Originals bring a starting average of $3,500 for florals and $4,500 to $7,500 for butterflies and hummingbirds. Rare lamps can bring more than $50,000. Chinese reproductions of Puffy lamps are available for $100 to $150 each.

Original Puffy shades were first acid-finished (frosted) before decorating. Any undecorated surface on both sides of an

New Puffy shade, raised roses, painted butterflies.

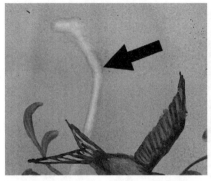 

New shade. Flaws like this large paint drip are common in the reproductions but virtually never found in originals.

New Puffy shade. New Puffy shades are fairly thin, 1/8 inch thick or less. The majority of originals are thicker, usually about ¼-inch thick.

original Puffy appears as frosted glass. Like other original re-verse painted shades, paint on authentic Puffy shades was fired and is permanent. Paint on new Puffy shades is not fired and has the same white coating as found on other new reverse-painted shades.

Large, obvious paint flaws like runs and bubbles are common in the reproductions, but virtually never found in originals. New glass shades also usually have imperfections in the glass blanks and crudely ground shade rims. New glass shades also have prominent mold seams; original glass shades were specially finished and do not have any signs of seams.

Original full-size Puffy shades, 10 to 12 inches in diameter, are fairly thick, usually approaching about ¼ inch at the rim. All the new puffy shades are approximately 1/8 inch or less in thickness at the rim's edge. The majority of Puffy shades with a squared-off bottom had a curved fitting rim to secure the shade. With only one exception, the new shades do not have a fitting rim.

There are lots of genuine old bases and bits of hardware available to "marry" with new shades. Anyone dishonest enough to deliberately misrepresent a new Puffy for old will probably have the new shade on an old base. Here are a few specific features to inspect to be sure you are getting original hardware. If the shade is supported by a spider (armed bracket), how is it attached to the lamp? New spiders that come with the new shades are notched. The new bases that come with the new shades are crude pot metal with low quality metallic finishes.

If an authentic shade is marked, it is with a dark ink applied with a rubber stamp (for authentic Pairpoint marks, see chapter on Art Glass). The mark may read in one of the following ways: "The Pairpoint Corp'n," "Patent Pending," or "Patent Applied For." Puffy shades are sometimes found marked "Patented July 9, 1907," also rubber-stamped. Original rubber-stamped marks are usually no more than 1/8- to 3/16-inch high at the most. No marks currently appear on the reproduction Puffy shades. This doesn't mean, however, that enterprising forgers won't add marks before reselling new pieces as old. Be suspicious of blotchy, smeared, or particularly large rubber stamp marks.

Virtually all original bases were marked. A number of original parts–such as spiders, metal rims, washers, and other pieces– were often, but not always, also marked. The most common mark in metal bases was the capital letter "P "inside a diamond. This mark was die-stamped below the surface of the metal.

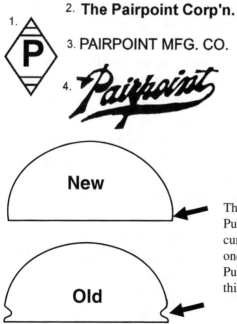

2. **The Pairpoint Corp'n.**

3. PAIRPOINT MFG. CO.

1.

4.

1) "P" in diamond trademark. Originally used on paper labels and stamped into metal only.

2) Original mark stamped in ink on shades only.

New

Old

The majority of original Puffy shades have a curved fitting rim. With one exception, most new Puffy shades do not have this feature.

Tiffany

New

New scarab desk lamp. Blue iridescent art glass shade, bronze base. No
marks on glass or base.

Old

Original Tiffany 9-inch scarab
desk lamp. Base marked "Tiffany
Studios New York" and "2138."

Scarab Lamp

Mention "Tiffany lamps" and most people immediately think
of leaded-glass shades. Tiffany, in fact, made many high-quality
lamps of all kinds, shapes, and uses. The scarab desk lamp shown
above is a typical example of those other lighting products.

The original scarab lamp has a molded iridescent art glass
shade (Favrile) mounted on a bronze base. Although the mark
varies, original bases are always marked. The most common
marks are "Tiffany Studios New York" or the "TGDC" (Tiffany
Glass and Decorating Company) monogram. The model number, "2138," always appears on authentic bases. Marks alone
aren't a guarantee of age, but authentic pieces should be clearly
marked with a model number. Original glass shades were available in a variety of colors.

There have been several reproductions of this lamp. This
particular version was purchased from the manufacturer in 1993.
It has a hollow, pressed-glass iridescent scarab shade. This particular manufacturer offered blue iridescence on green glass and
gold iridescence on amber glass. The new glass has a bright,

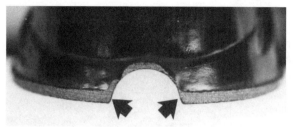

New shades are fit to new rims by grinding. Grinding marks are obvious around the bottom rim.

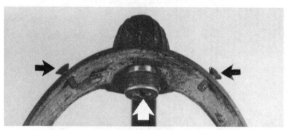

New shades are held by large set screws (black arrows) seen in this top view of lamp rim. The rim is attached to the base by bulky Phillips-head bolts (white arrow).

shiny gleam to the surface, plus obvious pressing flaws such as creases and pits. Original shades are flawless with a soft non-reflective surface. Ends of the new shades show ground edges where the shades have been fit around the new hardware.

Original bases are supported on ball feet; new bases do not have ball feet. Arms of the original base join in a ball connector; arms of the new base join in a Y-shaped yoke. The rim holding the shade on the new lamp has four large set screws visible on the outside of the rim; the old rims do not have set screws.

Leaded glass Tiffany lamps

The high prices of originals make Tiffany leaded lamps the targets of very sophisticated fakes and forgeries. There are lots of people willing to invest 10 to 40 hours of handwork with the hopes of passing a clever fake for $5,000, $10,000 or $20,000. These same people don't mind spending several hundred dollars or more to have dies and stamps made with which to forge Tiffany marks. Because the best fakes are individually made by hand,

Reproduction Tiffany
lamp with Oak Leaf
shade. Shade and base
both marked like
originals.

Original Oak Leaf
shade shown below for
comparison.

it's hard to categorize the kind of fakes you might encounter. Below are some general hints to help you separate the more obvious forgeries.

First, all high quality original leaded shades are made in the copper foil technique. That means each piece of glass has thin copper foil wrapped around the edges. Foil-wrapped pieces are laid together and soldered along the foil to join the pieces together. Many shades can be made of hundreds or even thousands of these small pieces.

Embossed markings in rim of faked Tiffany Oak Leaf lamp shade, "TIFFANY STUDIOS NEW YORK 1467." Shown about twice actual size. "1467" is the original Tiffany model number for Oak Leaf, low dome shade. Note that the model number is much larger than other lettering.

Almost without exception, some of these joints become loose on original shades. If you gently tap entirely around the shoulder of the shade with the knuckles of a closed fist, you'll almost always hear a rattle of the loose pieces in genuinely old leaded shades. New shades virtually never rattle because they have fresh tight joints.

Next, examine the shade from the outside with the light turned on. Look for cracks in the small pieces of glass. Almost all genuine lamps have at least some pieces of glass that have cracks. Most cracks are caused by heat (expansion and contraction) or being slightly twisted in the soldered joints. A few pieces of glass with cracks are actually a desirable sign of age and normal use. On the other hand, if you examine a shade with every piece of glass in perfect condition, it could be a warning sign of recent reproduction.

Marks are probably the most confusing aspect of reproductions. Originals are not marked in any consistent manner, so there are no clear right and wrong answers. Rather, you need to look for out-of-the-ordinary features that are beyond what's found in known originals.

For example, almost all original lamp bases were marked, and the marks were almost always die-stamped. Marks on many new bases are cast (in a mold), not stamped. Original stamped marks are generally much sharper than new cast marks. Original stamped marks were applied to the metal before patina was applied, so old marks are under the patina. Many forged marks, especially stamped forgeries, are applied after the patina. Bright

Bottom of new lamp base has two separate marks: "Tiffany Studios New York," and the "TGDCO" (Tiffany Glass & Decorating Company) monogram. These are copied from original marks. When they appear together on originals, however, they appear together (illus. at right), not separately.

TIFFANY STUDIOS
NEW YORK

TIFFANY STUDIOS NEW YORK

Correct style of lettering found on shade marks. All capital letters, all sans-serif letters of equal thickness and weight.

TIFFANY STUDIOS NEW YORK

Incorrect style of type made of thick and thin lines.

Tiffany Studios New York

Incorrect lettering, no lowercase letters are used in original marks.

shiny metal can frequently be seen in many new stamped marks because the new stamped mark cuts through the patina. Virtually all authentic Tiffany bases have model numbers die stamped into the metal. Model numbers should match the shapes shown in Tiffany catalog reprints.

Many original shades were not marked; those that were have a variety of marks. The most common was to stamp some form of the company name and a model number in the shade rim, or stamp the name on a metal tag or plate and solder that into the shade. Both of these techniques are widely copied by modern forgers. Fake signatures are found in both new lamps and genuinely old but originally unmarked lamps.

First, check the patina around such marks. Patina was applied after original marks were stamped. Marks should have the

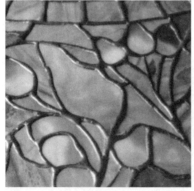

Dark film on shade makes glass appear opalescent when lamp is lighted.

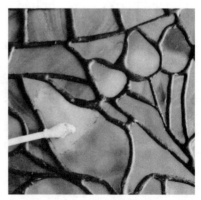

Spray removed showing low-quality white glass with streaks of green.

same even patina that appears on the entire shade. Be suspicious of silver colored solder near a mark. The mark could have been recently added. Virtually all old solder joints are covered by patina.

Next, compare the appearance of the lettering in the mark. All lettering in original shade marks is quite small, barely 1/8-inch in height. Letters are virtually always all capital letters, no lowercase letters. All letters should be impressed in the metal to an equal depth and should be the same height. Be suspicious if model numbers are different heights than the other letters. All original lettering is of equal weight and thickness (sans-serif).

Keeping up with all the ways Tiffany lamps can be faked is a challenge. One of the more interesting recent efforts is a spray that alters the appearance of the glass in new shades (see photos on opposite page). When the lamp is turned on or the shade is held to a light, the glass appears to be highly opalescent like original glass. This spray is quite different from ordinary dirt and grime occasionally found on undisturbed original lamps. It cannot be removed with soap and water. Only acetone or paint remover will take it off.

Approach any big ticket item like Tiffany lamps with a healthy amount of skepticism. There are just as many bad lamps sold in gallery auctions with champagne previews as from the trunks of cars in flea markets.

Motion Lamps

A number of classic motion lamps from the 1950s have been reproduced since late 1998. The designs are virtually identical to originals made by Econolite Co. during the 1950s. Four new examples are shown on the next page. They are, left to right: Sailing Ships, Train, Old Mill, and Antique Car. Originals of these models sell for $225 to $350 each. The reproductions, made in India, are retailing for $30 to $40 each.

There are several ways to help separate new from old:

• Bases on original Econolite lamps are pierced, brass-plated

Lamps and Lighting

Reproductions of classic motion lamps originally made in the 1950s. New lamps are $30 to $40. Originals of these same models are $225 to $350.

metal with three ball feet. Bases on new lamps are molded black plastic with the feet molded as part of the base.

• Tops of old Econolite lamps are cardboard; tops in new lamps are plastic. There is a single large hole in the center of old tops. New shades have four tiny holes around the edge of the top plus a large single hole in the center.

• The surface of new shades is shiny; the surface of old Econolite shades is a matte finish.

New shades fit on old bases, so be careful of marriages and switching.

Motion lamps get their name from a separate cylinder in the center of the lamp that rotates as heat from the light bulb rises. Designs on the inner cylinder combine with artwork on the outer walls of the lamp to create movement.

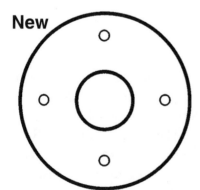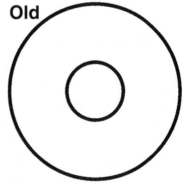

Comparison of new and old tops in motion lamp shades. Old tops have a single large hole in the center. New lamps have four small holes and a large hole. (Size of small holes exaggerated for illustration.)

Metal-overlay shades

New scenic metal-overlay shade (above) in windmill pattern. New lamp (right) with camels and palm trees in desert oasis .

Metal-overlay shades have a pierced design over glass. The metal creates a dark pattern against the glass when the lamp is lighted.

Pierced designs in original metal-overlay shades were cast. Designs on the great majority of new metal-overlay shades are stamped. The old cast designs have flat, solid backs. New stamped designs are half-rounded shells.

There are some exceptions. Some new metal overlay designs in simple geometric patterns like beading or scrolls do have cast designs just like old shades. Virtually all the new scenic designs, however, are stamped in half-round like the sample shown below.

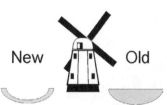

Cross-section of windmill overlay. New metal is stamped leaving thin shell. Old overlay is cast with solid metal, which forms a flat back.

Reverse side of new metal overlay showing thin shell hollow back.

Figural Napkin Rings

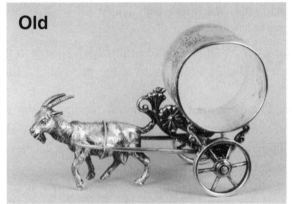

Original goat pulling ring on wheels made by Meriden Britannia Co.

Reproduction of Meriden ring. Wheels move just like wheels on original.

New

Reproduction boy feeding dog. Base has faked mark of Meriden Britannia Co.

Old

Original Meriden boy feeding dog. Original mark includes model number 199.

Silver plated figural napkin rings are exclusively an American product of the Victorian era. First patented in 1869, figural rings soon filled entire pages of Victorian silver plate catalogs. Figural rings remained popular until the turn of the century. After 1900, fewer and fewer were seen in silver plate catalogs until they were entirely gone by the first decade of the new century.

Each family member had his own ring, usually received as a gift, with his initials or name on it. Many figural rings were intended to represent certain aspects of the owner's personality, their pets, occupation, or interests. Other figures represent characters or themes in nursery rhymes and stories, popular sports and hobbies, and other Victorian interests.

New figural ring. A copy of original Meriden #202.

Prices for original figural rings can range from $75 for simple figures to $1,500 and higher for rare figures or elaborate rings that include containers for condiments or other accessories such as glass flower vases. Moving parts such as wheels increase the value.

Many reproductions in the market have been copied directly from old originals like the goat pulling ring, boy feeding

269

Napkin Rings

dog, and dog pulling ring shown here. Not only do the latest rings copy old shapes, but they also have fake marks with the same name as original makers, such as Meriden, Reed and Barton and Simpson, Hall, Miller. Prices for reproductions are a fraction of originals, with the majority of new pieces selling for $15 to $45.

Like many other reproductions, new napkin rings are best identified by comparing details of construction of both new and old. Once you become familiar with how old originals are made, it is fairly easy to detect the modern fakes and reproductions.

The vast majority of original figural napkin rings are made from a combination of casting and die stamping. A casting is made by pouring molten metal into a mold. Die stamping is rolling or striking an engraved image against cold metal to impress the engraved image into the metal's surface.

Original three-dimensional figures and most original bases were usually cast. Original napkin rings were almost always decorated by rolling or milling in dies. Original manufacturers' marks and model numbers were nearly always die stamped.

Many new figural napkin rings, both figure and ring, are entirely cast, most frequently as a single piece. Originals were almost always assembled from several pieces.

The first step in evaluating a figural napkin ring is to examine the ring itself. The vast majority of original rings have die-stamped or engine-turned designs and patterns that are clear and

File marks and grinding marks (lower arrow) are common on many new rings. Also be alert for mold seams (top arrow) on the rings.

Scratches from wire brush left these obvious tool marks. Such tool marks are frequently found on the outside and inside of many new rings.

Reproduction figural napkin ring: dog pulling napkin ring on wheels.

Original Victorian-era dog pulling napkin ring on wheels.

New napkin ring shows typical lack of detail. This ring and the vast majority of other new rings are cast in a mold and have little detail.

Original napkin ring pulled by dog. This and other original Victorian rings are stamped or turned and typically show very sharp detail.

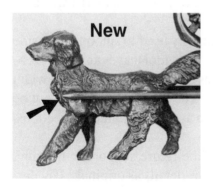

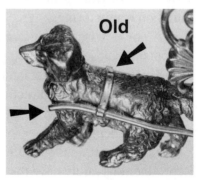

Harness gear on all original animals is very realistic and logical. Note there is no back pad (or cinch strap) on the new dog. Also note the new harness shafts are simply metal rods with the tips filed to sharp points.

Napkin Rings

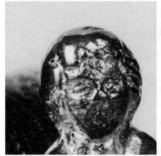

Close up of boy's face in ring at right. Poor detail is typical of new rings.

New Kate Greenaway-style ring. The new boy is 2¼ inches tall, much smaller than originals of this figure, which are rarely under 3 inches.

sharp. Reproduction rings are almost always cast in a mold, which produces weak and poorly defined details. Although reproductions vary, most new rings don't have the same fine detail found in originals.

Next, examine how the ring is finished. Because most new rings are cast, the vast majority have mold seams, pits, bumps, and other flaws. Attempts to remove the flaws also frequently show up as obvious grinding or file marks. Such marks are never found on original rings.

A power wire brush is commonly used to smooth the inside and outside surfaces of new rings. This tool leaves an easily identifiable pattern of parallel scratches of about equal depth and width that all run in the same direction. These scratches should not be confused with normal wear, which appears in random directions, widths, and depths.

Next, examine the detail in the figure supporting the ring. Reproductions rarely have the same details as originals. Pay particular attention to human faces, especially eyes, mouth, and nose. These features are usually well-defined in originals, but often blurred and frequently grotesque in many reproductions. Another

Cast (molded) Meriden mark in base of reproduction figural napkin ring includes model number 199.

Die-stamped Meriden mark in base of original. Model number 199 also die-stamped.

Cast Simpson, Hall, Miller mark in base of reproduction. Molded marks are less sharp.

Die-stamped Simpson, Hall, Miller mark in base of original. Die-stamped marks show more detail.

good indication of quality is the fur on animals. It is not unusual to be able to see individual hairs on originals; fur on many reproductions is virtually smooth without detail or texture.

The surface of many reproductions is pitted, rough and bumpy. Originals almost always have a smooth, evenly finished surface. Silver plating is not generally a good test of age. Plating on old originals can be worn, or originals can be replated. Plating varies from good to terrible on the reproductions.

On any ring pulled by animals, be sure to examine how the

Napkin Rings

animals are joined to the ring. The vast majority of original figures are joined with very realistic harnesses. Remember, originals were used in the last quarter of the 19th century when dog, goat, and horse carts were everyday sources of power. The average person had firsthand knowledge and experience with the parts of a harness and how it was made. Present day fakers and reproduction artists often forget this and make new harnesses that are unrealistic and illogical.

Almost all original harnesses on napkin rings, for example, include a realistic cinch rope or back pad on the animal's body. This was an essential part of any real harness because it transferred the pulling power of the animal to the shafts. Shafts, in turn, were connected to the wagon, cart, or load (or, in this case, a napkin ring). On napkin rings, cinch ropes are usually made of twisted wire; back pads are bars or straps.

Also, pay close attention to how wheels are constructed. Although wheels move freely on reproductions, that is not a test of age. A better test is to examine the overall construction of the wheel, especially the spokes and roundness of the rim. New spokes frequently show rough mold seams or grinding marks; new rims are often out-of-round and irregular.

Whether you're buying figural napkin rings, Gallé cameo glass, Nippon, Roseville, or any other antique or collectible, never rely on a mark alone as guarantee of age or authenticity. Marks can be copied and forged. You are much better off to base your tests of age on how a piece was assembled, constructed, or decorated.

So far, all new marks have been cast (molded) at the time the reproduction was made. Original marks are almost without exception die stamped as a separate step. Die-stamped marks are sharper, cleaner, and show more detail. Molded marks tend to be blurred and lack detail. The depth of the mark varies with some letters extending farther below the surface than other letters. A wide variety of original maker marks have been reproduced. There are no "safe" marks.

Several maker's marks that were originally stamped on discs then soldered to bases are also out in the market. The most fre-

Example of a very complicated new ring by modern silversmith James Mackie. Very similar in quality to Victorian original.

One of the hallmarks on high-quality figural reproductions by James Mackie. Actual size only about 1/8-inch wide.

New figural napkin ring by Mackie. JM hallmark on bottom of domed base.

Hallmarks found on new rings by Mackie. JM in shield (left); JM and crown (right).

quently seen forged marks on discs are Simpson, Hall, Miller; Meriden Britannia Co.; and Rogers Brothers.

A notable exception to the general run of poorly made reproductions is a line of very well-made copies by contemporary silversmith James Mackie. Mackie's rings are very close in quality to Victorian originals. All of Mackie's rings have his hallmark,

Napkin Rings

either a JM or JM and crown. Unfortunately, the hallmarks are very small and often hard to find. Although Mackie's rings are more expensive than the cheap imports–running $75 to $250– they are still only 1/3 to 1/5 of originals and still a tempting target for unethical resellers.

In addition to being reproduced, figural napkin rings are also frequently faked from genuinely old parts "married" together. Forgers will take figures from toothpick holders, vases, compotes, and other old objects and combine them with ordinary single napkin rings. After common rings have been joined to figures, the new piece is offered as a "figural napkin ring." Since these pieces are made from old parts, examining quality is often not a clear clue in detecting them.

One way to catch many of these fakes is by comparing model numbers in marks to original model numbers in reference books and catalog reprints. With rare exceptions, original manufacturers never used or repeated model numbers of figural napkin rings with other objects.

1161 Silver, $3.00
     Silver & Gold. 3.50

This figural ring is marked Tufts 1161. Is it authentic? Looking up the model number in a Tufts catalog reprint, you see the original 1161 is a vase holder not a napkin ring. Close inspection shows the vase holder was removed and an ordinary ring attached.

One group of new figural rings, which includes this kneeling boy, is mounted on thin pressed metal bases. Other figures on these thin bases include Kate Greenaway characters, animals and sporting figures including golfers.

Very thin, pressed bases clearly show a pattern on bottom as well as top. Original bases are much heavier and usually cast, not pressed. You rarely see a pattern on the underside of original bases.

Side view of thin pressed base.

277

Toys

New paper over wood farm set. Wood case (below, left) is 12-by-9 inches closed. Opens into barn (above). The artwork was scanned from reference book on antique toys into a computer. Artwork was then printed out on ink jet printer and pasted on new wood. Matching animals shown below (right.)

All the new paper fluoresces under black light. Original paper litho over wood does not fluoresce.

It seems like just a few years ago the only toys being reproduced were crude cast iron banks, cars and trucks. Now there are virtually exact copies of everything from space toys to Victorian litho over wood pieces, from prewar German tin to 1960s plastic playsets. The most confusing aspect of many new toys is the appearance of marks which are copies of old originals. Considering many new toys are also being made in original molds and dies, the collector needs a continuing flow of information to keep up with all the reissues and reproductions. The following pages show some of the most recently issued examples.

Cast iron

Reproduction cast iron goat with cart. Copied from early 20th century original by Hubley.

Cast iron was the 19th century equivalent of today's plastics: the raw ingredients were cheap, it could be made in almost any shape, and identical pieces could be mass-produced in molds. It was the perfect material for inexpensive toys. Those are the same reasons cast iron is so widely reproduced today–it's extremely cheap to make, especially overseas.

There are so many cast iron reproductions, it is impossible to learn specific differences between all the new and old cast iron toys. It is better to learn and understand how to evaluate cast iron in general and then use those general rules during your routine inspection. Handmade individual forgeries, of course, cannot easily be categorized, but the following guidelines will help you avoid the majority of factory-made reproductions currently in the market.

Old cast iron, for example, almost always has a much smoother surface than new castings. New cast iron generally has small prickly bumps that rise above the surface and holes or pits that go below the surface. The rough texture is the most obvious on unpainted surfaces, so try to look on the inside or underside of toys.

Old castings almost always have sharper detail; new castings are generally less sharp, blurred, and lack fine details found in old pieces. Most new molds don't fit together very well and molten metal runs out through gaps where mold halves meet. This is called "finning," seldom found on old pieces but is common among reproductions.

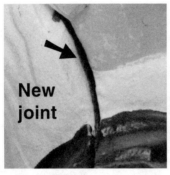
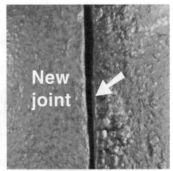

Reproduction cast iron almost always has wide poorly fitting joints where pieces meet. Original cast iron was usually hand fit and has very tightly fitting joints. Many old joints are too tight to pass a piece of paper through.

Joints of original cast iron toys were often fitted together by hand filing or at least had the edges tumbled smooth. This extra attention produced very tight joints in original cast iron toys. Seams in new cast iron are typically very loose and carelessly made; gaps in seams are frequently 1/8-inch and more in width. What little finishing work is done on reproductions is usually performed with modern high-speed production tools. Any visible grinding marks are usually positive proof a piece is a reproduction.

Old iron usually was decorated with fairly heavy paint, most frequently some type of oil-based enamel. New pieces are typically decorated with a much thinner paint that is usually a water-based acrylic. Old and new paints were also applied differently. Many old pieces were *dipped* in paint, not painted with a brush (although details may have been added by a brush). Many new pieces are painted with spray guns to speed production. Dipping deposits paint on inside surfaces like hidden angles and along the edges where seams meet–spots usually missed by spraying. Toy banks, for example, should usually show paint on both inner and outer edges of the coin slot.

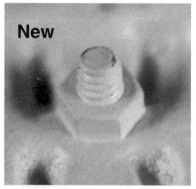 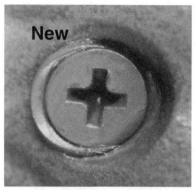

Hex nuts and Phillips head screws are used to join about 99% of cast iron reproductions. These fasteners are almost a guarantee of a reproduction.

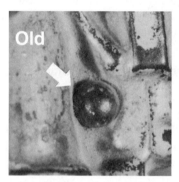 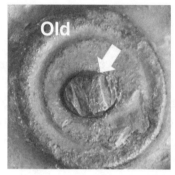

Virtually all original pre-1930 cast iron was joined by peened (left) or hammered (right) steel bolts or rivets. The only type of screw generally used had only a single slot in the head .

The unpainted surface of new cast iron is virtually always rough and pitted (left). Look inside banks and under toys to find unpainted areas. Grinding marks (right) are common on new cast iron, but rarely seen on old.

New

Old

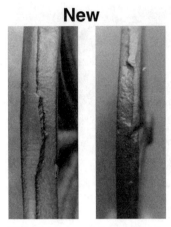
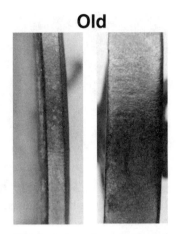

Wheels are a good place to check for quality. Note grind marks, misaligned mold seams, and roughness in new wheels (left). Old wheels (right) have relatively smooth surfaces, no mold seams, and no flaws.

Normal wear in original heavy enamel paint is characterized by sharp-edged paint chips. New, thin paint on the reproductions seldom produces chips (even if you deliberately gouge it). If you look at the chips in the photo on the opposite page, you'll see a lighter inner ring (arrows). This is another sign of the older, thicker paints; most chips reveal one or more additional colors underneath the top layer of paint.

Old unpainted iron usually looks dark brown or even black; new cast iron is typically gray or a dirty silver color. Rust on old cast iron is dark brown or black. Rust on new iron is red or reddish brown. Be wary of any painted pieces with an overall uniform appearance. High temperature can turn the surface of a new piece into

New

New molds seldom fit properly. The metal that runs through the gaps is called a fin or finning. Finning is rarely found on originals, but is typical of most cast iron reproductions. Finning is a particular problem with new cast iron wheels, as seen here.

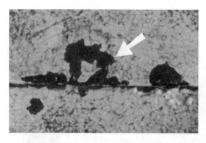

Thick, old enamel paint is very hard and produces deep, sharp, jagged-edged chips. Chips in old paint almost always show two or more colors because they expose multiple layers of paint.

a uniform dull brown or darker color. Burying a new piece or soaking it in chemicals can also change the color.

Old paint should logically show natural wear. Natural paint wear is characterized by scratches of random width and direction, varied length, and irregular depth. Artificial wear, applied with sandpaper, files, etc., is characterized by parallel lines in a regular, repeated pattern all aligned in the same direction.

Many new paints, especially red, fluoresce under long-wave black light. Black light is also helpful to detect repaints and repairs. Check for hidden repairs by going over the entire piece with a magnet. Many repairs and replacement parts are made with epoxies, brass, and aluminum, which have no magnetic attraction.

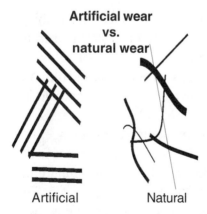

Artificial wear vs. natural wear

Artificial   Natural

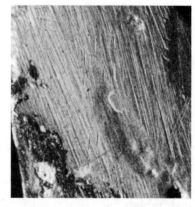

Scratches by natural wear are random in direction and vary in width and length. Artificial wear created with sandpaper, files, wire wheels, or other abrasives and power tools, generally leaves an evenly spaced pattern of parallel lines of almost identical width in the same direction.

Hubley

New

Reproduction 10¾-inch cast iron race car marked Hubley. Exhaust "flames" in hood rise and fall as car wheels turn. Nickel plated wheels.

Classic 1930s Hubley cast iron toys with fake Hubley marks are being reproduced. This includes the race car above, which features 12 exhaust flames that move up and down in the hood as the wheels turn. Originals bring $2,500 to $3,500. Hubley produced two sizes of the original racer, one 7-inch and the other 10¾-inch. The reproduction is of the larger 10¾-inch size.

Unlike most new cast iron, new Hubley racers are well made. The casting quality is generally very good, very close, if not equal, to original quality. Paint is thick and heavy, also very similar to original paint.

Marks on new and old are virtually identical. The "Hubley" mark is cast in raised letters on the bottom of the left rear frame on both new and old. Mold or part numbers are cast below the surface on the bottom of the car's steps on both new and old. As a practical matter, there is no difference between new and old lettering and marks in size, location, or sharpness.

The new paint is also very convincing at first glance. It is thick and heavy like the enamels used on originals. Because it is thick like the original paint, it produces the deep irregular chips that buyers normally look for to authenticate old cast iron. This test, which has been used for many years to separate new from old cast iron, *does not apply* to the new Hubley racers.

Unpainted surfaces of the great majority of cast iron reproductions are shiny silver or red with rust. In the new Hubley racers,

Bottom of new racer. Hubley mark, left arrow. Front axle, right arrow, raises and lowers cylinders in hood. New front axle, below, shows distinct hammer marks not found on original front axle.

unpainted metal–like axles and exposed metal under paint chips–appears a dark brown, almost black, color. These dark colors have traditionally been found only on originals, not reproductions. Like paint chips, the dark patinas and colors previously used as a test for old cast iron *do not apply* to this reproduction.

Separating new and old racers requires attention to some very small details. First, look at the front axle. The exhaust flames are raised and lowered by bends in the axle. Look closely and you'll see dents and flat spots in the *new* axle. New front axles have been *hammered* into shape. Old axles are smooth without dents. They were made in a power fixture by bending, not hammering.

Next, use a 10X loupe to examine areas of paint wear. Under the loupe, you'll see that every spot of bare metal resembling paint wear on the reproductions is surrounded by regularly spaced parallel scratches. Such marks indicate the wear is artificially created, most likely by sandpaper or a wire wheel. Normal wear appears as scratches of irregular width and random direction. Any patches or groups of evenly spaced parallel lines of regular width are virtually always a sign of artificially applied wear.

Lehmann copies

Marks of genuine factories and companies have appeared on reproductions of china, pottery and reproductions for some years. Now the mark of one of the most famous makers of tin toys, Lehmann, is being found on reproductions and knockoffs.

Lehmann Toys was started by Ernst Paul Lehmann in 1881 in Brandenburg, Prussia. The mark consists of an old style press with the initials EPL forming a monogram.

There are many variations of the basic press and monogram mark that commonly have trademark or patent information of the various foreign countries to which the toys were exported. The number 1881 also appears in a number of original marks. But keep in mind that 1881 represents the year the company was founded, not the year a particular toy was made.

Lehmann made many different types of toys but was perhaps best known for its painted clockwork toys and lithographed tin windups. Production ended in the mid-1920s. Originally selling for pennies, Lehmann items are now among the most highly sought antique toys with small 4- to 6-inch tin windups averaging $300 to $1,200.

New toys with old-appearing Lehmann marks are now being made in China. Lehmann look-alikes are also currently being made in Russia, but so far those pieces are not marked Lehmann like the Chinese toys.

Carefully inspect the mechanism of all metal windups. Springs, gears and other parts made 75 to 100 years ago, even toys with mint paint, almost always show at least traces of rust or discoloration on the unpainted steel parts.

The basic Lehmann mark (left) is a monogram of the initials E P L within a press. The mark appears alone or with words related to countries where toys were exported (center). The number   1881 appears in many marks (right) and refers to the year the company was founded, not when the toy was made.

Original Lehmann marks are being used on look-alike new metal windup toys made in China.

New

Old

New 8½-inch lithographed tin windup cart marked Lehmann. New retail, $35. Removable key.

Original Lehmann cart titled Zikra, 1910 to 1920s. Key permanently attached behind wheel (arrow).

New Lehmann toys and many other new metal toys have reinforcing washers (arrow) behind the tabs. These washers were never generally used on metal toys made before 1940. These washers are almost always a sure sign of a modern reproduction.

Keys on virtually all original Lehmann windups were permanently attached. The new Lehmann-marked toys have large removable keys. The position of the windup shaft (arrow) is the same in both old and new.

Marx playsets

Original Marx playsets were produced between 1949 and 1976. Many were based on popular television shows and movies from the 1950s and 1960s like "The Untouchables," "Yogi Bear Jellystone Park," "Zorro," "Ben Hur," "Davy Crockett," and "Robin Hood." Other good selling sets included gas stations, farms, airports, military themes of all kinds, and cowboys and Indians. Most sets from the '50s and '60s originally sold for about $5 to $10. Today, original playsets sell for $300 to $2,000, depending on title, number of original pieces, and condition.

Separate groups of plastic figures from Marx playsets have been reproduced since 1995. Complete boxed playsets including metal buildings, plastic figures and accessories, have been reproduced since 1997. At least four new sets were in production in the late 1990s, including: Davy Crockett at the Alamo, Fort Apache, Sears Service Station, and Cape Canaveral. Sets reproduced in the early 1990s included: Lassie's Heartland America, The Flintstones, Battle of Navarone, The Gold Rush Western Frontier, The Jetsons, and The Great Chariot Race.

The new Davy Crockett playset shown here highlights basic differences between new and old metal in all the sets. First, look for the original Marx trademark on the metal. Virtually without exception, the lithographed metal used in original pre-1970 playsets should include "Made in United States of America." Most,

New Marx Toys "Official Davy Crockett at the Alamo" playset with metal buildings and accessories. Reissue price, $99.

New sets do not include names of licensees like Walt Disney. Original gate above has "Walt Disney's Official" at top. Walt Disney name missing from new gate.

but not all, trademarks on metal also include "New York, NY." All the new metal so far is made overseas, mainly China, and is usually marked with the new "Marx Toys" trademark shown below. Many vintage metal pieces are also marked with the names of additional license or copyright holders such as Walt Disney, MGM, ABC, etc. Not all original metal pieces were marked. So far, every piece of new metal we have seen has the new circular trademark shown below.

Use marks only to evaluate metal buildings, but not plastic figures and accessories. Most plastic pieces with the new sets are made

New    **Old**

New Marx trademark on metal buildings made overseas does not include "Made in United States of America."

Original Marx trademark on original metal buildings includes "Made in United States of America, New York, NY." Marks on plastic and boxes may include "United States of America" but no new *metal* so far includes those words.

Toys

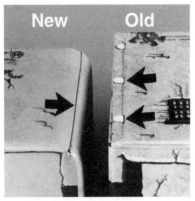

New buildings have rolled seams and rounded corners. Originals made with slots/tabs and square corners.

New plastic accessories made in the United States are packaged with the original Marx trademark.

from original molds, many of which have old-appearing dates and trademarks. Since a complete playset with most of its contents is worth about two to three times that of a set with only half or fewer of its pieces, there is strong temptation to mix in new figures and accessories to complete sets.

Many variations of original sets were made. There were at least 40 versions of authentic Fort Apache playsets; 12 or more authentic Cape Canaveral sets. Study and learn what markings, pieces, and assortments were offered in the original playsets.

New Mexican soldier, left, original Mexican solider, right. Original Mexican soldiers came with Zorro sets and Alamo sets.

Dates are not a reliable test of age for Marx figures or accessories. New pieces from original molds are marked with the original dates.

Lithographed tinplate

The vast majority of all tinplate toys, both new and old, are decorated by a process called offset lithography. This system of printing was invented about 1875. Unlike other methods of printing, the actual printing plate does

New litho tinplate horse and cart.

not touch the material on which ink will be printed. The ink from the printing plate is transferred, or *offset*, to a rubber roller that deposits the ink on sheets of metal (see illustration below). Printed sheets are then fed through a series of molds and cutters, which create three-dimensional pieces ready for final assembly.

Although the printing process is essentially the same for old and new tinplate, there have been important changes in how the color plates are prepared. In vintage tinplate toys made up to about 1960, each color was printed with a separate printing plate. Purple and green, for example, would each require their own plate. Some toys used up to 12 or more plates. Each separate color was printed solid.

Around the late 1970s, screened separations, long used in regular

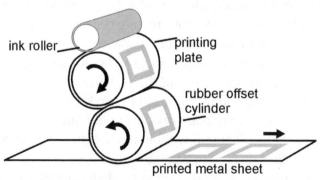

Simple illustration of offset lithography used to print metal toys. Printing plate picks up ink from ink roller, top. Plate transfers or offsets ink to rubber cylinder, center. Rubber cylinder transfers ink to metal sheet, bottom. Printed sheet is then stamped and formed into toy parts.

Toys

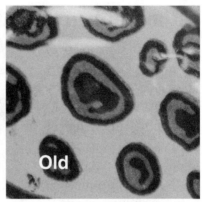

Close-up of horse's harness shown in toy on previous page. Multicolored surface on metal reproductions is composed of dots. Dots appear as regular, repeated pattern under 10X magnification.

Close-up of "skin" on 1930s tinplate snake. Multicolored typical old surface. Each color printed with a separate plate. No dot system evident under 10X magnification.

printing, begin to be used to create color on tinplate toys. In this process, the original full color image is broken down or *separated* into only four plates: black, red, blue, and yellow. By printing these four colors as tiny dots, an infinite variety of colors can be created. Green, for example, is formed by printing dots of yellow and blue; purple by printing dots of blue and red. Our eyes and brain mix the dots together so we "see" a single color.

This test is best used on areas that have two or more colors or areas that gradually change color. Large areas of solid primary colors may not show the dot structure because they are printed by a single ink (without mixing or separating). The cart shown on the previous page, for example, is a solid color and does not show the dot structure. However, the driver and horse, which both show gradual shading and multiple colors, do show the dot structure. Some very simple tinplate toys with only one or two colors are still being manufactured without the dot structure, so be sure to use more than one test to determine age.

Many inks on reproduction tinplate fluoresce under long-wave black light, especially red and white. Inks on tinplate before 1960 rarely fluoresce; inks used before 1940 virtually never fluoresce.

New litho tinplate tea set with Little Red Riding Hood shows regular dot pattern. Made in China.

New windup litho tinplate toy. White areas fluoresce under black light.

New litho tinplate toy. White and red areas fluoresce brightly under long-wave black light.

Reproduction of paper lithograph applied to wood. This new lithograph was made on a home ink jet printer. See the chapter on Paper for more details on lithographed paper reproductions, which includes toys.

Paya reissues

Since 1985, Paya, a Spanish toy maker, has been reissuing metal toys it originally made in the early 20th century. The new toys are made in the same molds and dies from which originals were produced.

The Paya company dates back to 1902. Emilio, Pascual, and Vincente Paya expanded the business into the company called Hermañós Paya (hermañós means brothers in Spanish). This name is represented by the trademark monogram "HP" used from 1906 to 1910. By the 1920s, Paya's mechanical toys were competing with the established toy companies of Germany and France.

Like the rest of the European toy industry, Paya essentially shut down during World War II. Following the war, it struggled financially. In 1985, a decision was made to reissue the early 20th century toys. According to a present day Paya sales brochure, 2,000 different toys were made between 1906 and 1940. Currently, 50 toys are being made as reissues.

Many original Paya toys are in the $200 to $2,000 price range in today's antique market. One of Paya's most sought after toys, a Bugatti race car from the 1930s, has sold for more than $10,000.

The new reissues are produced with the same trademarks that appeared on original pre-1940 Paya toys, so marks alone are not a test of age. Marks found on both new and old include the "HP" mark and a stylized version of the word "Paya," in which the "P" forms the body of a locomotive. Both old and new marks are in various sizes and color combinations.

Since old dies are being used, reissues appear to be identical with originals. Although there are slight differences in paint and the way the metal is finished, these clues are not easily recognized. Fortunately, Paya markets the new reissues as "limited editions" and permanently marks each piece by stamping an edition number into the metal.

Unfortunately, if unethical sellers want to misrepresent pieces, most buyers don't know what the stamped numbers mean; new numbers look like old model numbers or production codes.

New 11-inch windup metal motorcycle. Original was first made in 1936. New reissue price, $350; original sells for $1,400 to $2,200.

Hermañós Paya trademarks: "HP" monogram mark (left), and engine mark (right), appear on both old and new toys. P forms engine, other letters form wheels.

New Paya reissues have an edition number between 1 and 5,000 stamped into the metal. The location of the number varies and is not always obvious. Numbers are slightly more than 1/8-inch high.

Reissue windup rowboat by Paya, 14 inches. Same as the original, which was made in 1923.

Schylling

Schylling logo on key from new windup metal toy.

Schylling is a present-day toy maker/distributor specializing in "nostalgic" products. Any toy with the Schylling logo is new; no old company by this name ever existed.

Two examples of Schylling toys are shown below. The original Atomic Robot Man windup robot was made in Japan during the American Occupation following World War II. It is among the rarest of robots and space toys, with originals selling for $500 to $1,000. The Schylling copies, introduced in 1997, retail for $20 or less. Original keys are simple stamped steel. Keys in new robots are generic cast pot metal keys (shown above) used in a variety of new Schylling key-wind toys.

Schylling offers a wide range of new toys including comic character and personality toys like the Popeye speed boat shown below. A companion boat is made with a Felix the Cat figure.

New windup Popeye 7-inch speed boat by Schylling.

Reproduction 5-inch tin windup Atomic Robot Man by Schylling.

Tucher & Walther

Tucher & Walther is a modern German toy company founded in 1979. This company owns a number of molds and dies from pre-World War II German toy makers including the famous Tipp & Co. (Tippco) of Nuremburg, Germany. The motorcycle shown here, for example, is a classic 1950s design made by Tucher & Walther from original molds.

The mark of Tucher & Walther is a "T" and "W" as shown below. Fortunately, this mark is on most of its new toys. But you won't find it in any reference books on antique collectible toys for the simple reason that it's too new. Look in the same books, however, and you'll see toys made in the original molds Tucher & Walther now owns.

Any toy with the Tucher & Walther mark cannot be older than 1979, the year Tucher & Walther began making toys.

Mark of Tucher & Walther, a German toy company started in 1979. Any toy with this mark cannot have been made earlier than that date.

Silver

The use of "sterling" as a silver standard mark is unique to the United States. To be marked sterling, an item must have 925 parts silver for every 1,000 parts of total material. This is expressed as the ratio 925/1,000 or, more simply, .925. The great majority of original Victorian-era silver flatware and novelties made and sold in the U.S. that met this standard were marked "sterling," not .925. The same .925 standard was adopted by European nations in a 1975 treaty. This eliminated the expense of applying marks in each separate language. Almost all new and reproduction silver novelties made today are marked .925 so they can be sold in any country that has adopted the sterling standard. Any item marked .925 only is almost certain to have been made since 1975. While many original Victorian novelties have manufacturer's marks, many other originals do not. The absence of a factory mark does not necessarily have any bearing on age. The presence of a factory mark (whose years of use are known) and the word "sterling" generally, but not always, indicate a piece is authentic. Recently, some new pieces have begun appearing marked both .925 and "sterling." This combination of marks, although technically possible, would be extremely unusual on vintage pieces and should be viewed with suspicion. There are also several new hallmarks that appear exclusively on reproductions, including "DAB" and "CME" (shown opposite) and a number of forged English hallmarks that appear with .925. No authentic English hallmark will ever appear with .925. Many new pieces of silver are cast, which makes them thick and heavy. These pieces frequently have grinding marks and mold seams. Most originals were die-stamped and are lighter in weight with hand-finished seams. Many new pieces, like the cigar cutter (shown opposite), are entirely silver and too soft to be functional. Steel, not silver, was used for most original blades, pins, hooks, and other areas that required strength, a cutting edge or point.

Typical .925 mark found in new silver.

Mark on new silver with both .925 and STERLING.

DAB hallmark of David Bowles, present-day English silversmith who makes figural matchsafes.

Modern hallmark on new silver match safes, maker unknown.

New Art Nouveau 2½- by 1-inch wide chatelaine marked .925. One inch tall not including chains.

New 3¾-inch silver baby rattle and whistle, marked .925.

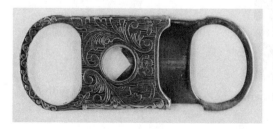

New silver cigar cutter. Blade is also silver, which is too soft to hold a cutting edge; original blades were almost always made of steel.

Silver

New silver match safe, left, marked with CME hallmark. Original, right, was never made in silver.

New silver match safe, red glass eyes; DAB hallmark.

New silver match safe, red glass eyes. Faked English hallmark.

New silver match safe, Punch character. Marked .925 and STERLING.

New silver match safe, mermaid, marked .925.

New silver match safe with Art Nouveau flowers. Marked .925.

Silver

A series of new sterling silver match safes with sports themes began showing up in mid-2001. All of these pieces have a previously unrecorded hallmark of the letters GJ in a diamond, shown below. Several of the new match safes are direct copies of vintage originals. The best way to avoid these new pieces is to keep in mind that any item with the GJ diamond hallmark is new. No sterling silver made prior to 2001 has this mark.

GJ in diamond hallmark found on new match safes with sports themes in 2001. May be found on other new pieces of silver.

Left, new 1½-inch sterling silver match safe with female golfer, GJ hallmark. Right, new 1¾-inch sterling silver match safe with male golfer, GJ hallmark. Piece on right copied from Gorham original.

New round match safe with GJ hallmark. Copied from old original English match safe. The original piece always has a full set of English hallmarks.

Silver

New silver figural pin cushions marked .925. Left, 1-inch chatelaine style with chain; right, 1¾-inch figural swan.

New silver thimbles marked .925. Left, horse head; right, figural pig.

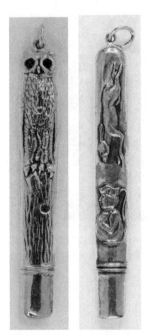 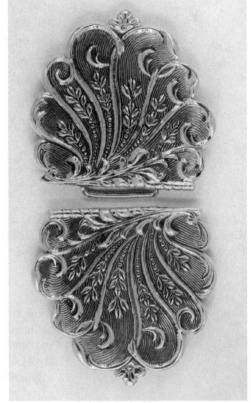

New silver needle cases marked .925. Left, owl with red glass eyes. Right, Alice in Wonderland with Queen of Hearts and White Rabbit.

New silver buckles marked .925. Clasp and fabric anchors on reverse side are also solid silver.

Silver

A number of small sterling silver boxes with confusing enamel inserts are being reproduced. A white enamel background is fired on a copper sheet. The sheet is then simply glued to the silver. The reverse side of a new insert is shown below with the copper sheet clearly visible under the poorly applied enamel. New decorations applied as transfers.

Vintage enamel work is applied directly to the silver; it is not a separate or applied piece. The practice of applying enamel to a separate sheet then attaching it to an object didn't occur until the mid-20th century. When that technique is used on quality pieces, the separate sheet is soldered or attached with a bezel, not glued. Decorations on vintage enamel pieces were hand-painted.

Two new sterling silver boxes with enamel sheets glued to top of lids. Left, 1½-inch figural horseshoe; right, 1½-inch box. Decorations on both boxes are transfers.

Back side of the glued enamel sheet with jockey decoration from above. Very low quality enamel doesn't reach to edges of copper sheet. New enamel is deeply pitted and uneven in coverage.

Scientific Instruments

Reproduction 5-inch sextant. One of many new brass scientific instruments now being made in India. New retail, $98. Authentic vintage sextants this size can bring more than $1,000. Many pieces have confusing marks that appear to be old dates and names of vintage manufacturers.

A major new category has recently been added to the ever-growing list of reproduced antiques–scientific instruments. Solid brass pieces with working knobs, gears, and glass lenses have been slowly seeping into the collectibles market since 1997. The group includes many types of sextants, various telescopes, surveying equipment, different kinds of compasses, various styles of levels, and other 19th century optical and measuring instruments. If authentic, average items of this type retail for about

Reproduction brass pocket sextant made in India; marked "Stanley London 1911." See photo below.

$100 to $1,000. The reproductions wholesale for $25 to $100.

What makes this new category of reproductions particularly confusing is that many pieces carry what appear to be legitimate Victorian-era markings. Despite being made in India, many (but not all) pieces are marked with European or English city names, such as London. Some new pieces are also marked with what appear to be authentic vintage makers' names, such as Stanley, Ross, and Thos. J. Evans. Many new pieces also carry a four-digit number, such as 1911, which suggests a year of production. Anyone looking in auction sales records or price guides could easily confuse similar names on originals with fakes having apparently the same name.

It's the same old problem. All legal requirements are met by the removable "Made in India" paper label, which identifies

Mark on new sextant from above. Mark seems to suggest the piece was made by Stanley in London in 1911. It is a reproduction made in India.

Scientific Instruments

Another version of the Stanley, London, mark on new pieces.

the country of origin. As long as a new mark does not say "Made in ...," any name is acceptable to U.S. Customs agents. "Made in England" would be illegal if the item were not made in England, but "Stanley, London," is technically legal because it does not include the name of a country. This is yet another case proving the point, "Never base evaluation of age or quality on marks alone." Marks are too easily copied and forged. Your best test of authenticity is to examine how a suspect piece is made.

As with all reproductions, one of the first tests you should apply is simple logic. Ask yourself, "Can this item perform the function it was supposedly designed for?" Does this mean you need to know how to use a sextant or theodolite to identify reproductions of those instruments? Of course not; just use common sense.

Simply stated, any part that is supposed to move, should

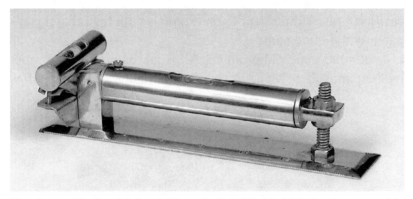

New brass 6-inch spirit level. Two alcohol filled bubble levels mounted in solid brass. Originals date to the mid-1800s.

This black plastic lens holder is virtually hidden deep inside the mechanism. You need a flashlight to see it.

Inspect carefully for small plastic parts. This plastic washer (arrow) is only about ¼-inch diameter and located at the bottom of a knob. It's easy to overlook.

move. Arms, levers, and dials should move freely. Knobs should not be frozen; they should tighten and loosen easily. If a piece has an optical system (like a sextant, theodolite, telescope, etc.), you should be able to bring the lens into focus. On pieces that measure angles, double-check all inscribed markings. For example, make sure 90 degrees is at a right angle from zero degrees, and 180 degrees is directly opposite the zero mark.

A detailed inspection of many of the new instruments reveals the use of modern materials. In the top photo next page, for example, a plastic washer has been used. In another example, a black plastic rim is used on a lens located deep inside a pocket sextant. Whatever you do, be thorough. These parts are smaller than ¼ inch and are easily overlooked, especially when they are

Scientific Instruments

located deep in an intricate mechanism. A small flashlight is often needed to see down into an instrument to identify the plastic parts.

Other typical clues to a reproduction are grinding marks and rough surfaces. Original instruments were skillfully made precision machines. Authentic originals may have some dents and scratches from normal wear, but these should be irregular in size and randomly placed. Modern grinding marks from power tools are generally regular in size and repeat in an obvious pattern.

Closely inspect all calibrated markings such as degrees, inches, angles, etc. Most originals were carefully scribed or engraved, and remain clear and easy to read even after years of normal use. Many markings on the reproductions are either faint, shallow, and hard to read, or grossly large, oversized, and crude. The crude mark-

New brass 9-inch theodolite, a surveying instrument.

ings are stamped rather than engraved, which distorts or "squashes" the outlines of the numbers.

The new instruments have been widely reported throughout the U.S. and in most of the tourist markets in England and

Reproduction clinometer, also known as an anglemeter. Typical uses were to measure angles of cannon, the tilt off vertical of sailing ships, slopes of hills in surveys, etc. This new piece is marked "G. Wright, Wm. Thomson (Baron Kelvin) Clark & Kelvin & J. White, London."

Typical rough, pitted surface on reproduction instrument. Old surfaces are finely machined and smooth.

Rough grinding marks on bezel around a glass vial in a new level. Tool marks are rarely seen on originals.

Europe. A number of the instruments are available in wood cases with brass hardware that also appears old and may have confusing markings.

Additional names found on new brass scientific instruments currently being imported from India and some of the pieces they have been found on include: Ross–telescopes; Ross Evans–Brunton-type compass and telescope; Thos J. Evans–Brunton-type compasses; Elliott–compass; Ottway; West–sundial; Ramsden–sundial.

Pickle Castors
Glass Inserts and Metal Frames

Reproduction metal pickle castor frames and new glass inserts have been sold since the 1960s. Buyers should be particularly alert to mixed and "married" castor sets: new inserts with genuinely old frames and genuinely old inserts in new frames.

Both frame and insert should be examined carefully. We'll discuss new frames first, then the inserts.

Frames

The great majority of new frames made since the 1960s are in one of only five styles. These are shown in Figs.1 through 5. In 2002, only three of these were in production. Learn these basic styles and you'll probably be able to avoid 95 percent of reproduction castor frames currently in the market.

Frame style #1 was introduced by L.G. Wright Glass Company in the 1960s. It was available with and without feet. It was discontinued about 1990. The Wright version was unmarked. This same style was put back in production in the year 2000. It is now being made in Canada and is permanently marked "Marlboro Pewter, Canada." There are now old counterparts with this mark.

All of Wright's metal lids were available with three types of finials: an eagle, a fleur-de-lis and an open wreath. The only lid currently offered with the Canadian frame is the eagle.

Frame style #2, with birds and vines, was introduced by AA Importing in the mid-late 1960s. The key to identifying this frame is the four Phillips head screws in the base. The finial on the lid is a flat disc embossed with a grape design. This frame is currently in production.

Frame style #3 is another frame introduced by AA Importing in the 1970s. It was advertised as a "mechanical" frame. The lid rises automatically as the handle is tilted back. There are no old counterparts to this frame. This frame was back in production in 2001.

1

2

Frame style #1 sold from ca. 1960s to present. Early versions were available with or without feet. Now sold with eagle finial on lid. Earlier finials were a wreath or fleur-de-lis.

Frame style #2 has been sold from the 1960s to the present. The finial is a flat disc with raised grapes and vines.

Above, detail of frame style #1 top. Below, marking on bottoms of frame #1 sold since 1999.

Above, frame #2 top with singing birds. Below, Phillips head screws on new #2 bases.

Pickle Castors

Frame style #3, so-called "mechanical" frame. As handle is pushed back, lid automatically rises. Sold from at least the 1970s through today. Front view shown on left; side view of frame style #3 on right.

The remaining frames, styles #4 and #5, were sold by L.G. Wright, ca. 1960-1990. Style #4 has a scroll and floral pattern in an arched top. Style #5 has a horizontal bar of flowers. As of early 2002, neither #4 nor #5 were in production.

The vast majority of original metal castor frames made ca. 1875-1910 were almost always made up from separate pieces soldered together. New frames are most often cast as one piece. About 90 to 95 percent of old frames are marked with the name of the silver plate manufacturer. None of the new frames shown in this chapter, with the exception of "Marlboro Pewter," is marked. However, the absence or presence of a factory name by itself does not prove a frame is new or old. Marks can be added or removed fairly easily.

New frame styles #4 and #5 were sold ca. 1960s-1990. Frames #4 and #5 were sold with and without claw feet. Claw feet shown on #5; base without feet shown on #4. Frames #1, #4, and #5 were sold with three styles of lids: eagle, shown with frames #1 and #5; wreath, on frame #4; and fleur-de-lis, above, far right. The fleur-de-lis and wreath were discontinued ca. 1990. The eagle lid is currrently sold with #1 frames made today.

Inserts

There are two general categories of reproduced inserts: American made and those made overseas. Inserts sold with Wright frames, ca. 1960-1990, were all made in America from new molds made to Wright's specifications. Wright owned the molds and jobbed production out to a number of glass houses including Fenton, Summit, Fostoria, Imperial and others.

Wright's most popular inserts were new opalescent patterns copied from original Victorian patterns such as Swirl, Dot Optic (Honeycomb), Fern and others. All of Wright's opalescent inserts were made as straight sided cylinders. Genuinely old opalescent pattern inserts were almost never made in that shape.

Wright closed in the mid-1990s. The company's molds were sold at auction in May 1999. Included in the sale were the insert shape and pattern molds which were purchased by Fenton. The insert molds went into production in mid-2001, when Fenton began making new inserts in opalescent patterns. Some of the patterns made so far include Fern, Dot Optic (Honeycomb), Swirl

Pickle Castors

New cranberry opalescent inserts. Virtually all opalescent inserts in this straight-sided cylindrical shape are new.

Two typical new pressed glass inserts. Mirror and Roses, left, Daisy and Button, right. Both examples available since 2000 in vaseline and other colors.

and others. The opalescent patterns have appeared in various colors of body glass including cranberry.

Although Fenton attempts to permanently mark each new opalescent insert, many marks are difficult to see. Most marks are faint because of the extensive blowing and shaping required to produce the inserts. Of the samples we've seen, only about one or two in every ten pieces have clear distinct mark like the one shown on the opposite page.

Two other insert molds sold at the Wright auction were for the pressed glass patterns Mirror and Roses and Daisy and Button shown above. These were purchased by Rosso Glass and went back into production in 2000. Rosso's R in a keystone

Fenton mark on bottom of new opalescent castor inserts. Fenton logo with decade code "0" for decade of 2000. Most marks on new Fenton opalescent inserts are very faint and hard to find.

Molded mark of Rosso Glass. Very faintly molded on inside bottoms of Mirror and Roses and Daisy and Button pressed glass inserts.

Scalloped rim on new Daisy and Button insert shown on opposite page. Original castor inserts virtually never had decorative effects around the top rim. They would only get damaged in daily use. Decorative top rims almost always indicate a new insert or a mismatched piece of glass being used for an insert.

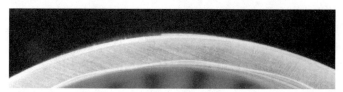

Top rim on new Fenton insert shows obvious grinding marks which produce a frosted, almost gray, appearance. Top rims on original Victorian glass inserts were usually wheel polished or fire polished (held to the furnace to smooth the surface).

trademark is molded on the inside bottom of these inserts but is usually very hard to find, especially on the Daisy and Button pieces.

The Daisy and Button insert is made from an old mold. If you look at the top rim, though, you'll see it is scalloped. That's because this shape was originally sold as a spoon holder, not a castor insert. Top rims on original castor insert are virtually always flat. Saw teeth, scallops or other decorative effects in the

Pickle Castors

The four most common styles of new inserts offered by AA Importing since the 1960s. All of these inserts have shoulders, or a narrowing, where the lid rests. From upper left, clockwise: inverted thumbprint (ITP), cut crystal, Nailsea and cut to clear. The overlay, Nailsea and ITP sold in a variety of colors.

glass would get broken and chipped by the metal castor lid. If a piece with teeth, scallops or other decorative effect in the top rim is offered to you as an insert, it is almost certainly a replacement or reproduction.

While Wright's castor inserts are limited to a relatively small number of molds, reproduction inserts sold by AA Importing show considerable variation over the years. So much so, it is hard to summarize all the styles made. The AA Importing insert most frequently found in new frames or mixed with genuinely old frames is a cut to clear overlay style. A relatively simple floral pattern is cut through an overlay of either ruby, cranberry or cobalt blue. The next most common AA Importing inserts are clear glass with cut patterns, a Nailsea loop-type pattern and an inverted thumbprint pattern in various colors. These four basic styles have appeared continuously in AA Importing catalogs for nearly 40-plus years, beginning in the 1960s.

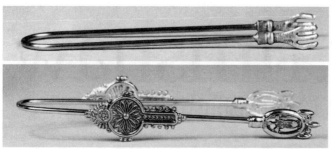

The two most commonly seen new castor tongs. The bottom set, made in a Victorian style, has been sold since the 1960s.

AA Importing insert shapes are generally more similar to original inserts than Wright insert shapes. Most AA inserts, for example, have a shallow shoulder around the top, while Wright's shapes are straight cylinders.

Mixed and married pieces

Castor sets made up of mixed and married parts are often harder to detect than all new sets. Here are a few suggestions: First, pick up the tongs and go through the motions of taking a pickle from the insert. If all parts are original, you shouldn't have any problems. Can you remove the lid easily or does the lid get caught in the metal frame? Can the lid be passed easily through the frame? Is there a logical amount of space between the top of the insert and the top of the frame or has too large an insert been placed in a small frame or vice versa? Does the metal lid match the frame? Virtually all original lid finials repeat some major design theme of the frame. Both frame and metal lid should have approximately the same finish and the same amount of wear. Finally, do all the pieces look balanced and complement each other–does everything appear to be the right proportion and simply look well together?

Some collectors may decide that the new reproduction pickle castors, particularly the new Fenton and 1960s Wright, are collectible for their own merits. That decision, and what price to pay, is up to the buyer. But don't confuse late 20th century copies with Victorian-era originals. Keep in mind that all of Wright's molds were purchased by modern glass companies and are being put back into production.

Scrimshaw

and Other Nautical Carvings

Rachel Pringle of Barbadoes, 5½-inch plastic imitation of carved sperm whale tooth, called scrimshaw.

When scrimshaw is mentioned, almost all non-scrimshaw collectors and dealers think of carving on sperm whale teeth only. But scrimshaw also includes engravings on skeletal whale bone–such as the jaw bone, called panbone–and ivory from other marine mammals such as walrus. Although scrimshaw is widely associated with nautical themes and designs of the 19th century whaling industry, vintage scrimshaw was also produced as tribal art in many cultures. Today, scrimshaw is recognized as a unique medium in which present-day artists have developed their own modern themes.

Scrimshaw reproductions and imitations may take several

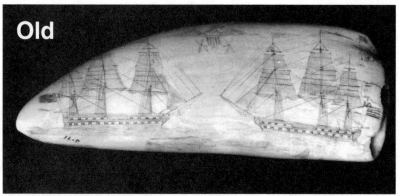

New Bedford Whaling Museum.

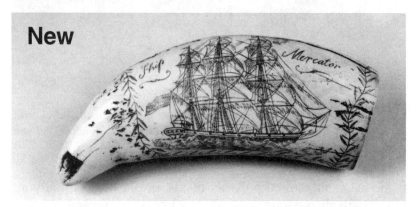

The most commonly faked scrimshaw is the sperm whale tooth. In recent years, the latest generation plastic copies have become somewhat closer in general appearance to 19th century originals. New and old shown above.

forms. There are new carvings on genuine ivory or bone with the deliberate intent to create an "antique"; new carvings on genuine ivory or bone sold as signed and dated contemporary art, clearly marked synthetic museum reproductions, and mass marketed, unmarked synthetic replicas.

Painstakingly carved deliberate fakes are directed towards the scrimshaw collector and seldom appear in the general market. Pieces of contemporary art and museum copies are usually clearly marked and openly sold for what they are. The biggest problem in the general antiques market are the mass-produced synthetic pieces and are the focus of this chapter.

Synthetic or natural?

The great majority of synthetic scrimshaw reproductions are

Scrimshaw

Eagle, arctic whaling scene on reverse. Plastic imitation 5½-inch sperm whale tooth.

Plastic imitation of 3¾-inch walrus tusk section marked, *Steam Whaler William Lewis.*

made of manufactured polymer resins, or plastic. Virtually all plastic will absorb long wave ultraviolet (UV) light and appear a dull matte blue under black light or appear the same color under black light as it appears under room lighting, or white light. This is regardless of the surface color of the plastic. Natural bone and ivory appear white to yellowish-white under long wave black light regardless of their surface color in white light.

Do not use heated pins or open flame, apply acetone, or scratch the surface of the test object. Not only are such tests largely ineffective, they are destructive and potentially harmful. Many plastics emit toxic fumes if heated or dissolved in acetone.

Bone or ivory?

Carvers in China are now using bones of water buffaloes and fish to imitate scrimshaw and antique bone. Many of these new carvings on bone include 19th century whaling and nautical themes, especially on small boxes. Most of these pieces of new bone fluoresce white or yellowish-white like ivory under long wave black light. But according to the staff of the Kendall

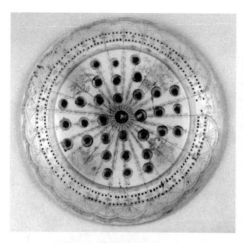

New plastic game board and calendar; 9-inch diameter disc. Center for marbles, cribbage holes around border. Border also inscribed with months. Marked and dated, *Henry Sadler, 1832.*

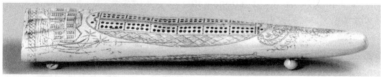

New 12½-inch plastic "tusk" cribbage board with plantation scene.

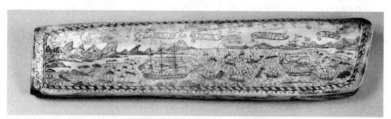

New 17-inch panbone (whale jaw bone) with whaling scene.

"Certificate of authenticity" came with imitation crimshaw sold by Offstage Auctions ca. 1990s.

Scrimshaw

New 2-inch box carved in bone, basketweave pattern on sides.

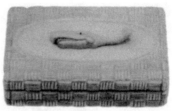

New 3½-inch box carved in bone, basketweave sides, whale on lid.

New 3-inch box carved in bone with whaling scenes on lid.

New 3-inch so-called puzzle box carved in bone.

This foot on a cribbage board is cast as one piece with the board. Authentic feet and other added details were virtually always carved separately and attached.

Many plastic pieces have construction details, wear and weathering cast in the mold to create an appearance of natural aging. Left, wear and cracks cast in tip of a new tooth. Right, wear and weathering in the base of a new tooth.

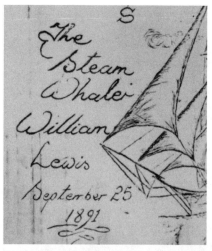

It is common to find inscriptions, dates and other personal information on imitation scrimshaw and nautical carvings. Two typical examples shown here.
Left: *The Steam Whaler William Lewis, September 1891* molded on plastic walrus tusk.
Below: *Taken in the Arctic Ocean 1850*, molded on reverse of plastic sperm whale tooth.

Whaling Museum, no similar authentic boxes were ever made in the 19th century. All the boxes and other novelty shapes are called "fantasy" pieces; no originals ever existed.

You can separate bone from ivory by examining the surface. All true ivory comes from a tooth–a tusk is simply a large tooth. The part of ivory that is carved is composed primarily of dentine, a nearly perfectly solid mass. A microscope is required to observe any cavities in ivory, called dentinal tubules, which average one micron in diameter (1/25,400th of an inch). By contrast, cavities in bone through which fluids pass, the Halversian System, are easily visible with the unaided eye or a loupe. They form a typical pattern of dark pits and grooves.

But be careful. Molds of the better quality synthetic pieces now include the pits and grooves of natural bone. A black light test still proves the more accurate fakes to be made of synthetic material, not true bone.

Remember, guidelines in this article are for detecting the mass produced synthetic pieces, not individually crafted forgeries on old bone or ivory, which require professional inspection.

Genuine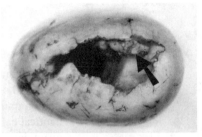

Pulp cavities in genuine teeth frequently, but not always, have small nodules known as pulp stones (arrow). Pulp stones are a sign of genuine sperm whale teeth. The base of this genuine tooth is more closed than typical teeth. The amount of closure visible may be affected by where, if at all, the base of the tooth is cut or sawed. *New Bedford Whaling Museum.*

Bases of two molded plastic sperm whale teeth. The cavity in these bases is a simple cylinder and doesn't attempt to duplicate an original pulp cavity.

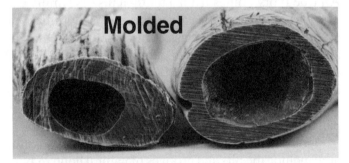

Another set of new molded plastic teeth with pulp cavities deliberately designed to imitate original pulp cavities. These cavities are very irregular in shape, not conical like pulp cavities in genuine teeth. Genuine teeth were frequently sawed off on the base so the piece could be displayed upright. Note the molded "saw" marks on these bases which imitate old saw marks.

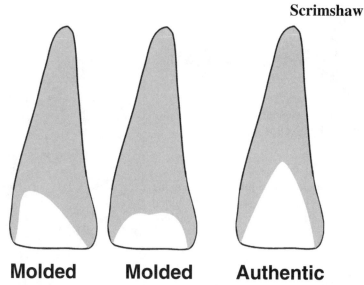

Molded   Molded   Authentic

Vertical cross sections of sperm whale teeth. The bottom of genuine sperm whale teeth have a hollow space in the base called a pulp cavity (shown in white in the illustration). The pulp cavity is distinctly conical in genuine teeth. This conical section is hard to duplicate in the molded plastic teeth. The cavity in most new teeth is a flat-topped dome or an off-center, irregular shape.

Three new imitation plastic sperm whale teeth. These examples show the variation in surface color found among new teeth. Most new teeth are colored at the factory to resemble age.

Scrimshaw

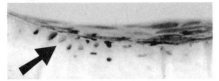

End view of genuine bone showing dark pits left by blood vessels.

Top view of genuine bone showing pits and grooves left by blood vessels.

Reverse side of new molded plastic panbone, or jaw bone. Very realistic imitation of Halversian System that appears in genuine bone, dark pitting interspersed with dark grooves. The surface is also realistically "splintered" like genuine bone.

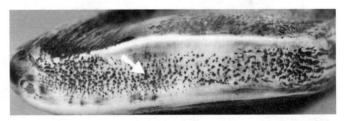

End view of the cast plastic panbone shown above. The dark pits in this view are a realistic imitation of an end view of genuine bone.

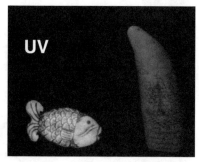

Fish carved from new bone on left; new scrimshaw in synthetic material on right. Under room light, or white light, left, surfaces look the same. Under long wave ultraviolet light, right. Virtually all synthetic materials absorb untraviolet and appear black or a deep dark blue that is nearly black. Bone, new or old, will fluoresce white. This test only separates bone from synthetic materials. It does not prove age.

sperm & killer whales

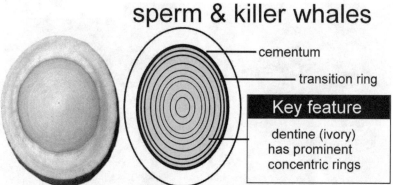

cementum

transition ring

Key feature

dentine (ivory) has prominent concentric rings

Parts or portions of a sperm or killer whale tooth can be identified by examining a cross section. The ivory, or dentine, is deposited as concentric rings. Photo left, line drawing right.

walrus

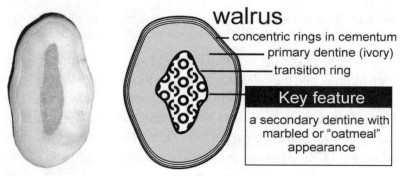

concentric rings in cementum

primary dentine (ivory)

transition ring

Key feature

a secondary dentine with marbled or "oatmeal" appearance

Walrus is today legally carved by native peoples of several nations. Walrus is identified by an "oatmeal" or marbleized-like texture in the center of a cross section. Photo left, line drawing, right.

Little Red Riding Hood

Size is one of the best clues to a Little Red Riding Hood pottery reproduction. So far, all the reproductions are considerably smaller than originals. The new cracker jar, left, is 7½ inches tall; the original jar, right, is over 8 inches tall.

Reproductions of Little Red Riding Hood (LRRH) pottery have been filtering into the collectibles market since the mid-1990s.

The basic design for original LRRH pottery was created by Louise Bauer. Bauer received Design Patent #135,889 for LRRH on June 29, 1943. She assigned the patent to the Hull Pottery Company which sold LRRH pottery products between 1943 and 1957. Hull never did any of the LRRH decorating and made virtually none of the pottery blanks. All decorating and almost all the blanks were produced by Royal China and Novelty, a part of Regal China Corp.

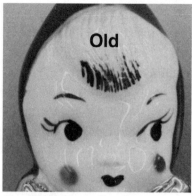

Typical reproduction and original faces. On new faces, small green eyes stare straight ahead; no spots of blush on cheeks. Poorly molded mouth and lips lack detail. Original faces have large blue pupils in the corner of the eyes and spots of blush on cheeks.

Although many original pieces are marked with the patent number, the Hull name or some combination of both, many other original pieces are unmarked. Therefore, marks are not a reliable test of age. Further, many reproductions are marked in the identical manner as old originals. The best test of age is to closely examine how a piece is decorated and formed.

Comparing the sizes of suspected reproductions to known originals is especially helpful. All the reproductions have been made from molds taken from originals. During this process, shrinkage occurs. Although originals can vary slightly in size from piece to piece, all reproductions made so far are have been substantially smaller than originals.

Original pottery is made of vitrified (high fired) china. Reproductions are made of a low-fired soft clay like that commonly used in china painting and ceramic classes. Originals were made for functional, everyday use. Reproductions are made as "antiques." Check the fit of lids, shape of spouts and placement of handles. Ask yourself, "Could this piece be used for the purpose it was intended?" Many reproductions cannot function in a practical, logical manner.

Original faces have lifelike eyes and human facial expression. Eyes of the reproductions stare zombie-like straight ahead. Eyes of originals are looking to the side. Original eyes are virtually always blue; new eyes are almost always pale green.

Little Red Riding Hood

The hair on reproductions is a thick, heavy, pale, yellow with a few thick strokes of brown to suggest single hair strands. Original hair is a crisp sharp yellow with generally very fine brush strokes to suggest a few single strands.

New gold trim shows no normal wear; original gold trim almost always shows at least some normal wear around handles, knobs, rims and lids. New gold trim also tends to have a mirrorlike reflective surface. Original gold trim is softer and less reflective.

In addition to the new pieces listed here, reproductions are also being made of the spice jars, kitchen cannisters, stringholder, and large and medium sized shakers. There may be other new pieces as well. Most all the other new pieces can be detected by using the guidelines listed in this article.

The base of new butter dish is 6½ inches left to right; original, 67/8 inches. Opening in the new cover is 6-by-4¼ inches; opening in old, 6¼-by-4½ inches.

New batter pitcher, left, measures 7½ inches from tip of spout to back edge of handle. The original, right, is 8 inches. Note the difference in facial details.

330

Smaller new teapot, left, 7½ inches tall. Original teapot, right, is almost 8½ inches tall. See details of new and old lids below.

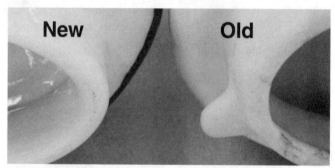

Lids from new and old teapots. The original lid, right, has a catch on the rim to keep the lid on the pot. Reproduction lid, left, does not have the catch.

Many features on the reproductions are not functional. The tiny spout on the new teapot won't allow much tea to flow.

Little Red Riding Hood

New wall hanging planter, about 8½ inches top to bottom.

Original wall hanging planter, about 9½ inches top to bottom.

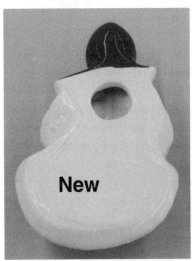

Back of new hanging wall planter. Back is glazed. Hole is 1½-inch diameter, about the size of a 50-cent piece.

Back of original hanging wall planter. Back is unglazed. Hole is 5/8-inch diameter, about the size of a dime.

New

Old

New bank is about the same size as original bank. Casting holes in base are about dime sized and almost always nearly perfect circles.

Both new and old banks are about 7 inches tall, 5 inches across at base. Irregular casting holes in old base are only about the size of a wood pencil.

New   Old

New wall match box holder is crudely made with virtually no molded or painted details in face, clothing and body. New window is simply divided by a vertical and horizontal line with diagonal lines to suggest shutters. Much less of the surface is painted compared to the original. Less than 5 inches tall. Original wall match box holder has sharply molded and painted details on house, clothing and face. The dress is entirely painted. Original window has four distinct panes and fully painted shutters; painted flowers appear under the window. About 5¼ inches tall.

333

Lawn and Garden Cast Iron

Three new pieces of cast iron. Left: 34-inch cast iron chair; right: 24-inch lion wall fountain; center: 25-inch rooster.

Cast iron outdoor furniture and lawn ornaments were at their height of popularity from 1850-1890 during the Victorian gardening craze. Molded cast iron was relatively cheap and replaced the more expensive handmade wrought iron used largely from the early 1800s to the mid-1840s. By the 1890s, cast iron was, in turn, replaced by steel, which was lighter, stronger, and less brittle. A resurgence of interest in gardening since the mid-1990s has brought out reproductions inspired by the Victorian originals.

New cast iron 25-inch table top, left; complete 26-inch tall table with cast iron base, right. Assembled with threaded studs (discussed on page 339) typical of reproduction cast iron furniture.

A few one-of-a-kind cast iron pieces were individually designed and made for wealthy customers, but the majority of pieces were mass produced in molds and sold to the general public. Victorian manufacturers overcame the weight problems posed by cast iron by simply dividing a large design into a number of smaller castings. The small castings were individually boxed, shipped and then assembled into the final form on the grounds or backyards of customers.

Original cast iron urns up to five or six feet in height, for example, are typically created from four to five separate castings, all generally under 12 inches tall and weighing no more than 50 to 100 pounds. Original garden benches can be made from as many as eight to 10 pieces usually in the five-to 50-pound range. While not exactly

New 38-inch cast iron chair. Portrait medallion in center of back; bearded man's head lower back; clusters of grapes at sides.

Lawn and Garden Cast Iron

lightweight, these sizes and weights could be handled by a Victorian home owner and a helper fairly easily. Although these pieces look massive and imposing when assembled, most can be taken apart and easily moved.

Some of the companies that made Victorian-era cast iron furniture and ornaments include: J.W. Fiske, New York City; Janes, Kirtland & Co., Manhattan, NY; Westervelt, New York City; Lorio Iron Work, New Orleans; F.P. Smith, Chicago; Kramer Bros., Dayton, OH; and Robert Wood & Co., Philadelphia.

The new furniture and ornaments suffer from the same general problems found in the majority of reproduced cast iron whether it's toys or doorstops. These typical problems are: 1) a generally rough, pitted surface; 2) poorly fitting joints and seams, 3) grinding and other modern tool marks; 4) major differences in construction between new and old; 5) the reproduction is not as practical as the original.

Problems one through three–rough surface, loose fit and grinding marks–are about the same on lawn and garden pieces as other new pieces of cast iron. These problems are discussed in detail in the text and close-up photos found on pages 279-281 in the Toys chapter of this book and here on the opposite page. Rather than repeat that information here, we will devote the text to the specific problems unique to garden and lawn pieces.

Benches, chairs and tables

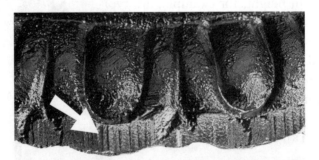

Detail of the regular parallel lines left by modern grinding tools on most pieces of new cast iron. Shown about actual size. Also note the rough, grainy surface that shows through the paint.

336

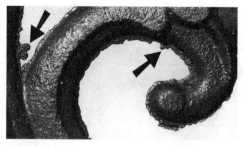

If molds do not fit properly, molten iron runs out and produces "finning" along the mold seams (arrows). Finning is rare in original cast iron furniture and ornaments, but almost always present in reproductions.

A good way to catch casting flaws is to compare details in repeated patterns. Note the repeated openings around the semi-circle in this example found on the new planter, above right. Each opening is slightly different. Repeated patterns in original castings are almost always crisp and clean with nearly perfect repeats of pattern details.

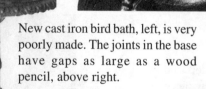

New cast iron bird bath, left, is very poorly made. The joints in the base have gaps as large as a wood pencil, above right.

Joints in vintage cast iron, right, are uniformly tight. Some old joints are so tight, paper cannot be passed through the joint.

Lawn and Garden Cast Iron

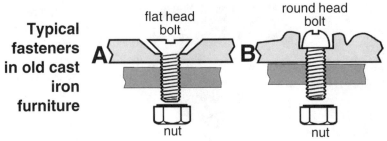

Typical fasteners in old cast iron furniture

flat head bolt

round head bolt

A

B

nut

nut

Parts and pieces of typical vintage cast iron furniture were assembled with nuts and bolts, not threaded studs or threaded pockets. Bolts were generally made of steel, much stronger and more flexible than cast iron. If a bolt would break, it was easily replaced. Surfaces subject to human contact–such as seats and table tops–generally have a bevelled hole to accept flat head bolts (A). Where body contact wasn't a concern, round head bolts (B) were generally used. Round head bolts were often hidden in raised designs.

All typical old cast iron furniture was constructed of a number of parts. Holes were either cast or drilled completely through the pieces to be joined. Old joints were almost always fastened together with nuts and bolts. There were two basic types of bolts used: a flat head straight slot bolt and round head straight slot bolts (see illustrations above).

Flat head bolts were used on horizontal surfaces such as bench and chair seats, and table tops which needed a smooth surface. The bevelled flat head bolt fits into a matching bevelled hole in the furniture, which makes the bolt head flush with the surface. If you find a piece that you believe is old but has another type of bolt or fastener, inspect the holes. Original flat top bolts could have been replaced over the years, but the bevelled hole

A typical threaded stud in the frame of a new piece of cast iron furniture.

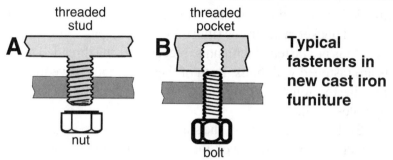

threaded
stud

threaded
pocket

**Typical
fasteners in
new cast iron
furniture**

nut

bolt

Many new pieces of cast iron furniture have threaded studs rising from the frame (A) or internal threading in a hole, or pocket, in the frame (B). If the relatively brittle cast iron breaks, the joint can't be repaired.

should still remain in seats and tabletops.

The other fastener you could reasonably expect to find in an old piece is a round head bolt. These bolts were generally used only in a deep recess of the three dimensional cast design where they would not catch on clothing or pinch the body. They are usually found in backs, armrests, side panels and structural supports in low areas between leaves, branches, flowers, fruit, etc. With rare exceptions, all original bolts and nuts on American cast iron are based on English inches such as one-half, five-sixteenths, etc., not metric sizes.

The new reproductions are made quite differently. Rather than make a hole in both pieces to be joined, the new pieces only have a hole in one of the mating pieces. This hole then fits over a

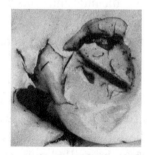

Two typical old flat head bolts as found in vintage pieces of cast iron furniture. Many vintage bolt heads are sealed in by layers of paint, right. Although painted-in bolts are no guarantee of age, mutiple layers of aged paint are consistent with vintage cast iron furniture.

Lawn and Garden Cast Iron

threaded stud permanently embedded in the frame or an inside threaded pocket in the frame (illustration, top of page 339). Pieces over studs are fastened with nuts; pieces over the threaded pockets are fastened with bolts. Both of these methods leave the side opposite the joint not only flush but perfectly smooth without any holes at all.

Both of these methods, the stud and internal pocket, are easy to detect because only one of the pieces being joined has a hole. In other words, if you looked on the opposite side of any new joint, the surface would be perfectly smooth. The hole or bolt would not be visible. This is unlike old furniture which has clear open holes in both pieces being joined together. For every original bolt head or nut you see on one side, there will be a matching nut or bolt head on the opposite side.

Another difference is that the threading on the new pieces is based on the metric system, not English inches. The new hex head bolts, for example, have 14mm heads; the hex nuts are 10mm wide. Since the threaded studs are embedded in the frame and the internal threads are also part of the frame, it will be very difficult to switch the new metric fasteners with the correct English nuts and bolts.

Does it really matter how old and new pieces are held together? Yes, it certainly does; it's an important matter of function and practicality. Original pieces were made to be used as outdoor furniture and were designed accordingly. Exposed to the weather, the nuts and bolts which hold the furniture together could become rusty and break. What then? Just replace it with a new nut and bolt which cost pennies and the piece of furniture is repaired.

A piece designed as a reproduction, however, is seldom as practical and functional as the original it copies. If the nuts or studs rusted together in these new pieces and broke, how could they be repaired? The studs and internal threads would have to somehow be drilled out and new studs installed or new threads cut in. Both very difficult and lengthy operations compared to replacing a simple nut and bolt on an original.

We were unable to find any references, examples, or

Lawn and Garden Cast Iron

personal observations of American-made cast iron garden furniture with these studs and threaded pockets. A fast inspection of the bolts and holes may be a quick way to eliminate the benches, chairs and tables in this new group of reproductions. Keep in mind, however, that earlier reproductions may use a removable bolt like the originals–don't ever use just one test for judging age or authenticity.

Urns and vases

Virtually every original Victorian period urn or lawn vase was assembled from two or more separate castings. The original urn shown below, for example, is 27 inches tall overall and is made from four sections. Each casting fits snugly into adjoining castings by the use of interlocking rims and projections. Although nuts and bolts were sometimes used to fasten urn handles, they were very rarely used to connect the large castings. Nuts and bolts were not practical because they rusted quickly in the soil and water inside the planter. Victorian designers relied on rims, grooves and gravity alone to hold the major castings together.

Another distinguishing feature on most original urns is an overflow opening. An overflow opening was necessary to drain water out of the planter. If there was no opening, the urn could fill with water and wash out the soil and plants. The overflow

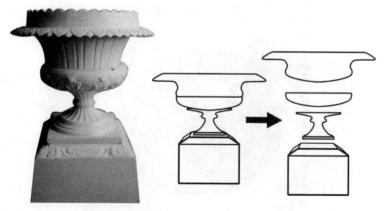

Nearly all original cast iron urns, like the one shown above, were stacked together from three, four, or more, separate pieces. Bolts were rarely used; gravity held the pieces together. This original is only 27 inches tall but weighs a total of almost 200 pounds. If not made in several pieces, it would be extremely difficult to move.

Lawn and Garden Cast Iron

The vintage urn from the previous page taken apart to show the four separate castings from which it is assembled. The pieces are arranged in order with the top (1) on the left, the base (4) on the right.

opening is usually in the ring casting just below the main casting (see photo at the bottom of this page).

The large new urn on the opposite page is typical of most reproduction urns. Unlike originals, new urns are generally made up of only one or two castings. This particular urn is made from only two castings. The large top casting is extremely difficult to handle because of its size and weight.

This reproduction urn is held together with nuts and bolts. It does not have an interlocking system of boltless grooves and ridges like originals. Nor is there an overflow opening for excess water or a hole for filling the urn with water. Another clue to its recent manufacture are the threaded studs embedded in the handles which are fastened to the side of the urn.

Overhead view of piece number 2 from the vintage urn shown at the top of page. Old urns generally have overflow drains (white arrow) for excess rainwater and fill holes (black arrow) to add water in dry times. Reproductions virtually never include these two features.

342

Reproduction urn, 17 inches tall, 32 inches in diameter, upper left. Unlike vintage urns, which would be made in several or more pieces, this new urn is made in only two pieces, bottom. Old urns are stacked together and generally held together only by gravity, not nuts and bolts. The two halves of this new urn are bolted together with modern hex head bolts, upper right.

Another Victorian garden piece being heavily reproduced is the gazing ball stand. Vintage gazing, or reflecting, balls were used as lawn and garden ornaments from the late 18th century to the first third of the 20th century. Balls were made of blown glass with a mirror. The spherical shape provided a unique 360 degree reflection view of sky, garden and surrounding buildings.

One of the more elaborate gazing ball reproductions features three Art Nouveau-styled mermaids. The 30-inch tall cast iron base includes tridents, sea weed and shells. A bronze-colored paint with an artificial patina covers the metal surface. The base supports a 10-inch diameter mirrored ball.

Careful examination shows that the metal has been fastened with Phillips head screws, a modern type of fastener. The poorly made cast iron shows the same problems found in the great majority of new lawn and garden pieces–finning, tool marks and a very rough, pitted surface.

This same mermaid base is now also being sold with table

Lawn and Garden Cast Iron

top. Both the table and the gazing ball version are available through antique reproduction wholesalers for under $70 each.

Summary of guidelines to reproductions

As a general rule, all vintage cast iron has sharp, clear detail with relatively smooth surfaces and tightly fitting seams. Casting flaws such as finning, pits, bumps and seams with wide gaps are almost always evidence of new work. Old pieces should show evidence of normal aging and wear. Old rust is usually dark brown, almost black; new rust is usually red or reddish brown.

Be suspicious of any bench, chair or table that is not fastened with removable English threaded, not metric threaded, nuts and bolts. Vintage seats and tabletops should have flat head bolts in bevelled holes for a flush surface.

New mermaid cast iron gazing ball stand. Base is 30 inches tall; mirrored ball, 10 inches diameter. The base is decorated with sea weed, shells and tridents.

Phillips head screws are used to fasten this reproduction cast iron pedestal.

Be suspicious of larger pieces, those over 24 to 30 inches, especially urns and vases, that are not cast in three or more separate pieces. Most original multi-piece urns, with the exception of some handles, were held in place by gravity, not nuts and bolts. Urns 12 inches and more in diameter should generally have cast drainage holes.

Some original pieces are marked with the names of the foundry, but many originals are unmarked. New pieces made from molds taken from old original marked pieces will also be marked. Marks alone are not a reliable test of age.

And don't overlook the obvious–carry a magnet to make sure you're really looking at cast iron and not cast aluminum or cast resin.

Old foundry marks are nice but are not necessarily a guarantee of either age or quality. The mark of Kramer Bros., Dayton, OH, shown here is on an original pre-1900 urn. Original foundry marks only appear on about 30% to 40% of urns; on only about 10% to 25% of furniture.

New two-piece 8-inch cast iron bird , one of a pair. Sold with "distressed" surface; rust shows through heavily chipped white painted surface.

Modern hex-head bolts, like this one in the base of the new cast iron bird, are generally the sign of a reproduction.

Bakelite

Today's market is filled with Bakelite look-alikes. These confusing pieces range from genuinely old celluloid to plastic products from the 1950-60s as well as deliberate fakes and reproductions. Only four of the seven pieces shown above are genuine Bakelite.

In 1984, a so-called "Philadelphia" Bakelite bracelet–a hinged style with multicolored wedges on top–sold for $250. That same style of bracelet can now sell for $4,000 and more. Relatively common Bakelite bangles and pins, which brought only $10 to $50 in the mid-1990s, are now priced $50 to $200.

As prices have risen, so has the tendency for sellers, either through lack of knowledge or deliberate intent, to call any piece of plastic "Bakelite." There has also been a steady increase in reworked and "married" pieces, items made by joining bits and piece of several pieces into a complete object. Old Bakelite stock has been fashioned into new pieces and reproductions have become more common.

This chapater will examine how originals were made, the simple tests anyone can use to separate genuine Bakelite from the lookalikes, and the common warning signs of new, fake and reproduction pieces.

A page from a 1930s catalog showing a selection of stock shapes. This photo from a catalog issued by Catalin, a manufacturer of Bakelite.

Bakelite is a trade name derived from its inventor, Leo Baekeland, who invented Bakelite in 1907. Bakelite is made from carbolic acid (phenol) and formaldehyde and is referred to as a phenolic resin. Bakelite was the first thermosetting plastic. That means once a Bakelite product is formed, it will not change shape or melt under heat. Plastics formed from other formulas can be reshaped after reheating or will burst into flame if reheated.

Bakelite was first used as an insulator against heat and electricity. As ways were found to manufacture Bakelite in bright colors, it began to be used for all sorts of decorative objects,

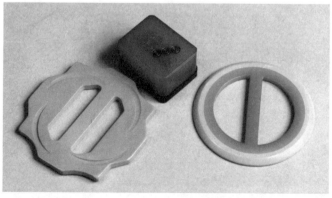

Pieces sliced from preformed stock shapes like those shown in the catalog at the top of this page. Hand-finished into buckles and a Mah Jong tile.

Bakelite

Genuine Bakelite develops a patina over time and changes the color of the surface. Image, left, shows exterior surface color of 1930s block of Bakelite. Right, piece sliced from block on left showing original color concealed below the now oxized original surface.

especially jewelry.

Although Bakelite was the trade name of the first thermo-setting phenolic resin, it was not the only one. Other important trade or brand names include Catalin, Marblette, Prystal, Phenolia and a number of others. Since brand names rarely appear on the products, collectors generally use "Bakelite" to refer to all of the thermosetting phenolic resins, not just to the Bakelite brand products and that's how we'll use the term. Throughout this chapter, "Bakelite" will refer to all phenolic resin pieces regardless of their original brand name.

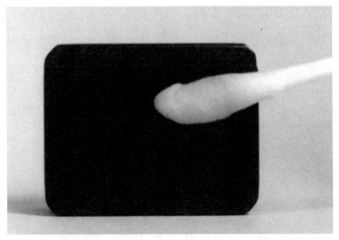

Dark green Bakelite. Test swab shows ivory or pale yellow.

The three most widely used materials to test Bakelite: 409 household cleaner, Scrubbing Bubbles bathroom cleaner and Simichrome Polish.

When testing with hot water, heat only the edge of an article. Use the thinnest edge available for best results.

How Bakelite was made

One of the keys to identifying original Bakelite is to understand how it was manufactured. Modern hard plastics, which are often confused with Bakelite, were generally produced by injecting or pouring a liquid resin into a mold which produced the final product. In other words, to get a dog pin, you'd pour molten plastic into a dog-shaped mold. The mold would create all the details of the finished product such as fur, eyes, collar, etc. When the mold was opened, the final piece was essentially ready for sale.

Typical findings, or hardware, found on vintage Bakelite. Left to right: old pin catch driven into Baklite; old pin catch screwed into Bakelite; hinge fastened with tiny nails.

Bakelite

By contrast, the majority of vintage Bakelite jewelry was not individually molded, but assembled by hand from simple stock shapes–such as cylinders, tubes, sheets, blocks and cubes. If you wanted to make a bracelet, for example, you'd typically begin with a preformed tube. Workers then sliced off sections which could be carved, set with stones or laminated with other pieces. The pieces shown in the bottom of page 347, for example, were all sliced from raw preformed stock.

Because finishing and assembly of Bakelite was done by hand, special designs and small custom orders could easily be made without the overhead of expensive molds required by hard plastics. Anyone could buy the raw Bakelite material and small studios and amateurs could afford to experiment with their own colors and designs.

Tests for genuine Bakelite

Unlike other plastics, authentic Bakelite oxidizes over the

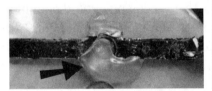

Typical findings on plastic and common "married" pieces or old Bakelite. Left: a new fastener glued to the back of typical 1960-70s plastic brooch. Right: a new metal fastener glued (arrow) to a Bakelite clothing button to make a piece of "jewelry."

Any molded findings, like the pin catch shown at right on this dog brooch, are a sign of molded plastic, not Bakelite. Findings on authentic Bakelite are made and applied separately, not molded.

years developing a patina which changes the surface color. Exposure to sunlight, body fluids, cosmetics and other factors contribute to patinas and color changes associated with normal age and wear.

Normal oxidation provides a valuable clue whether a suspected piece is true Bakelite (phenolic resin) or a lookalike material. All true Bakelite, regardless of surface color, will leave an ivory or pale yellow smear on a cotton swab wetted with one of several common products: the cleaning fluids 409 and Scrubbing Bubbles and the paste-form Simichrome Polish. Lookalike materials, such as modern hard plastics, will not leave any color on the swab or will leave a smear in the same the color as the plastic (blue plastic will leave a blue smear, etc.,).

All the testing products cause eye and skin irritation and should be used carefully; rubber gloves are recommended. Use a

Two typical vintage Bakelite bangles with simple hand carving. Note the lighter color (arrow) on the inside surface. The outer surface has darkened from normal oxidation.

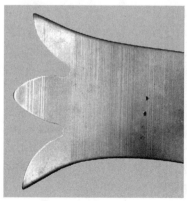

Tool marks on the back side of a typical vintage pin. Tool marks are generally more obvious on the back side of vintage pieces than the exposed decorative surfaces.

Bakelite

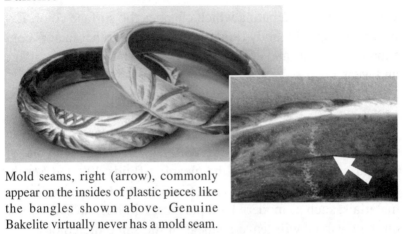

Mold seams, right (arrow), commonly appear on the insides of plastic pieces like the bangles shown above. Genuine Bakelite virtually never has a mold seam.

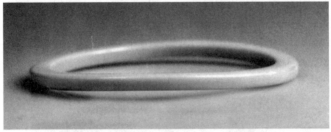

No authentic Bakelite will warp, bend or lose its original shape due to heat or moisture. Any warped or misshaped piece like the bangle above cannot be authentic Bakelite. This example is made of plastic and has deformed under heat.

tiny amount of material; it doesn't take much. Apply to a small, hidden area such as the back side of a pin or inside of a bracelet. Scrubbing Bubbles can dull the original finish; Simichrome will leave the tested area with a higher shine; 409 leaves the surface virtually unchanged and is the best choice.

Most non-Bakelite products are not affected by the products, but you should always be careful and carefully wash and wipe dry all tested areas to prevent any possible long-term changes.

The swab test is effective on virtually all Bakelite. The most common exceptions are pieces of genuine Bakelite that have recently been completely polished or cleaned and the original patina has been removed. Certain colors, particularly black and some reds, can also occasionally give confusing results.

VINTAGE BAKELITE

Catalog offer for "vintage" Bakelite jewelry carved today from old 1930s stock. New pieces have no oxidation or patina.

Another easy, simple test is to place a suspected piece under hot water from your household faucet. Hold the piece so an edge is in the middle of the flow. After 20 to 30 seconds, most genuine Bakelite gives off a strong phenol odor similar to paint remover or varnish. Modern plastics and other lookalikes do not generally produce any odor when held under hot water produced by the average household hot water heater.

Other considerations

Once you determine a piece is made from genuine Bakelite, it doesn't mean you have proved the piece is necessarily old. There is a surprising amount of original unfinished Bakelite stock that has survived. This old but never-used stock can be carved today and offered as vintage Bakelite. Genuine vintage jewelry

New 1¾-inch wide Bakelite bracelet carved from old stock, left. Most new carvings are very coarse and generally appear gray, right.

that is plain and low value, is frequently recarved into more desirable and higher priced designs. Old stock and recarved pieces will both pass the swab and hot water tests because the pieces are genuine Bakelite.

One way to confirm age is to carefully examine the findings, or hardware, such as pins, hinges, etc. Findings on genuine vintage Bakelite jewelry are generally attached with mechanical fasteners such as tiny screws, pins and nails. Findings in modern plastic are typically formed in the mold or glued on later. Original metal findings almost always shows some tarnish or even rust. Be wary of shiny hardware with no sign of normal age or wear.

Since genuine Bakelite produces a patina, outer surfaces on truly vintage pieces should normally be darker than protected inner surfaces. Insides of bracelets, for example, should be lighter in color than the exposed outer surfaces. Backs of pins and earrings should also be lighter than exposed outer surfaces.

Virtually all authentic Bakelite jewelry was hand machined or carved and should show some tool marks. Vintage tool marks are, however, at the very least, tumbled and rounded off, never jagged or sharp. Grinding marks with a frosted, chalky appearance are typical signs of recent carving.

Tool marks should also be logical. An original carver, working by the hour or piece-rate, would spend more time finishing exposed surfaces rather than finishing hidden surfaces that were not exposed. Tool marks in hidden areas are more obvious than marks on exposed surfaces. Surfaces of reworked or newly carved pieces are sometimes completely polished on all sides, regardless if the surface is exposed or hidden.

Warnings signs of typical reproductions, copies and lookalikes are shown at the top of the next page. One of the more obvious signs that a piece could not possibly be a piece of Bakelite is a mold seam. Authentic Bakelite, made piece by piece with hand finishing, never has a mold seam. Modern hard plastics produced in a mold, virtually always have a mold seam.

Glued hardware is a also a sign of modern pieces, or at the very least, a repair. New pins are commonly glued to inexpensive Bakelite clothing buttons to make a piece of "jewelry." Remember, even if a piece passes the cotton swab test, it doesn't mean the hardware is original. New hardware is frequently glued to odd, broken and mismatched bits and pieces of low value old Bakelite which is then offered as more expensive "jewelry."

No original Bakelite will warp or bend under heat or exposure to moisture. Any warped or distorted piece is not Bakelite but some other material such as modern hard plastic or 19th century celluloid.

Brightly colored vintage Bakelite was used for many items other than jewelry. Some of those items include napkin rings, pencil sharpeners and handles on a vast assortment of kitchen flatware, gadgets and tools. The same tests described in this article for Bakelite jewelry also apply to these other objects. When testing Bakelite, always use safe, nondestructive tests like those described in this article. Always ask the seller's permission before making any tests.

New   Old

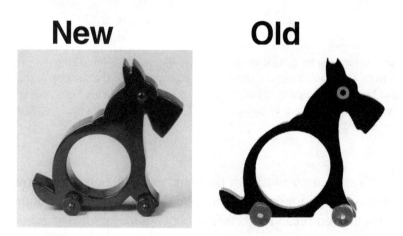

A new Scottie dog "Bakelite" napkin ring on wheels, left, is selling for $4 each. The original, right, sells for $75 to $100. The new and old Scotties shown here both have black bodies. Colors of wheels and eyes vary in each. The new Scottie is black plastic, not true Bakelite. The new pieces fails the cotton swab and hot water tests.

Halloween
Lanterns and Candy Containers

New paper mâché 7-inch devil lantern. Orange with green trim and black details, printed paper eyes and mouth insert. Retailing for around $30.

New paper mâché 8-inch "singing" jack-o'-lantern, so-called because of the shape of the mouth. One in a set of three sizes, each with a different singing face. Three-piece set about $40.

Very few categories of fakes and reproductions have shown the growth in numbers and improved manufacturing techniques as Halloween-related objects. The rather crude lanterns and candy containers that first starting appearing in the early 1990s have evolved into very carefully planned, well-made creations which are virtually exact copies of vintage originals.

Where most Halloween reproductions of the 1990s were simple generic jack-o'-lanterns–copies of originals typically worth less than $100–the current generation features many copies of very specific rare and scarce originals worth $500 and up.

Separating new from old has become much more difficult.

Although most reproductions are mass produced overseas, they are being made by hand in much the same manner as vintage originals. New pieces from China, India and the Philippines have the random irregularities and flaws collectors have previously used to authenticate genuine pieces.

The wide range of vintage pieces, as well as the ever growing number of reproductions, makes it difficult to offer a list of hard and fast rules for separating new and old. So many new and improved reproductions keep coming into the market, what's true today may be incorrect next week. At this point in time, the following suggestions are some of the general guidelines to help you detect a good majority, but certainly far from all, of the reproductions currently in the market.

The dull flat paint on the latest reproductions is nearly identical to that found on vintage pieces. Many new colors are close matches for vintage colors. Long wave black light will fluoresce some, but far from all, new paint, particularly reds and most white.

One of the best tests of age for paint is simply to smell the surface. Many reproductions still have a strong paint odor for a year or more after manufacture. If the paint stinks, so does the seller if they're offering the item as old.

Two new cat lanterns. Left, black cat cardboard pulp 6-inch cat head with handpainted trim and paper insert behind eyes, nose and mouth. Right, standing 7½-inch paper mâché cat, orange with black trim. Each currently retails for less than $30.

Paper mâché candy containers/party favor cups. Black cat left, pumpkin, right; each about 2½-inch diameter. Handpainted trim, artificial wear to rims and surface. Note pipecleaner "ears" on cat. Steel wire handle painted black. New retail, $9 each.

The great majority of vintage pre-1940 paper mâché and composition lanterns and candy containers have a relatively smooth dull exterior surface. A rough exterior surface is often a sign of a reproduction. One series of new pumpkin lanterns, for example, has a deeply crackled exterior surface (page 361). Any piece with this deeply crackled surface is suspicious and is almost certainly new.

Another warning sign of a potential reproduction is the presence of clean white chips in the surface (page 361). Since many new pieces, like the originals, are coated with gesso–a mixture of water and plaster–before painting, the white plaster shows through the new chips. Chips in vintage pieces made 50 to 80 years ago have darkened from absorbing dust and dirt. Of course, you need to be alert for artificially darkened new chips.

Lantern paper, the paper behind the eyes, nose and mouth in lanterns, can provide important clues to age. Original lantern paper is translucent; it helped spread and diffuse the light from the candle flame. Bright ink or paint on the papers also provided extra color to the lighted lantern.

New 4-inch diameter pressed cardboard candy containers with modern mylar (plastic) sparkling glitter. Note three-dimensional objects on wire handles. Retail price in 2000, $12 each. No vintage pre-1930 lanterns are decorated with mylar glitter.

Recently-made lantern papers are very often produced on laser or inkjet printers. These types of digital printers almost always create distinct patterns in the color. Inkjets, for example, form fields of color made up of randomly shaped blobs, or drops, of colored ink. Both lasers and inkjet printers deposit inks and toners in relatively narrow horizontal rows, one row at a time. If the rows become slightly misaligned it can produce "banding," a horizontal striping obvious to the unaided eye. New lantern papers made on home inkjet printers are particularly common as replacement papers.

Some mass-produced lantern papers are printed on traditional printing presses. These are identified by solid colors broken into a regular repeated network of similar sized dots, or screen pattern. The human brain fuses the separate dots together to create the illusion of a solid mass of color. The typical dot pattern can usually be detected with a 10X loupe; some coarse patterns may even be observed with the unaided eye. See page 363 for a chart outlining the differences between various lantern papers.

Nearly all original lantern paper is translucent. A number

Halloween

Above, new 10-inch paper mâché black cat combination lantern and candy container. Shown with lid removed. Right, detail of the cat's head. Note the scuff marks applied at the factory to suggest wear and age (white arrows). Colored lantern paper behind eyes, nose and mouth.

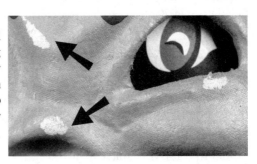

Another example of artificial wear on a new pulp, or egg carton, lantern. The new painted surface has been rubbed away at the factory to let the raw pulp below show through (black arrows).

of reproductions and modern replacements are made from ordinary office-quality white opaque paper. This is especially true of replacement papers made on home inkjet printers. Inkjet papers are specially designed to be opaque in order to prevent bleed-through of the inkjet droplets of color.

Most new papers, especially inkjet and laser papers, will fluoresce under long wave black light. Original papers rarely, if ever, fluoresce. Modern synthetic glues used to attach new papers to new lanterns generally fluoresce. Most old glues made of natural materials do not fluoresce. Of course, you might find a repair where a genuinely old paper has been reattached to an old lantern with new glue.

The deeply crackled surface shown on this pumpkin lantern is widely used on reproductions of all kinds to suggest age. The cracks are fingernail size and wider. Vintage Halloween paper mâché and pulp lanterns virtually never have such a finish.

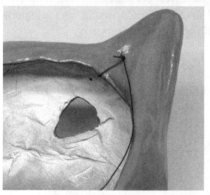

Be suspicious if the inside of a lantern is not painted or is bright white like this new example. Vintage lanterns were generally painted and have darkened over the years with normal aging.

Mists or droplets of sprayed paint are generally the sign of a new lantern. Overspray paint mists are virtually never seen on pre-1930 lanterns.

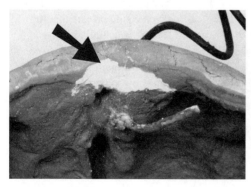

After a piece of paper mâché is shaped, it is generally smoothed with gesso, a mixture of water and plaster, before being painted. Bright white plaster under paint chips (arrow) is a warning sign of a reproduction lantern.

Using lantern papers as a test of age

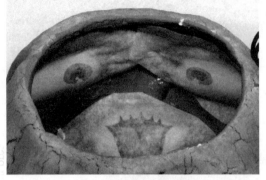

Lantern papers are applied to the inside of lanterns behind the eyes, nose and mouth (see example above). The paper diffuses the light of the candle flame. Although most lantern papers are one piece, it is not unusual to find more than one piece of paper in either new or old lanterns. The more complex the lantern shape, the less likely a single piece of paper could fit properly.

This new lantern paper has been stained on the front side to suggest the darkening associated with age. The reverse side of the same new lantern paper is shown below.

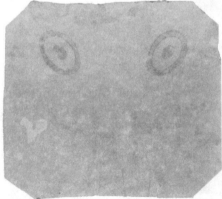

The perfectly clean, spotless reverse side proves that the "stain" is actually only a surface coating on the front side. Although vintage papers can show some slight variation front to back, like smoke blacking on the inside, an extreme illogical difference generally indicates artificial aging.

Printing on lantern papers

The colored features on the great majority of old lantern papers appear as smooth continuous fields of solid color.

Colored features on many new lantern papers are applied by laser and inkjet printers. Characterized by randomly spaced fuzzy dots of various colors. May include misaligned bands of color.

Colored features produced on a printing press are arranged in a consistent repeating pattern of similarly sized dots.

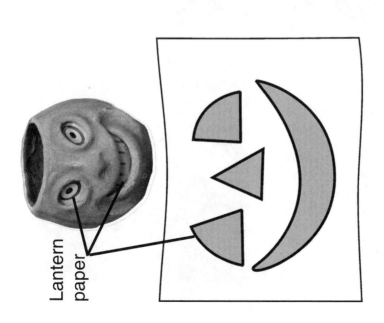

Lantern paper

New versions of cardboard jack-o'-lanterns with tab and slot construction. Pumpkin is 8 inches wide by 6 inches high; cat is 6 inches wide by 8 inches high. Wholesale price, $7.75 each.

Pieces of a typical new tab/slot cardboard lantern before assembly. Old tab and slot lanterns are made from similarly shaped pieces. Like most other lanterns, this style also uses separate lantern papers behind openings for eyes, nose and mouth.

Original cardboard tab and slot lanterns like this example date to the 1940s-early 1950s. Original lantern paper missing from behind eyes, nose and mouth. Many, but not all originals, had some type of metal candle holder (see opposite page) in the base.

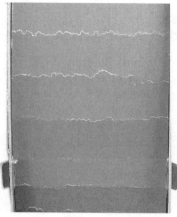

The curved side of the new tab and slot pumpkin. The curve is so irregular the painted finish is cracked and torn.

The curved side of old tab and slot pumpkin is smooth and continuous. No distubance of the surface finish.

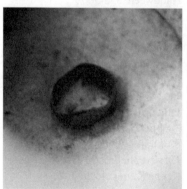

The bottoms of three typical old cardboard tab and slot lanterns. Clockwise from upper left: metal fish hook-shaped socket; clip-type socket; circular socket. So far, the new tab and slot lanterns have flat, plain bottoms without sockets or holes for candles.

Index

Tools to catch
fakes and reproductions

6" black light

Take anywhere in your pocket or purse; 4 watt longwave, 90-day month warranty on circuitry, 30 day warranty on bulb. Uses 4AA batteries (not included)

$24.00 $3 shipping

mini black light

A pocket powerhouse that flouresces vaseline glass and many other materials in room lighting. Use for bone, ivory, glue, invisible inks and most credit cards and currency. 2¾-inch virtually crushproof metal case; true longwave, includes key loop and snap swivel, includes removable 30-inch all weather neck loop, SIX FREE BATTERIES

$14.00 ea. $2.95 shipping
two for $23.00, FREE shipping

Black Light Book

Enlarged 4th edition. Complete tests for fakes, reproductions, damages and repairs; 112 pgs; 109 illus. 6x9-inches, softcover. China, pottery, ivory, paper, textiles, gemstones, glass, paintings, prints, etc. How to use invisible inks for secret marks, to prevent returns, readmission, etc. **$14.95** $2.95 shipping
($9.95 plus shipping with any black light)

Diamond loupe 10X color corrected, distortion free triplet 5/8-inch dia. (18mm) glass lens Leather case and hanging loop. Compare at $30-$45.
$19.95 + $2.95 shipping

satisfaction guaranteed–same day shipping

Antique & Collectors Reproduction News

$20 minimur **Community Library of Allegheny Valley** ntral time
1522 Broadview Boulevard
Natrona Heights, PA 15065
HARRISON